This book is an interesting integration of bibli politics, and development. This approach to fo daring, exciting, fresh, and most welcoming. There is much to the methodology, analysis, and application of global principles of theological enterprises to a particular culture – transformation, the holistic development of individual persons and society at large is the goal of the gospel. When this development is examined, explored, and elaborated as peace it becomes more fascinating. Thank you Wole, you have given us a good example of how to do Christian theology in the African context. I am proud of this book and wholeheartedly recommend it to all.

Emiola Nihinlola, PhD
Professor of Christian Theological Studies and President,
Nigerian Baptist Theological Seminary, Ogbomosho

Dr. Wole Adegbile's book, *Development as Peace* explores a contextual political theology of development using Yoruba traditional culture. The work is well researched and it makes a seminal contribution to the quest for development that is rooted in the African heritage, and one that is relevant and meets the aspirations of Africans. Adegbile argues the current modernization theory that undergirds the idea of African nation-state and development has not served Africa's development agenda well. He proposes a contextual alternative to development, which draws on Yoruba political wisdom, that sees "development as peace." The book's strength lies in Adegbile's skills in engaging the Yoruba culture by exploring its political thoughts and practices, by seeing Scripture as the main source for theological reflection, and offering a biblical, theological, and cultural critique of the modernization theory of development. He sees a correlation between both *alaafia* as the underlying Yoruba philosophy of "development as peace" and the biblical idea of *shalom* as the foundation for a biblical view of development and politics. I recommend the book for all development practitioners, students of development, development agencies engaged in community and government institutions, and policy makers on national development programmes, who want to do development that transforms communities.

James Nkansah-Obrempong, PhD
Dean, Nairobi Evangelical School of Theology,
Africa International University, Kenya

Development as Peace

A Contextual Political Theology of Development from Yoruba Culture

Wole Adegbile

Langham
MONOGRAPHS

© 2023 Wole Adegbile

Published 2023 by Langham Monographs
An imprint of Langham Publishing
www.langhampublishing.org

Langham Publishing and its imprints are a ministry of Langham Partnership

Langham Partnership
PO Box 296, Carlisle, Cumbria, CA3 9WZ, UK
www.langham.org

ISBNs:
978-1-83973-645-2 Print
978-1-83973-884-5 ePub
978-1-83973-885-2 PDF

Wole Adegbile has asserted his right under the Copyright, Designs and Patents Act, 1988 to be identified as the Author of this work.

All rights reserved. No part of this publication may be reproduced, stored in a retrieval system or transmitted, in any form or by any means, electronic, mechanical, photocopying, recording or otherwise, without the prior written permission of the publisher or the Copyright Licensing Agency.

Requests to reuse content from Langham Publishing are processed through PLSclear. Please visit www.plsclear.com to complete your request.

Scripture quotations marked (NKJV) are taken from the New King James Version (NKJV). Copyright © 1982 by Thomas Nelson, Inc. Used by permission. All rights reserved.

Scripture quotations marked (TLB) are taken from The Living Bible copyright © 1971. Used by permission of Tyndale House Publishers, a Division of Tyndale House Ministries, Carol Stream, Illinois 60188. All rights reserved.

Scripture quotations marked (NLT) are taken from the Holy Bible, New Living Translation, copyright © 1996, 2004, 2007, 2013, 2015 by Tyndale House Foundation. Used by permission of Tyndale House Publishers, Inc., Carol Stream, Illinois 60188. All rights reserved.

Scripture quotations marked (NASB) are taken from the New American Standard Bible®, Copyright © 1960, 1962, 1963, 1968, 1971, 1972, 1973, 1975, 1977, 1995 by The Lockman Foundation. Used by permission.

Scripture quotations marked (AMP) are taken from the Amplified® Bible (AMP), Copyright © 2015 by The Lockman Foundation. Used by permission. www.Lockman.org.

British Library Cataloguing-in-Publication Data
A catalogue record for this book is available from the British Library

ISBN: 978-1-83973-645-2

Cover & Book Design: projectluz.com

Langham Partnership actively supports theological dialogue and an author's right to publish but does not necessarily endorse the views and opinions set forth here or in works referenced within this publication, nor can we guarantee technical and grammatical correctness. Langham Partnership does not accept any responsibility or liability to persons or property as a consequence of the reading, use or interpretation of its published content.

*To all my teachers, instructors, and mentors,
from primary to graduate school*

Contents

Preface xiii

Chapter 1 1
Introduction
    Africa's Situation Characterised by "Chaos" 1
    Failed Politics as a Cause of Poverty in Africa............................... 5
    The Uniqueness of the Book 8
    Methodology and the Making of the Book................................... 9
    A Brief Note about the Yoruba People... 14
    Conclusion 16

Chapter 2 17
The Contextual Political Theology of Development
    Introduction 17
    The Emphasis on Relationship with God in Holistic Development
        Practice 17
        The Meaning of Holistic Development Practice 18
        Deficiency in Human Existential Domains and Poverty Breeders... 21
        The Interplay of Bad Politics and Poverty Trap as
            Underdevelopment Breeders... 23
        The Vitality of Human Spiritual Domain in Development
            and Politics... 27
    Review of Models of Development Practices and Poverty
        Eradication in the Christian Church 29
        The City on the Hill: Community as a Way to Change........ 30
        The Idea of Christendom: Building a Christian Cultural
            Consensus 31
        The Gospel of Liberation: Restructuring Power Relations 32
        Practice of Compassion: The Development Model 33
    Christian Evangelism and Social Services 33
    Prosperity Gospel as a Means of Development Intervention.... 34
        Prosperity Gospel as Directed against Ignorance................ 35
        Prosperity Gospel Teaches Entrepreneurship in the Face of
            National Sociopolitical and Economic Breakdown......... 36
        Variation in Pentecostalism and Prosperity Theology 37
        The Central Focus of Prosperity Theology in Africa........... 38
        Theological Evaluation of the Tenet of Prosperity Gospel 39

  The Church and Political Theology and Development 42
    How the African Political Past Haunts Its Political Present 43
    Revising the African False Political Ideals 45
    The Church as the Hope of African Sociopolitical and
      Economic Liberation 46
    The Implication of Political Theology 47
    A Call for Contextual Political Theology of Development 48
    Conclusion 51

Chapter 3 53
Àlàáfíà Lójù: *Yoruba Traditional Developmental-Political Thoughts*
  Introduction 53
  Life and Wellbeing in Yoruba Traditional Thought 54
  Related Words for Wellbeing and Development in Yoruba
    Traditional Thought 57
  The Concept of Sin and Its Implication on Wellbeing in the
    Yoruba Traditional Thought 58
    The Meaning of Sin in Yoruba Traditional Thought 59
  The Essence of Iwa in Human Wellbeing in the Yoruba
    Traditional Thoughts 60
    Sources of Moral Codes in Yoruba Traditional Thoughts 62
    Some Specific Sins among Yoruba People 64
    Causes of Sin according to Yoruba Traditional Thought 67
    Dealing with Sin in the Yoruba Traditional Thoughts and
      Practices: Kingship Involvement 69
    Theological Reflection of Yoruba Concept of Sin in Light of
      Human Wellbeing and Political Responsibility 72
  Yoruba Educational Philosophy and Its Implication for Development ... 74
    Education towards Social Life, Vocation and Trade in Yoruba
      Traditional Thoughts 76
    Theological Reflections on Yoruba Educational Philosophy 79
  The Role of Yoruba Politics in Development 80
  Conclusion 84

Chapter 4 87
Kábíyèsí, Aláṣẹ Èkejì Òrìṣà: *Yoruba Traditional Developmental-Political Practices*
  Introduction 87
  The Political History of Yoruba 88
  The Political Administration of Oyo Empire 92
  Theological Reflection on the Political Administration of Oyo Empire ... 96
  Kábíyèsí, Aláṣẹ Èkejì Òrìṣà: The Sacred Kingship in Yorubaland 98

  Relationship with *Oduduwa* 100
  The Essence of Yoruba Sacred Kingship 104
 Theological Reflection on Yoruba Sacred Kingship 105
 Religion, Rituals, and Community Wellbeing 106
 King's Role in Religion, Ritual, and Wellbeing 109
 Theological Reflection on King's Role in Religion, Ritual, and
  Wellbeing 114
 The Yoruba Political Structure of Maintaining Peace, Justice, and
  Conflict Resolution 116
  Yoruba Concept of Justice 117
  Yoruba Reconciliation: Process of Upholding Justice and
   Maintaining Peace 118
  Assessing the Approaches of Ensuring Peace, Justice, and
   Reconciliation 120
 Conclusion 122

Chapter 5 125
Modernization Theory of Development and its Implications for African Nation-State Politics
 Introduction 125
 Modernization Theory and Development 126
  Modernization and Colonialism in Africa 127
  Modernization Theory, Globalization, and Colonialism ... 128
 The Positive Aspects of Modernization Theory 131
 Negative Effects of Modernization on African Developmental-
  Political Life 134
  Deviation from Divinity 134
  Overgeneralized Idea of Prosperity 136
  Crisis of Identity 137
  Psychological and Evolutionary Implication of Modern-day
   African Politics 139
 Conclusion 141

Chapter 6 143
Politics that Fosters Development: Lessons from Yoruba Traditional Developmental-Political Thoughts and Practices
 Introduction 143
 Biblical Order of Developmental-Politics 143
  God's Agenda for the Wellbeing of the Nations 144
  The Spiritual and Sociophysical Dimensions of God's
   Commandments 145
  The Kingship Role in Israelites' Political Setting 148

  Human Wellbeing Is Intrinsic to Kingdom Lifestyle 151
 Review of Modernization Theory and Its Implications for
  Development in Africa 154
   Operations, Benefits, and Biblical Correlations 154
   Negative Effects and Biblical Antitheses 155
  Implications from Yoruba Traditional Developmental-Political
   Thoughts and Practices 156
   Political Society Built on the Idea of *Àlàáfíà* 156
   Political Society That Demands *Ìwà Rere* from Society Members ... 159
   Political Society Built on Spiritual, Value-Based Educational
    System 164
   Political Society Built on Sacred Kingship 170
  Conclusion 178

Chapter 7 181
 Way Forward
  Lessons from Biblically Correlated Yoruba Developmental-
   Political Thoughts and Practices 181
   A King Must Ensure Proper Political Coordination 182
   A King Must Seek Spiritual Guidance and Help 183
   A King Must Ensure Righteous Judgement 183
   A King Must Be Divinely Appointed 183
  Major Biblical Antitheses of Yoruba Traditional Developmental-
   Political Thoughts and Practices 183
   Human Effort and Victory over Sin 184
   The Place of the Ancestors and the Traditional Deities in
    Securing God's Help 184
  Lessons and Biblical Correlations of Modernization Theory 184
  Negative Effects and Biblical Antitheses of Modernization Theory 184
  Way Forward 185
   For the General African Society 185
   For the African Church and Church Leaders 185
   For National Policymaking in Africa 187

Bibliography 189

Glossary of Yoruba Terms Used 205

Appendix 207
 Some Yoruba Cities in the Middle Ages

List of Figures

Figure 1. Use of Critical Correlation in Constructing Contextual Political Theology of Development 14

Figure 2. *Àlàáfià* as based on on Good Moral Standing Marked by a Four-Dimensional Relationship..56

Figure 3. Yoruba Political Involvement of the Divinity for the Sake of Wellbeing 110

Figure 4. Yoruba Petitions to the Traditional Deities on Development............113

Figure 5. The Clash between Traditional and Modern Africas.........................139

Figure 6. The Two Dimensions of God's Law 147

Figure 7. Biblical Order for Development 152

Figure 8. The Contextual Framework for Contextual Political Theology of Development...154

Preface

Africa has learned so much from the West, especially through modernization. Meanwhile, the West also has something to learn from Africa. And more importantly, Africa has so much to learn from itself, from its own traditional way of life. My hope is that with this book, contemporary Africa, the West, and the entire world will learn something from traditional Africa.

I have undertaken this study on theology, politics, culture, and development with the aim to *do* and *advocate* a "contextual political theology of development." I hold that **politics** should be done in God's way, and **development** should be carried out from a holistic perspective, and that both political and developmental endeavours should be of relevance to cultural identity. If there exists a favourable political environment that promotes human wellbeing and growth, then development always ensues. Establishing the right political environment entails following God's purposes and fulfilling the aspirations of the common people.

I initially wanted to write about Africa, but Africa is vast. I therefore resolved to write about the portion of Africa that I am most familiar with by virtue of birth, a portion of Africa occupied by the Yoruba people of Nigeria. I am aware that the discussion would be richer if I brought different perspectives from different African contexts rather than limiting myself to the Yoruba context. But I believe that my brothers and sisters from other parts of Africa can further enrich the discussion if they also undertake a similar writing project and stir up the same discussion from their traditional contexts. That is why I have developed a framework that I believe can work for any writer who wants to take the same path as I have taken in this book.

What I have done in the book is recount the wisdom of the Yoruba people as to how politics could be done to foster development. First, I have done this in relation to modernization theory. I write from the perspective that the idea of nation-state in Africa is undergirded by modernization theory. I have advocated authentic African thoughts and practices, against the background that modernization theory has not served Africa well. Still, brief as it is, I have pointed out the good things of the theory, which I regard as a good lesson for the contemporary African political leadership. For some, this may sound as if I contradict myself. I have done this as a respect for the wisdom of the Yoruba people, the wisdom that forms the basis for my discussion in this book. The Yoruba wisely say that *Ogbọ́n ò pin síbì kan* (wisdom is not limited to one place), and that *Ọmọdé gbọ́n, àgbà gbọ́n lafi dá'lẹ̀ Ifẹ̀* (Ile Ife, the ancestral origin of Yoruba people, was built by the wisdom of the young and the old). The idea behind these two proverbs is that if we are sober enough, we can acquire wisdom from anywhere, anyone, and any situation. Therefore, my primary intention is not just to critique the Western practices that have been imbibed in Africa, but also to commend them for their beneficial elements.

Second, as I recount the wisdom of the Yoruba people as to how politics could be done to foster development, I do so in relation to Scripture. As much as my discussion in this book may appear to romanticize Yoruba thoughts and practices, I do not by any means intend to equate them with the authority of the Scripture. I have affirmed Yoruba traditional thoughts and practices that are in line with the Scripture and condemned the ones that are not. One remarkable area where Yoruba political thoughts and practices fall below the biblical standard is in the engagement of deities as intermediaries between humans and God.

In my use of the Scripture, I have mostly quoted from eight translations: King James Version (KJV), New King James Version (NKJV), New Living Translation (NLT), The Living Bible (TLB), New International Version (NIV), Good News Translation (GNT), New American Standard Bible (NASB), and Amplified Bible (AMP). Selection of the translation for each quote is based on which of them, (1) best translate the particular text, in my view, and (2) use the most familiar language to contemporary readers.

Like other researchers, as I undertook the study I stumbled on many facts. Central to all the facts I stumbled upon is that, for the Yoruba people, development is peace. Placing this realization side-by-side with the Scripture, I have inferred that Yoruba traditional thoughts and practices about politics and development are strongly correlated with those of the biblical context.

Yoruba fundamental thoughts on development, which is *àlàáfíà,* are similar to that of biblical thoughts on the same – *shalom*. Relating development to politics, Yoruba traditional developmental-political thoughts and practices are built on ethical living, borne out of the spirituality enforced and promoted by the king. This also has a strong correlation with the biblical developmental-political view.

Chapter 1 of the book provides the general overview of the study. In chapter 2, I argue for holistic development that caters for all human existential components. In connection to holistic development, I stress the need for Christian political theology that aims at development, with relevance to a cultural context, which is what contextual political theology of development is all about. In chapter 3, I begin the exploration of Yoruba thoughts and practices about development, and link this with chapter 4, where I discuss Yoruba developmental-political practices. In chapter 5, I discuss the distortion to the African political thoughts and practices by virtue of modernization. I also highlight lessons from modernization. In chapter 6, I discuss the implications of Yoruba developmental-political thoughts and practices, as opposed to modernization using the Scripture as the measuring rod. I conclude the study in chapter 7 by proposing some way forward for developmental-political practices in contemporary Africa.

This book is an outcome from my doctoral dissertation at Africa International University, Nairobi. When I got the opportunity to have it published with Langham Publishing, I felt a bit uncomfortable publishing it in a dissertation form. My discomfort was basically for two reasons: (1) Reading the dissertation all over again, I realised I had outgrown it. For instance, I realised some arguments that needed to be strengthened. (2) Reading a dissertation is sometimes like reading someone else's old examination booklet. The examiners are the writer's primary audience and therefore the work is largely presented with them in mind. For these two reasons, I took time to tighten some of my arguments and rework the presentation of the work so that it can naturally flow like a book.

I am grateful for the good environment provided for the foundation of the work by Africa International University. My gratitude goes to my supervisors, Prof. James Nkansah-Obrempong and Dr. Sicily Muriithi, who challenged me to explore something significant about my culture and who did not take substandard work from me. I appreciate all the professors who facilitated my doctoral seminars and those who examined my work; they all sharpened my thinking as I conducted and concluded the study. Thank you, Prof. Mark Shaw, Prof. Samuel Ngewa, Prof. William Dyrness, Dr. Grace Dyrness, Prof. Eric Aseka, Prof. Gyang Pam, and Prof. Yusufu Turaki.

I am also grateful for the personal interaction I had with Prof. Dankit Nassiuma, the university vice chancellor and Prof. Samuel Katia, the then deputy vice chancellor (Academic Affairs and Research). After I completed my term as student council president in the university as a master's student, both of them would not stop talking about what I should do as my contribution to the state of politics in Africa. When I enrolled for PhD, I resolved to write something related to politics partly due to the influence both had on me. And here is my contribution to African politics.

I went back to Nigeria with my wife to carry out this research after five years of continuous stay in Kenya. I truly enjoyed the blessing of being received by Grace Baptist Church Meiran, Lagos. Thank you, Rev. Ben Tella and the entire church membership for the love of Christ that you demonstrated towards us during our stay. Mr. Zion and Mrs. Olubunmi Oke hosted us in their house and took good care of us for all the four months we spent in Nigeria. Many of the church members volunteered their time and material resources to be of help to my study. I cannot thank all of you enough.

I finalised the book as a faculty member at Africa College of Theology, Kigali, Rwanda, where I still currently serve. I appreciate Dr. Charles Mugisha, college chancellor, my friend Johnson Karamuzi, who was then the college principal, and Prof. Nathan Chiroma, the current principal, for the good environment their leadership provided for research and writing. Special appreciation also goes to the Langham team for the opportunity to publish this work. They have worked tirelessly in making the final copy better than the first manuscript.

To all my extended family, the Adegbiles and the Ajuwons, I am grateful that you are all always there for me. *Alájọbí á gbè wá o.* To Jackie Adegbile, my beautiful wife. I conducted the field research for this study shortly after we got married. We went together to Nigeria to do it. And that was our honeymoon. I am deeply grateful for the love and friendship we share. They put a spring in my step as I undertook this work. *Nakupenda sana!*

CHAPTER 1

Introduction

Before we proceed into this chapter, I will give a general overview of what it entails. First, I echo George Ayittey's voice: Africa is in chaos because it got its socioeconomic and political ideologies wrong.[1] Following this, I also echo the voices of other writers who have made a similar claim. Adding to Ayittey's recommendations on how Africa can match up in terms of development, I propose a sociopolitical solution that places a premium on spirituality. I make this addition because spirituality is a vital (and biblically related) African identity. And there is no other way to pursue authenticity than to be who we really are, by living out our ontological identity. In the rest of the chapters in this book, I elaborate how African spirituality plays a critical role in African political settings and consequently brings about development. But let us begin with the dilemma of contemporary Africa, and why Africa finds itself in it.

Africa's Situation Characterised by "Chaos"

In his book *Africa in Chaos*,[2] George Ayittey provides a vivid picture of the state of the dilemma in Africa. What he had at the back of his mind as he wrote the book "is to examine why Africa has been imploding and remains intractably mired in poverty."[3] He began to lay the foundation for his argument in the book by highlighting the departed souls in Africa, people

---

1. Ayittey, *Africa in Chaos*, this is not a direct citation, but it is the general force of Ayittey's writings.
2. Ayittey, *Africa in Chaos*.
3. Ayittey, 24.

1

who lost their lives through assassination while fighting a cause that has to do with their homeland. Therefore, the book is dedicated to the murdered heroes in twenty-three African nations. The content of the book entails a critical analysis of how things have fallen apart in Africa, the chaotic state of its politics, economy, and even education, all of them taking a negative toll on development.

One of the questions that subtly echo as one reads the pages of the book is whether Africa has what it takes in terms of human resources to combat its chaotic state. The answer is yes. Africa has human power, the most important of all assets that can surmount its mountain. However, the challenge is that Africa does not duly appreciate the human power, the creative minds, at its disposal.

In this book, Ayittey portrays Africa as a lost continent. First, because of the way it lags behind its counterparts on the world stage; second, because of the contention between two Africas. African past and present coexist together and clash with each other. "There are two Africas that are constantly clashing. The first is traditional or indigenous Africa that historically has been castigated as backward and primitive.... The second Africa is the modern one, which is lost. Most of Africa's problems emanate from its modern sector."[4]

According to Ayittey, Africa is a lost continent, lost from the international scene where all other continents are having their voices heard, having strayed away from its original identity in the battle between traditional and modern Africa. The root cause of the chaos on the continent can be traced to several sources. Some of these sources were of African origin, for instance reckless politics and governance. Others were caused by the contribution and interference of some international entities or agencies such as the World Bank and International Monetary Fund.

Ayittey goes on to argue that the social, political, and economic mess is largely borne out of the fact that Africa has lost its originality. Africa took upon itself the ways of life borrowed from outside its jurisdiction, particularly from the West, at the expense of its original identity. In the pre-colonial era, Africa had its system running through a traditional means that was embraced by all the people of the land, and which were functional and efficient. For

---

4. Ayittey, 14.

instance, Africa had always had a democracy that is marked by free participation, accountability, and rule of law.

In Ayittey's view, Africa had something that it can take pride in. It had a social system that was inferior to none. Meanwhile, its exposure to European life stripped away its natural ways of life and it therefore lost its true colour. African governments keep adopting policies that are shaped by Western philosophies and worldviews, and therefore, have not been effective in their deliveries. Not only do African leaders enforce policies that are not true to African identity, they also follow the evil practices of their colonial masters. Therefore, in Ayittey's view, African poverty was borne out of the inability to get rid of corrupt and ineffective leadership that does more harm than good, or the inability to peacefully compel their governments to apply appropriate policies.

Ayittey opines that the chaos in Africa would have been resolved if African leaders thought critically about how they put policies in place and how they responded to national matters. He believes that this shortcoming is not only attributed to the African political leaders; even the so-called intellectuals are guilty of the same. He points out that the problem of Africa can simply be attributed to the fact that the responsible stakeholders are not applying "commonsense" as much as possible; therefore, "What modern Africa needs, perhaps more than anything else, is a commonsense revolution."[5]

In his argument, Ayittey notes that all the sociopolitical ideologies employed by African leaders are, in one way or the other, not favourable to the situation of the land. Such ideologies include "African socialism, political pragmatism, military nationalism, and Afro-Marxism."[6] By this Ayittey implies that, in their uncritical and careless application of ideologies, African political leaders end up destroying the good in the land. In his analysis, all the causes of poverty in Africa are connected to bad governance.

Ayittey's closing remarks come as a challenge to the African intellectuals. He gives them ten commandments that indicate their specific role in fixing the wrecked vehicle of the African states. The commandments for the intellectuals are:

---

5. Ayittey, 21.
6. Ayittey, 157.

1. Never forget your roots.
2. Seek ye first the economic kingdom in the private sector.
3. Privatize the universities.
4. Demand and defend freedom of expression/media.
5. Practice intellectual solidarity.
6. Demand national conferences.
7. Disband the military or cut it in half.
8. Practice pan-Africanism.
9. Set up a rival Organization of African Unity (OAU), now African Union (AU).
10. Selectively repudiate foreign debt.

In his recommendations, Ayittey has done well to challenge Africa to never forget its "roots." By "African roots," he certainly means that Africa should embrace what makes it authentically Africa. While Ayittey passionately calls Africa back to its root in the socioeconomic and political sense, he left out one fundamental factor that characterizes traditional African socioeconomic and political life – spirituality. In chapters 3 and 4, I shall extensively explore how spirituality plays into Yoruba sociopolitical life.

Since this book is written from a Christian theological perspective, my connotation for spirituality underscores the human relationship with God. As much as science, philosophy, and common sense have a relevant place in solving the underdevelopment problem, God must, however, take a prominent place in all African affairs. Hence, as I echo Ayittey's voice in this section of this book, I do so with the addition that God must be at the centre of a development endeavour. If we go merely by common sense and human philosophy, we may end up being victims of idolatry; since the exclusive application of common sense and human philosophies leads us to employ the means that are contrary to the will of God and his order.[7]

In this section, I have discussed African development and failed political leadership based on an exclusive interaction with Ayittey. In the section that follows, I shall maintain a general discussion on the same theme, with wider scholarly interactions. In the same section, I will also introduce how subsequent chapters build on this theme.

---

7. Goudzwaard, *Idols of Our Time*, 23.

Failed Politics as a Cause of Poverty in Africa

As I interact with Ayittey's work in the previous section, I indicated that the form of politics practiced in Africa is one that hampers development, because the political ideologies and institutions are not true to the African identity and worldview. It is also important to note that not only is it true that African political systems are not authentic to African context, so also are most national institutions – social, economic, and educational institutions.[8] The majority (if not all) of these institutions are structured according to European patterns.

However, my emphasis in this book is on the inauthenticity of African political systems. George Kinoti, Samuel Kobia, and Jesse Mugambi all agree and argue that the political system of Africa is unfavourable to development, because it is a replica of the Western political system, which does not suit Africa.[9] The obvious effect of this is the problem of underdevelopment, which leaves many people in Africa in situations of abject poverty.

Good political administration enhances the development of a state, whereas a bad one hampers it. "Poverty is a political condition." Many people find themselves in a state of poverty not of their own making but because they "have little or no control over the material and institutional conditions under which they exist."[10] This is one crucial challenge facing Africa today. Africa is in a political mess and its people consequently living in abject poverty.

Africa is in political crises that result in underdevelopment because of the identity crisis posed by the colonial imposition of nation-state politics. As I shall argue in chapter 5, nation-state politics is a form of Western developmental-political theory. Nation-state politics and other Western developmental-political formulae find no root in African traditional developmental-political thought. These Western formulae have become a way of life that Africa is struggling to live by. In his discussion about the problem of the nation-state in Africa, Kobia uses the words of Basil Davidson to condemn its emergence, noting that, "The predicament of Africa is 'the curse of the nation-state.'"[11] Kobia himself personally argues thus:

---

8. Collier, "Poverty Reduction in Africa," 16763.

9. Kinoti, *Hope for Africa*, 25–26; Kobia, *Courage to Hope*, 42; Mugambi, "Religion and Social Reconstruction," 21–22.

10. Phiri, *Proclaiming Political Pluralism*, 5.

11. Kobia, *Courage to Hope*, 53.

> We are witnessing a kind of political and economic dispensation that is linked to the Europeanization of Africa and Africanization of European institutions in Africa. We are therefore confronted with the problems of authenticity and legitimacy. The former is indicative of the fact that the historical progression of the nation-state in the continent was not rooted; therefore, it does not reflect the soul of Africa. The issue of legitimacy has to do with the question of consent given that the people of Africa did not give and so do not participate fully in the state. An exercise in ethical discernment is therefore indispensable in confronting the dual dilemma of the so-called disfunctionality and disorderliness of the state in Africa.[12]

The core of Kobia's argument in his statement above is that institutions in Africa have problems of "authenticity and legitimacy."[13] Particularly applying this to the African political institutions, Kobia argues that the political institutions in Africa are operated in ways that are not true to African identity. They are a *replica* of something *real* in another (European) political context.

In agreement with Kobia's claim, Kinoti also opines that the way by which an African government goes about its economic activities is still colonial. He states that, "A major reason for Africa's failure to develop since independence is the failure of untested development policies . . . developed in the West and applied to Africa."[14] Again in this section, I echo the voices of Kobia and Kinoti who hold that Africa's interaction with the West through colonialism is the undoing of Africa's modern politics. The problem of modern Africa resides in the ideas, knowledge, and practices that Africa borrowed or inherited from the West. While I will paint more pictures in chapter 4 to illustrate this reality, one picture that comes to mind here is the biblical image of David in Saul's military attire (1 Sam 17). David was in a war outfit that hampered his free movement as a young soldier of Yahweh.

Presently, Africa is fighting the battle of underdevelopment, but with unsuitable political weaponry. As such, the economic backwardness of the African nations is traced to political decisions and actions that are alien to its

---

12. Kobia, 52.
13. Kobia, 52.
14. Kinoti, *Hope for Africa*, 26.

people.¹⁵ For Africa's political system to win the battle against underdevelopment, it must be robed in war attire that is cut to its size and employ the use of ammunition that it is skilful with.

As we shall see in chapter 5, the development theory that underlies nation-state political practices in contemporary Africa has brought about critical deviation in African developmental-political worldview. The development theory that underlies traditional African developmental-political practices does not fundamentally regard development as physical and material sophistication.¹⁶ As we shall see in chapter 3, in Yoruba development thoughts, development is simply having peace. Hence, to pursue peace is to pursue development. When there is peace, there is development. Whereas this peace has to do with physical and material possession, it basically entails, and is based on a four-dimensional relationship – good relationship with the supreme being, self, community, and environment. This is one fundamental distortion in African developmental-political thought by virtue of African contact with the West.

Another distortion that occurred has to do with the role of a political leader. From the African perspective of politics, as I shall discuss in chapter 4, a political leader exists solely to ensure peace, which is the foundation and synonym of development. He ensures peace in the society by safeguarding the four-dimensional relationship; a leader's failure to do this results in a chaotic society. Hence, the critical African developmental-political thought is that pursuit of peace (development) is the essence of political leadership. Meanwhile, this thought is encapsulated in African spirituality that manifests in beliefs and practices that give deep reference to the spiritual universe. In chapter 5, I argue that modernization theory that underlies African nation-state politics has brought about remarkable distortion to this African spiritual identity.

The African developmental-political thoughts, which translate into daily practices and rooted in spirituality, have some biblical correlation. This is my argument in chapter 6. This point therefore culminated into my central argument that, the biblical restoration of African spiritual identity, defined

---

15. Kinoti, 25–26; Kobia, *Courage to Hope*, 42; Mugambi, "Religion and Social Reconstruction," 21–22.

16. Njoh, *Tradition, Culture and Development*, 2.

by a four-dimensional relationship, manifested in daily life, and ensured by political leadership, will serve Africa well in its quest against underdevelopment. The spiritual identity that pursues peace – peace that is based on a four-dimensional relationship – is a biblical development principle that the African traditional political system could relate with. But this has been distorted by the development theory underlying contemporary nation-state politics.

This book talks about a "biblical restoration" of this identity. In themselves, and their "raw" traditional form, I observe in this study that Yoruba traditional political thoughts and practices are not without significant flaws. When critically examined in the light of God's word, some traditional political thoughts and practices have negative long- or short-term effects on development. Hence, in my call for the restoration of African political identity for the sake of ensuring development, I only advocate for the ones that survive the scrutiny of the holy word of God, which is used as a corrective measure for the flawed Yoruba thoughts and practices.

The Uniqueness of the Book

Many scholars have undertaken studies similar to my intention here. For instance, Emmanuel Katongole wrote a book titled *The Sacrifice of Africa* which he subtitled "Political theology for Africa,"[17] where he dedicated a good number of pages to appraising, and praising many people who have engaged themselves in development works in Africa, "in a small way."[18] He left a message of hope for his readers that development is possible in Africa. It can happen if each person (particularly Christians) can make their contribution in a small way.

Interestingly, the majority of the people Katongole appraises and praises in his book are nonpoliticians in the popular sense of politics. By doing this he left his reader with an implication that each of us has to be our own politician in our own way, taking necessary actions when required, without waiting for the intervention of the political leadership. Meanwhile, in his work that can be regarded as political theology of development, Katongole's attention as a

---

17. Katongole, *Sacrifice of Africa*.
18. Katongole, loc. 21, 369, 1562, 1565, 1643, 1645, 2170, Kindle.

theologian is only directed towards politics and development. The scope of the book does not put any notable focus on cultural thoughts and practices.

Another example of scholarly work that seeks to address the issue of development by applying African philosophical thought was carried out by Adeyemi Ademowo and Noah Balogun. In their work titled "Proverbs, Value and the Development Question in Contemporary Africa: A Case Study of Yoruba Proverbs," they made a collection of some Yoruba proverbs from which they addressed the issue of development. While Ademowo and Balogun's work employed Yoruba proverbs (which partly inform Yoruba philosophical thoughts on development) to recommend theories of development that are African in nature, it does not have any recognisable link with theology, nor does it obviously relate to politics.

These two works are examples of similar Africanised development approaches I use in this book. As seen in these two cases, many writers (both theological and nontheological scholars) have attempted to address the issue of development in Africa using this similar approach.[19] Meanwhile, relatively little has been done in bringing African traditional political flavour (particularly in Yoruba culture) purged and forged in the furnace of the holy Scripture, to formulate a quintessentially African political theology of development. It is therefore important to provide a theological voice that speaks to the issue of development in Africa by promoting native political thinking about development.

Methodology and the Making of the Book

In this book, I do a theological construct (a contextual political theology of development) from three sources: (1) Yoruba people's traditional political practices and philosophical thoughts, (2) Contemporary political-development theory in modernization, and (3) the Scripture. There are two Yoruba cultural phenomena under study to formulate this contextual political theology of development – (1) their fundamental thoughts on development and politics; and (2) historical political practices and thoughts. The formulation

---

19. Examples of such scholars are: Opande and Barasa, "Locating Sustainable Development"; Ndlovu and Ncube, "Philosophy of Sustainable Development"; Okullu, *Church and State*.

of the contextual political theology of development as intended in this study is based on these two phenomena.

Three related theological works serve as the primary inspiration behind this study:

(1) Joseph Healey and Donald Sybertz's *Towards an African Narrative Theology*, which is a cultural, linguistic work that gathered Sukuma (of Tanzania) proverbs, myths, and stories to develop Christian theology such as Christology and Ecclesiology;[20]

(2) James Nkansah-Obrempong's doctoral dissertation, "Visual Theology: Some Akan Cultural Symbols, Metaphors, Proverbs and Myths about God and Their Implications for Doing Christian Theology,"[21] which draws some significant implications of Akan cultural symbols, metaphors, proverbs, and myths about God, for the purpose of doing a Christian doctrine of God;

(3) Emmanuel Katongole's *Sacrifice of Africa*, which tells stories that redirected Christian involvement in development.

The first two works are similar in that they both draw their theological formulations from African cultural elements, that is, proverbs, myths, stories, symbols, etc. While Healey and Sybertz apply these elements in the formulation of some selected Christian doctrines, Nkansah-Obrempong focuses his applications only on the doctrine of God. I have followed in their footsteps by drawing theological implications from Yoruba cultural elements (historical political narratives, traditional practices, proverbs, sayings, and common words) to formulate a Christian doctrine on development-oriented politics.

Katongole's *Sacrifice of Africa* paints a critical perspective in this study in the way it gives a new definition to politics. Although not directly stated, one of the messages that Katongole passes across is that everybody has a political role of bringing about development in society. We must first serve the justice we expect to see in society. We must first deal with any threat to human wellbeing in our community in our own way. If we find ourselves in political offices like Thomas Sankara, we should strive for a revolutionary leadership that is marked by intellectual clarity, revolutionary madness,

---

20. Healey and Sybertz, *Towards an African Narrative*.
21. Nkansah-Obrempong, *Visual Theology*.

commitment, and sacrifice.[22] More especially, the church should not be left out in sociopolitical actions that will bring about the wellbeing of the society.

The first Yoruba cultural phenomenon under study was Yoruba philosophical thoughts provided in their proverbs and oral traditions, as Mbiti asserted that proverbs are one of the places where a people's philosophy can be known.[23] Over two thousand proverbs were collated both on the field and in the literature. The literature I will use include: *Egberun Ijinle Owe Yoruba Pelu Itumo ati Iloo Won ni Ede Geesi: 1000 Yoruba Proverbs with Their Translation and Usage in English Language;*[24] *Akojopo Owe Yoruba fun Orundun Kokanlelogun: A Compendium of Yoruba Proverbs for the 21st Century;*[25] and *Alo Ninu Asa Yoruba.*[26]

The available proverbs were screened and analysed using Healey and Sybertz's technique. The use of this methodology entails that original proverbs are gathered indiscriminately and then screened into themes that are relevant to the discussion at hand.[27] The proverbs and sayings serve as a source of illumination into Yoruba developmental-political thoughts discussed in this study.

The second phenomenon under study of Yoruba traditional political practices is historical in nature. Therefore, I will delve into this by tracing Yoruba political practices from the story of their origin to the present-day traditional political practice. Hence, "traditional practices" in this study are not limited to the practices of the past. It also entails some practices that are peculiar to Yoruba people in the present time. This is because "it would be wrong to imagine that everything traditional has been changed or forgotten so much that no traces of it are to be found."[28] Information was largely gathered through library resources; however, supplementary information was also acquired through interviews, participant observations, and focus groups. Among other library resources, some texts that largely served as my sources of information are:

---

22. Katongole, *Sacrifice of Africa*, location 1047.
23. Mbiti, *African Religions and Philosophy*, 1.
24. Babade, *Egberun Ijinle Owe Yoruba*.
25. Jejeniwa and Babatunde, *Akojopo Owe Yoruba Fun*.
26. Agbaje, *Alo Ninu Asa Yoruba*.
27. Healey and Sybertz, *Towards an African Narrative*, 43–47.
28. Mbiti, *African Religions and Philosophy*, xii.

Samuel Johnson's *The History of the Yorubas: From the Earliest Time to the beginning of the British Protectorate*, which, according to Professor Toyin Falola (a Yoruba Professor) of the University of Texas, "has acquired the stature of a 'standard text.'"[29] In the layout and analysis of the book, one can liken Samuel Johnson's work on Yoruba people to that of Josephus about the Jewish people.

Samuel Ajayi Crowther's *A Brief History of the Yoruba People*:[30] Crowther was the first African Anglican bishop, and known for the first translation of the Bible to the Yoruba language. Although this is a very small book, Crowther's personality in the history of the Yoruba race makes the book a significant tool for this study.

G. J. Afolabi Ojo's *Yoruba Culture: A Geographical Analysis*:[31] Unlike Johnson and Crowther who based their discussion on Yoruba people up to the nineteenth century, Ojo goes as far as discussing the Yoruba culture up to the contemporary time particularly until 1971 when the book was published. The discussion of the book covers the following areas: the area of Yoruba culture, their economies, settlements, layout, and morphology of their towns, religion, philosophy, and art.

In addition to the texts highlighted above, I also consulted some current literature. More especially, works of scholars such as Toyin Falola were of great importance. Falola is an accomplished and celebrated Nigerian-trained professor of history.[32] Although his historical works transcend Yoruba culture, a good number of his works focus on Yoruba people. In addition to his works, some other modern Yoruba history books were also consulted.

In addition to the library resources, movies by Yoruba filmmakers, both secular and Christian, were also examined. Some of these movies include: *Oduduwa*[33] which narrates the story of Oduduwa's descent to Ile Ife and his intervention in the people's predicaments of the time; *Opa Oramiyan*[34] which depicts the danger of manipulating the oracle in the selection of a king; *Esin*

---

29. Falola, *Yoruba Gurus*, 32.
30. Crowther, *Brief History of the Yoruba*.
31. Ojo, *Yoruba Culture*.
32. "Professor Toyin Falola | Centre for African Studies," accessed 29 October 2019, http://www.africanstudies.uct.ac.za/cas/professor-toyin-falola.
33. Andy, *Oduduwa*.
34. Quadri, *Opa Oranmiyan*.

Ajoji which provides Christian insight into the implication of traditional political practice for development.

Intensive and semi-intensive interviews and informal conversations were conducted with fifty people with career and social status such as academic historians, politicians, traditional ruler (king), clergies, legal practitioner, and traditional chiefs serving in kings' palaces. A focus group session was conducted at the palace of Alaafin of Oyo, which is considered the ancient political headquarters of the Yoruba people.[35] For the participant observations, visits were made to five Yoruba palaces: Ooni of Ife (historical and spiritual headquarters of the Yoruba people), Oluwo of Iwo, Onimeiran of Meiran, Alajasa of Ajasa, and Alaafin of Oyo.

In addition to participant observations in kings' palaces, visits were also made to some prominent Yoruba ancient towns such as Ogbomosho, Ilorin, Ibadan, Abeokuta, Oyo, Iwo, and Ejigbo. Unlike the participant observations carried out in the palaces whose aim was to observe the practices in the palace courts by the traditional rulers, the second form of observation aimed at studying the traditional way of life of the common people.

The theological method to be used in this theological formulation shall be Critical Correlation. According to David Tracy, the critical correlation approach, otherwise called the revisionist model, has to do with "the dramatic confrontation, the mutual illuminations, and corrections, the possible basic reconciliation between the principal values, cognitive claims, and existential faiths of both reinterpreted post-modern consciousness and a reinterpreted Christianity."[36]

In this study, I mean to critique the modernization theory, which is the theory behind African nation-state politics, by placing it side by side with the African traditional political system and African understanding of development. However, this does not imply that every bit of the theory would be discarded. The use of Critical Correlation approach in the study sheds the light of God's word on Yoruba culture and contemporary developmental-political theories embedded in modernization theory to formulate a contextual political theology of development (Figure 1).

---

35. Johnson, *History of the Yorubas*, 11; Falola and Heaton, *History of Nigeria*, 24.
36. Tracy, *Blessed Rage for Order*, 32.

```
          The Scripture
         ↙      ↓      ↘
  Yoruba Culture ↔ Modernization Theory
         ↘      ↓      ↙
   Contextual Political Theology of
              Development
```

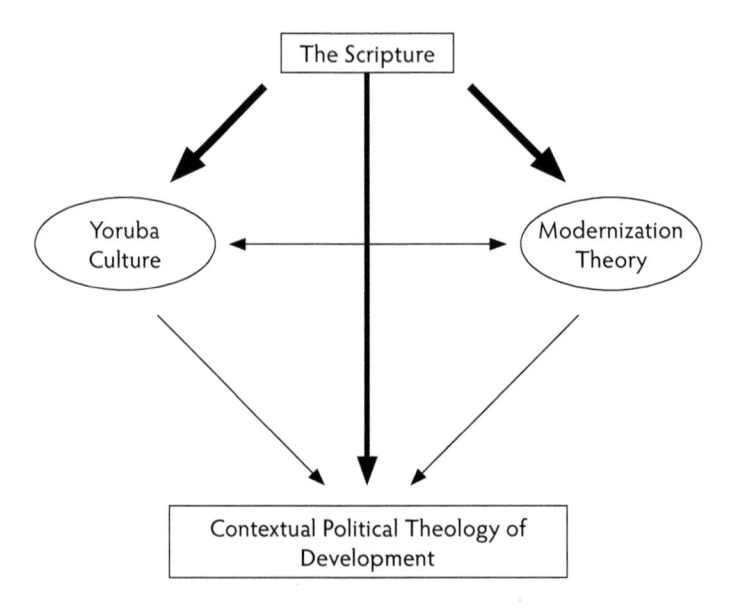

Figure 1. Use of Critical Correlation in Constructing Contextual Political Theology of Development

A Brief Note about the Yoruba People

Yoruba is one of Nigeria's largest ethnic groups. The other two largest ethnic groups in the country are Igbo and Hausa/Fulani. Nigeria is said to be the most populous country in Africa with an estimated population of 206,139,587 million in 2020.[37] Christianity and Islam are the two major religions in the country. Islam is widely practiced in the north among the Hausa/Fulani people, while Christianity is the dominant religion among the Igbo people in the east.

Ever since its independence from British rule in 1960, Nigeria has consistently experienced political instability. This political instability led the nation into a civil war that lasted from 1967 to 1970.[38] The nature of politics in Nigeria is one that is usually divided along religious, ethnic, and regional identities. "Christians from the south fear domination by the slightly more

---

37. "Population, total - Nigeria," accessed October 18, 2021, https://data.worldbank.org/indicator/SP.POP.TOTL?locations=NG.

38. Falola and Heaton, *History of Nigeria*, 8.

populous northern Muslims at the federal level. At the state level, ethnic minorities fear domination by larger ethnic groups: the Hausa-Fulani in the north, the Yoruba in the southwest, and Igbo in the southeast."[39]

Nigeria is grouped into six geopolitical zones, clusters of states with people of the same or similar ethnicity. These are southeast, south-south, southwest, northeast, northwest, and north-central. The population of Yoruba people cut across the six states of southwest geopolitical zones, namely, Oyo, Osun, Ondo, Ekiti, Ogun, and Lagos. They can also be found in parts of Kwara and Kogi states, as well as parts of Nigeria's two neighbouring countries, Benin Republic and Togo.

Among the Yoruba, Christianity, Islam, and traditional religion constitute 59.75 percent, 39.43 percent, and 0.26 percent respectively.[40] Despite the significant number of Muslims coexisting with Christians, it is widely noted that Yorubaland rarely experiences religious crises.[41] This implies that the Yoruba society is relatively characterised by peace. According to a statistical report from the office of the Nigerian inspector general of police, Mohammed Adamu, it is also remarked that southwestern Nigeria records the lowest crime rate.[42]

In this book, I have capitalised on the peace-loving nature of the Yoruba people, built on their traditional thought that wellbeing, or rather development, is primarily about peace. As I have noted earlier, in the Yoruba traditional thought, development is fundamentally defined as presence of peace in individual lives and society. Therefore, I shall explore their traditional political thoughts and practices in their pursuit of peace and wellbeing in the society.

Yoruba is a tonal language. Two words with different meanings and pronunciations may be spelt the same way, for example, *owó* (money) and *òwò* (trade). Accents are therefore used to indicate differences in pronunciations. Vowels with a grave accent are pronounced in a low tone, ones in acute accent are pronounced in a high tone, while the ones with no accent are pronounced in a middle tone. For the Yoruba expressions in this book, I follow the modern orthography of the language. All translations are done in such

---

39. Falola and Heaton, 8.
40. "Yoruba in Nigeria," *Joshua Project*, 2021, accessed 18 October 2021, https://joshuaproject.net/people_groups/16057/NI.
41. Akinade, "Enduring Legacy," 138–53.
42. Sowole, "Nigeria"; Dada, "South-West Records."

a way that the exact meaning in Yoruba is retained and at the same time are readable in English.

Conclusion

In this chapter, I drew a line of correlation between Africa's underdevelopment and inauthentic political practices and thoughts. I gave a preview of the contribution of subsequent chapters to this theme. I discussed the uniqueness of the work, the inspiration behind it, and how the information therein was put together. I ended the chapter with a brief note about the Yoruba people. In the chapter that follows, I will elaborate the framework within which the book is written – contextual political theology of development.

CHAPTER 2

The Contextual Political Theology of Development

Introduction

The aim of this chapter is to etch out the peculiarity and the need for contextual political theology of development. I shall discuss its nature as it pursues the holistic wellbeing of humanity. The chapter also reviews Christian development practices, both from political and nonpolitical points of view, in light of the contextual political theology of development. In the review of Christian development practices, I make a special reference to the prosperity gospel. The chapter closes with a call for contextual political theology of development.

The Emphasis on Relationship with God in Holistic Development Practice

In this section, my argument is that a development agenda must cater to all the existential components of human life. When one domain is left uncatered to, a form of poverty is bred. The human existential domain that has mostly been left unaddressed is the spiritual domain. Popular development practices have often overlooked this critical aspect of human life. Much has been done to ensure the wellbeing of human nonspiritual domains at the expense of the spiritual domain. In this section I will define holistic development in relation to all the human existential domains. I will indicate how these domains are interrelated and why special emphasis should be given to the spiritual domain. I will first begin the section by explaining the narrow and broad views of development.

The Meaning of Holistic Development Practice

Development thinkers have tried to define poverty both in the narrow and broad sense. The narrow view of poverty is exemplified in Abhijit Banerjee and Esther Duflo's description of poverty. They describe poor people as people who live on 99 cents daily, with "limited access to information – newspaper, television, and books," and do not know any viable cure for the disease in their ailing children.[1]

Also talking of the narrow view of poverty, Nkansah-Obrempong sees poverty "as a condition where people are involuntarily deprived of certain basic human needs essential for life such as food, clothing, medical care, and housing and such conditions reduce them to become beggars."[2] As such, the narrow view of poverty is that people lack physical needs that are necessary for quality human survival. To talk about the narrow view of poverty is to talk about physical poverty.

On the other hand, there is also a development perspective that deals with poverty in a broader sense. Taking a broad view of poverty, Elizondo remarks, "Poverty means the lack of something. It means not having the basic necessities of life, such as shelter, food, drink, clothing, *a space of belonging*, and a *space of freedom*"[3] (italics added). With this, he points out that poverty is not just the lack of physical needs, but also nonphysical needs.[4]

Also speaking about a broader view of poverty, Myers says, "Poverty is a complicated social issue involving all areas of life – physical, social, cultural, and spiritual."[5] As I shall discuss in the subsequent paragraphs, human life is complex. Nevertheless, in the complexity of human life, poverty simply entails lack of something that is needed – physical or nonphysical. A human life requires physical and nonphysical needs. These two categories of need are interrelated and interdependent. I shall discuss this interrelation and

---

1. Banerjee and Duflo, *Poor Economics*, ix.
2. Nkansah-Obrempong, *Foundations for African Theological*, 178.
3. Elizondo, "Culture, the Option," 158.
4. Elizondo, 158–61.
5. Myers, *Walking with the Poor*, 132.

interdependence in the paragraphs that follow, from which I shall establish my definition of holistic development.

When we consider their existential components, all human beings possess both physical and nonphysical domains. Put together, human beings have the following domains: physical domain, intellectual domain, emotional domain, domain of the will, and spiritual domain. Each of the domains requires certain needs to sustain the proper chain of human existence.

The physical domain requires certain aspects such as feeding, exercise, respiration, shelter, sex, and health. The intellectual domain requires the need for knowledge and information acquisition. The emotional domain requires love, peace, and sense of fulfilment. The domain of the will longs for freedom, ability to make choices, and power (a certain territory of dominion). The spiritual domain is the central part of a human that seeks to know what life is all about; it is the part of humans that seeks an affinity with something powerful and beyond humans; it is the part of humans seeking freedom from evil, and the desire for good. Narayan et al. affirm this in their findings about human voices on poverty and development:

> Across continents, countries, contexts, and types of people, a good quality of life includes *material wellbeing* [physical], which is often expressed as having enough; *bodily wellbeing* [physical], which includes being strong, well and looking good; *social wellbeing*, including caring for and settling children; *having self-respect, peace and good relations* [emotional] in the family and community; *having security*, including civil peace, a safe and secure environment, personal physical security and *confidence in the future* [spiritual]; and *having freedom of choice and action* [intellectual and will], including being able to help other people in the community.[6] (Italics added)

All the phrases I have put in italics are the needs that Narayan et al. have identified as the essential needs for a good quality life, which development aims to attain. They are the basic needs required by each of the human existential domains.

---

6. Narayan et al., *Crying Out for Change*, 21.

In his discourse on the definition and perspectives on poverty, Bryant Myers does a review of the works of four development scholars: Robert Chambers, John Friedman, Jayakumar Christian, and Ravi Jayakaran.[7] In Chambers' perspective, poverty is seen as entanglement. The poor household has a "'cluster of disadvantages.' This cluster has five elements: the household is poor, physically weak [deficiency in the physical domain], isolated [deficiency in the emotional domain], vulnerable, and powerless [deficiency in the domain of the will]." All these are an interactive system that Chamber calls "the deprivation or poverty trap."[8]

According to Friedman, poverty is seen as lack of access to social power (deficiency in the domain of the will), and he claims that "poor households are excluded and need to be empowered."[9] Talking of Jayakumar Christian's perspective on poverty, Myers summarizes him as seeing poverty as disempowerment.

> Christian sees the poor household embedded in a complex framework of interacting systems. These systems include a personal system that includes psychology and self-understanding; a social system, similar to Friedman's; a spiritual system [deficiency in the spiritual domain], which is personal and social; a cultural system, which includes worldview, and a biophysical system. Christian argues that the poor find themselves trapped inside a system of disempowerment [deficiency in the domain of the will] made up of these interacting systems.[10]

Ravi Jayakaran's perspective of poverty is that poverty is a lack of freedom to grow, and that the poor are "wrapped in a series of restrictions and limitations in four areas of life: physical [deficiency in the physical domain], mental [deficiency in the intellectual domain], social, and spiritual [deficiency in the spiritual domain]."[11] As I have indicated in the square brackets, the perspectives of poverty as offered by these four scholars all refer to a deficiency of a need in one or more areas of human existential components.

---

7. Myers, *Walking with the Poor*, 115–32.
8. Myers, "Poverty," 689.
9. Myers, 690.
10. Myers, 691.
11. Myers, *Walking with the Poor*, 131.

Deficiency in Human Existential Domains and Poverty Breeders

The effective way to address the problem of poverty is to ensure that all human existential domains are catered for. This is because if an aspect of human existential component is not addressed, it creates a void that consequently leads to a form of poverty, which in turn can create another form of poverty.

The void triggers other forms of poverty like this: a person who lacks proper education has poverty of the mind (a deficiency in one domain of his/her existential being). This can translate into a lack of productivity in making material wealth. Consequently, such person is said to be materially poor. This is an example of how the intellectual domain can affect physical domain resulting in material poverty. Another consequence can be that lack of finance (deficiency of physical domain) for someone else can lead to intellectual poverty in that such a person may not be able to afford any means of education by virtue of not having the means to have his/her education paid for.

To cite another example, it has been realised that negative emotions (for instance anger, poverty of the emotional domain) often have negative effects on human physical health.[12] In this way, the emotional domain affects the physical domain, causing physical sickness, another form of poverty.

The cyclic effect is also applicable when we consider the common saying, "A hungry man is an angry man." The "hungry man" gets angry and this provokes a reaction in him leading to an uproar in the society. Ayittey refers to this kind of reaction when he indicates that in African nation-state politics, the angry peasants (angry because they are hungry) are withdrawing their commitment to the national leadership and fighting back, "sabotaging the property of the predatory state and attacking its officials."[13] In this way, the poverty of physical domain – hunger – has led to a reaction in the emotional domain, culminating in crisis. The cyclic effect repeats itself. This gives a clear indication that humans' physical and nonphysical domains are interrelated and interdependent.

---

12. The connection between human mental state and wellness of the physical body is broadly discussed in books such as *When the Body Says No: Understanding the Stress-Disease Connection* by Gabor Maté.

13. Ayittey, *Africa in Chaos*, 222.

One important thing to know from the foregoing discussion is that deficiencies in any human existential domain can translate to physical poverty. In addition to causing physical poverty, deficiencies in any of the human existential domains also cause other underdevelopment breeders. What are underdevelopment breeders?

Since I hold a broader perspective of development in this study, I view development as a state whereby all factors of human holistic wellbeing are in place. When any of these factors is missing, it breeds underdevelopment. Economic prosperity is one of the factors of development; lack of it breeds underdevelopment. Intellectual wellbeing is another factor of development; lack of it breeds underdevelopment.

Ademowo and Balogun are right when they noted that "ethnic/religious violence, political unrest, lack of moral value, lack of visionary leadership and wanton poverty" are critical factors that bring about underdevelopment.[14] For Amartya Sen, underdevelopment is bred where there is lack of "basic opportunity of healthcare, or functional education, or gainful employment, or economic or social security."[15] For Paul Collier, underdevelopment is bred when a nation is trapped in conflict, insufficient natural resources, bad governance and being landlocked with hostile neighbours.[16]

All negative factors (majority of which are mentioned above) that create unfavourable condition for holistic human wellbeing are said to be underdevelopment breeders. Meanwhile, all these negative factors, as I have argued earlier in this subsection, are mostly as a result of deficiency in one or more human existential domains.

Talking about poverty in physical terms, we cannot effectively address physical poverty without addressing it from the broader perspective. There are certain conditions (underdevelopment breeders) that create a good environment for physical poverty to thrive. In other words, dealing with poverty is best achieved when we deal with it by also dealing with other underdevelopment breeders. This is because looking at poverty in a broader sense, it goes with a web of many things – injustices, sickness, limitations, bad governance, war, etc. As such, it is strongly asserted in this study that, poverty can be the

---

14. Ademowo and Balogun, "Proverbs, Value and Development," 149–50.
15. Sen, *Development as Freedom*, 3.
16. Collier, *Bottom Billion*.

cause of the other underdevelopment breeders and vice versa; and that the way to effectively address the problem of underdevelopment is, to a large extent, by addressing all the other factors that negatively affect human wellbeing. In the subsection that follows, I shall consider the interplay of underdevelopment breeders, focusing on the example of bad governance and poverty trap. I focus on these two examples because of their centrality to this study.

The Interplay of Bad Politics and Poverty Trap as Underdevelopment Breeders

Scholars have intensely debated the role politics plays in African development. While some thinkers believe that bad governance is the undoing of African development, others hold the contrary opinion. Jeffery Sachs is a development thinker who argues that the problem of underdevelopment in Africa is not a result of bad political governance.

> Both the critics of African governance and the critics of Western violence and meddling have it wrong. Politics, at the end of the day, simply cannot explain Africa's prolonged economic crisis. The claim that Africa's corruption is the basic source of the problem does not withstand practical experience or serious scrutiny. During the past decade I witnessed close at hand how relatively well-governed countries in Africa, such as Ghana, Malawi, Mali, and Senegal, failed to prosper, whereas societies in Asia perceived to have extensive corruption, such as Bangladesh, India, Indonesia, and Pakistan, enjoyed rapid economic growth. . . . African countries lag behind in economic growth even when they are perceived to be less corrupt than their Asian counterparts.[17]

Sachs notes that politics (i.e. bad governance) is not the fundamental cause of poverty in Africa as many thinkers have asserted. As he talks about the relationship between bad governance and poverty, Sachs also notes that bad governance has the possibility to thwart the prosperity of a nation. But more importantly is the effect of poverty trap: "I realised that although predatory government can soundly trounce economic development, good governance

---

17. Sachs, *End of Poverty*, 190–91.

and market reforms are not sufficient to guarantee growth if the country is in a poverty trap."[18] Rather than always blame leadership for all poverty issues in Africa, Sachs blames the poverty trap. So, what is poverty trap?

According to Sachs, the poverty trap is a series of unfortunate phenomena that people do not have power over, but which moves them from poverty to poverty in a vicious cycle. He writes, "Many African governments are desperately trying to do the right thing, but they face enormous obstacles of poverty, disease, ecological crisis, and geopolitical neglect or worse."[19] In Sachs' view, one fundamental thing that needs to be fixed for Africa to overcome poverty is the poverty trap.

In his response to Sachs's argument, Easterly goes back to a 1984 corruption report from International Country Risk Guide, and a democracy rating reported by the University of Maryland called Polity IV. Studying these reports, Easterly categorizes the countries with the worst rating in both corruption and democracy as "bad governments," and analyzes their growth rate. He finds that "While poor countries did worse, it's also true that the twenty-four countries with bad governments in 1984 had significantly lower growth in 1985 to the present: 1.3 percentage points slower than the rest."[20] With this, Easterly argues that bad governance has a significant negative effect on the economic poverty level of a nation.

However, Easterly acknowledges that, as it is true that bad government is likely to create poor countries, so also "poor countries are much more likely to have bad government." He then wonders as to which one is the cause and which one is the effect. He writes:

> When we control for both initial poverty and bad government, it is bad government that explains the slower growth. The coefficient on initial per capita is not significantly different from zero, once we control for bad government, this is still true if we limit the definition of bad governance to corruption alone. The recent stagnation of the poorest countries appears to have more

---

18. Sachs, 195.
19. Sachs, 207.
20. Easterly, "Big Push Déjà Vu," 100–101.

to do with awful government than with a poverty trap, contrary to Sachs' hypothesis.[21]

Therefore, in Easterly's view, one fundamental thing that needs to be fixed for Africa to overcome poverty is bad governance.

I have presented the arguments and views of Sachs and Easterly on whether poverty trap or bad governance is the cause of poverty in Africa. Meanwhile, everything that Sachs considers as poverty traps are all in themselves underdevelopment breeders. For instance, disease, ecological crisis, and geopolitical neglect which are examples of poverty traps in Sachs's view, have in themselves the tendency to create a good environment for underdevelopment to thrive.

Likewise, when we consider the sting of bad governance in Africa, how this has been unfavourable to a nation's development, bad governance also fits into the category of underdevelopment breeders within the context of this study. Poverty is bred when a society is badly governed. Hence, bad governance itself is an underdevelopment breeder.

Therefore, poverty traps and bad governance should not be categorised as if they are members of two different sports teams, as Sachs and Easterly seem to be doing; but members of the same team working together towards the same goal. The end result of bad governance is underdevelopment. Also, the end result of poverty traps is underdevelopment. All of these factors interplay with one another and create the atmosphere for underdevelopment. And this fact is scripturally supported. If we bring poverty trap and bad governance to the Scripture, what is the biblical theological view of the fundamental problem of poverty in Africa?

The Scripture affirms the "bad governance creates poverty" theory when it says, "A wicked ruler is as dangerous to the poor as a lion or bear attacking them" (Prov 28:15, TLB). Wickedness in biblical terms implies "a mental disregard for justice, righteousness, truth, honour, virtue."[22] A wicked ruler is therefore a political leader who does not have regard for godly principles that are necessary to foster people's wellbeing. Relating this biblical insight to an instance cited by Jeffery Sachs above, where he notes that some Asian countries thrive in spite of having corrupt leaders, it is an obvious fact that such countries would have attained a greater potential if they had been fortunate

---

21. Easterly, 101.
22. Elwell, "Wickedness."

to have political leaders or systems that were not corrupt. Thus, Proverbs 28:15 is one of the biblical texts that support the view that bad governance creates poverty.

Logically speaking, a nation that thrives in spite of corruption in the political system would have done better if it were free of corruption. One can affirm the greater level of development fortune the nation would have enjoyed if all government funds were rightly spent and duly accounted for, and fairness was embraced in all national affairs. Bad politics or governance is therefore in no way beneficial to the wellbeing of the people of a nation. The bad choices and actions of political leaders consequently turn things upside down and bring about poverty in the lives of the masses.[23]

Then when I place Sachs's "poverty trap causes poverty" theory side-by-side with the Scripture, I note that this argument also finds a biblical basis. My understanding of Sachs's poverty trap theory is that there are natural or unnatural circumstances that are beyond human control, circumstances such as "disease, ecological crisis, and geopolitical neglect or worse."[24]

Meanwhile, some of Sachs's "poverty traps" are circumstances that can be avoided by upholding necessary ethical values. Problems such as corruption and geopolitical neglect can be avoided when citizens of a nation and stakeholders of the international community choose to have respect for the rights of their fellow human beings. Other poverty traps such as diseases and ecological problems can be avoided simply by maintaining a good ethical relationship with the environment. Development practitioners of all orientations agree that "what is morally good and right is bound to the flourishing of human persons and human communities."[25]

Considering the obstacles to development as mentioned by Sachs (i.e. poverty trap), I conclude that they are largely because of human disregard for moral principles, which in biblical terms are regarded as sin. When people fail to do what is good and right, this is biblically regarded as sin (Jas 4:17), and it hampers the wellbeing of a nation (Prov 13:34). Thus, the view that poverty trap causes poverty can be said to be biblically supported.

---

23. Acemoglu and Robinson, *Why Nations Fail*, 68.
24. Sachs, *End of Poverty*, 207.
25. Schweiker, "Theological Ethics," 359.

When we talk about bad governance, we talk about leaders who make moral decisions that are detrimental to society's wellbeing, moral choices such as greed, wickedness, selfishness, revenge and corruption. Likewise, when we talk about poverty traps, we talk about circumstances such as conflicts, poor international relations, national corruption, natural disasters and the like.[26] Also, we talk about moral deficiency that manifests itself in disregard for fundamental human rights, environmental stewardship, tolerance, etc. which are the prime cause of poverty traps.

From the biblical theological point of view, wrong moral choice is the inferred common factor between Sachs's and Easterly's arguments. To talk about both bad governance and poverty trap is largely to talk about choices that are morally wrong; that is, human disregard for what is right and wrong. The biblical theological view asserts that sin is the fundamental cause of poverty. Sin is the fundamental force behind bad governance, and it results in poverty. Likewise, sin is the fundamental force behind, at least, most of the poverty traps, and they also lead to poverty.

Meanwhile, this is not to insinuate that Africans are the only or most sinful people in the world. I have discussed the problem of poverty in this study in terms of material poverty. It is important to note that there is also the immaterial aspect of poverty. If we consider poverty in a broader sense, the entire humanity experiences either material or immaterial poverty or both, as a result of sin.[27] Therefore, one fundamental issue that needs to be resolved in a society that suffers any form of poverty is sin. Meanwhile, sin is a result of the deficiency in the human spiritual domain. How is it so?

The Vitality of Human Spiritual Domain in Development and Politics

The vitality of the spiritual domain of human beings lies in the fact that it is the domain "that most directly relates to God."[28] An individual who suffers poverty of the spiritual domain simply does not have relationship with God. This translates into adverse effects on other domains particularly the domain of the will (Phil 2:13). Such an individual has a deficiency in his capacity to

---

26. Sachs, *End of Poverty*; Collier, *Bottom Billion*.
27. Myers, "Poverty of the Non-Poor," in *Walking with the Poor*, 145–48.
28. Grudem, *Systematic Theology*, 472.

make right moral decisions and ability to love truly, to administer justice, to live at peace with all people, as opposed to an individual who has a quality relationship with God. The quality of humans' relationship with God determines their level of moral standing (Rom 7:15–25).

Relationship with God is a critical human need. When this fails to happen, it is tantamount to the deficiency in the human spiritual domain. A need is not met in the domain and this creates a vacuum, a vacuum that weakens human will to resist moral temptations, and consequently make them yield to sin, the foundation of underdevelopment breeders. Therefore, Bryant Myers is right when he notes that, "the fundamental cause of poverty is spiritual in nature."[29]

> What causes the distortion and injustice in our relationship?.... What separates us within our community, with some doing well and others suffering? . . . Why do we abuse the earth? . . . The answers to these fundamental questions provide us with an explanation for the fundamental cause of poverty. Sin is the root cause of deception, distortion and domination. When God is on the sideline or written out of our story, we do not treat others well. We work instead for what we think life is for.[30]

Every human being needs God to be complete. Humanity is naturally sinful, and this has been the undoing of development fuelled by modernization. God has dealt with the problem of sin by making his Son "who has no sin to be sin for us, so that in him we might become the righteousness of God" (2 Cor 5:21, NIV). Nothing else can fill up the emptiness in the human spiritual domain. Only God can. This vital aspect of development is often left out, and therefore leaves us in the vicious cycle created by all underdevelopment breeders.

Christian theology and the church can find their relevance in playing an important role fighting everything that keeps humanity in spiritual poverty; a fight against "sin, the world, and the devil,"[31] as Henry Okullu rightly states.

The discussion of poverty traps and bad governance in this study has indicated to us that both political officeholders and individual African citizens

---

29. Myers, "Poverty," 694.
30. Myers.
31. Okullu, *Church and State*, xv.

have something they contributed to the state of underdevelopment in Africa. It has been noted in the general discussion on effective development practice that the development agenda will be complete only if it caters for all the existential domains of humanity – material, will, emotion, intellectual, and spiritual.

Through contemporary development practices, so much has been done in Africa to ensure human material and emotional wellbeing – relief, aid, donation and so forth; so much has been done to ensure that people freely express their free will and are happy – fight for justice, freedom of religion and so forth; so much has been done in enriching the human intellect – quality education, accessible information and so forth. Meanwhile, as I shall discuss in chapter 5, contemporary development endeavours cater to all other human existential domains but leave out the spiritual domain.

Contextual political theology of development, in its attempt to address the problem of underdevelopment from the political perspective, acknowledges the role of human spiritual domain as far as wellbeing is concerned. It therefore holds that human spiritual development is as important as sociophysical development. True wellbeing is realised with cordial relationship with God, and relationship with God that manifests in all our human activities. What does African culture teach us about relationship with God in terms of development-oriented politics? Chapters 3 and 4 focus on this, with a case study of the Yoruba people. Meanwhile, in the sections that follow, I shall review other Christian models of development practice and poverty eradication.

Review of Models of Development Practices and Poverty Eradication in the Christian Church

The church at large has always embarked on development programmes. The questions I want to consider in this section are: (1) As the ecumenical body of Christ, what are the approaches that have been in place to combat the challenge of poverty in the world? (2) How holistic are these approaches, in light of the holistic development pursuit of the contextual political theology of development described in the previous section?

As I seek to discuss some of the approaches the church has employed in its fight against poverty, I shall largely do so based on an insight given by Melba Padilla Maggay. According to her, there are four broad models through which the church all around the world seeks to involve itself in rising to the help of the poor and downtrodden.[32]

The City on the Hill: Community as a Way to Change

In this model, Maggay explains the attempts of churches to bring about the apostolic practice in Acts 2:45 where all the believers had everything in common by selling off their personal possessions and bringing their money to the apostles' feet. In this model, the church seeks to bring its members to the level of having their material things in common. It entails that the church models oneness as it serves as an example to the world. Examples of Christian communities who apply this model are "groups such as Sojourners among the urban poor of Washington, DC, Corrymeela in Northern Ireland, some charismatic churches in inner-city London and basic Christian communities (BCC) in Catholic countries such as the Philippines and Latin America."[33]

This model brings us close to the biblical teaching of giving and sharing one another's burden. None of the disciples lacked anything because all those who had money gave to those who did not (Act 4:34). However, for the churches that have settled for this model, they will always have the experience similar to the one the apostolic church had with Ananias and Sapphira. They will have people in their midst whose character and attitude are full of deception.

The weakness of this practice, in the light of holistic development, has to do with the problem of sustainability. This is because this kind of solution naturally reduces human productivity, in that the have-nots are being prevented from using their mental capacity to produce. Talking about this experience in the apostolic time, tradition holds that this practice "was responsible for the later economic collapse of the church at Jerusalem, [so that] much of the ministry of Paul was concerned with raising money in the Gentile churches to assist the poor Christians in Jerusalem (Rom 15:25–29; Gal 2:10)."[34]

---

32. Maggay, *Transforming the Kingdom*, 64–92.
33. Maggay, 64–68.
34. Nixon, "Poverty," 945.

The Idea of Christendom: Building a Christian Cultural Consensus

The idea behind this model is to make "Christian principles dominate as a framework for organizing society."[35] It is a practice of the church to get involved in the sociopolitical affair of the state with the intention of bringing to light its corrupt system. The biblical basis for this model is found in the earthly ministry of Christ. During his earthly ministry, he confronted the powers of his time – Herod and the religiopolitical leaders such as the Pharisees and the Sadducees in his teaching. He also taught people a new way of life that would enhance their social and political wellbeing.[36]

This model is an attempt of the church not to detach itself from how the government treats the poor but to make herself part of the state policy-making that would favour the poor. This has become the culture of the Catholic church in the Philippines and Latin America.[37] One of the possible challenges of Christianity in its ideological involvement in sociopolitical atmosphere, for example as Alan Storkey sets out to do in his work *A Christian Social Perspective*,[38] is how to make the Christian principles relevant to the pluralistic, secular society. How would Christianity claim that its principles are more viable than that of other religions?

Katongole borrows an insight from Villa-Vicencio, offering a practical suggestion to Christianity as it involves itself in the sociopolitical sphere:

> In the end, it seems the only relevant contribution that theology can make is through insights, programmes, and processes shared by all. This is the reason Villa-Vicencio insists that "In a radically pluralistic society the church . . . needs to learn with Bonhoeffer what it means to speak of its most fundamental values in a religionless or secular way. This is perhaps the only way in which it will be heard".[39]

---

35. Maggay, *Transforming the Kingdom*, 71.
36. Storkey, *Jesus and Politics*, 10.
37. Storkey, 74.
38. Storkey, *Christian Social Perspective*.
39. Villa-Vicention, *A Theology of Reconstruction*, 116. Cited in: Katongole, *Sacrifice of Africa*, location 589.

The appeal here is to avoid presenting in a religious term a proposition from the church to the society. In my view, the danger of not using a religious term will lead to the danger of negligence of the human spiritual domain in the long run. The avoidance of spiritual terms would imply that at some point we do not talk about God. That poses a danger to the holistic development endeavour that caters to all human existential domains.

The Gospel of Liberation: Restructuring Power Relations

This model puts much emphasis on liberation theology, which is the quest of the church to provide a teaching that stresses the freedom of the oppressed from the oppressor. It can be otherwise called solidarity with the poor. The church developed this model based on the belief that the poor find themselves in poverty not necessarily due to their laziness or fatalism but occasionally by oppression. The story of the Israelites and Pharaoh in Exodus forms a basic biblical root for this model. A contemporary example of liberation theology is black theology in South Africa.

From the example of black theology in South Africa (which the Anglican archbishop and theologian Desmond Tutu was identified with),[40] one shortcoming of liberation theology is how it can deal with the issue of injustice in society but fails to ensure true reconciliation. The pressure of liberation theology formed part of what liberated the nation of South Africa from apartheid. More so, Tutu's advocacy for liberation and message of reconciliation went hand-in-hand. However, one would doubt the genuineness of reconciliation that took place between the former "oppressors" (the whites) and the former "oppressed" (the blacks). Today there is still an element of tension between the racial communities of South Africa. A look into a website article by the South African Human Rights Commission (SAHRC).[41]

The article titled "Whites are not an Oppressed Minority Group in SA, says SAHRC" is a response to the accusation by minority white South Africans against majority black South Africans. Through a careful reading of the article,

---

40. Francis Anekwe Oborji, "Archbishop Tutu & South African Black Theology," *TheCable*, last modified December 27, 2021, accessed April 18, 2023, https://www.thecable.ng/archbishop-tutu-south-african-black-theology.

41. SAHRC, "Whites Are Not an Oppressed Minority Group in SA, Says SAHRC," last modified November 23, 2020, accessed April 1, 2023, https://www.sahrc.org.za/index.php/sahrc-media/news/item/2525-whites-are-not-an-oppressed-minority-group-in-sa-says-sahrc.

one will be able to identify the bottom line of the story, which is that the white minority still harbours some sense of insecurity towards the black, evidence that the journey of reconciliation has not led to the final destination.

Practice of Compassion: The Development Model

This model is the most widely practised model by the Christian church in alleviating poverty. It is modelled on Jesus's teaching about the good Samaritan who attended to the immediate need of the wounded traveller (Luke 20:25–37). Many missionaries who travelled to Africa to propagate the gospel used this approach. For instance, Christian figures like Mother Teresa became a symbol of compassion to the poor, using this model.

This approach brings immediate relief and instant provision for the poor. Churches are faced with the temptation of opting for the easy way of ensuring temporal solutions to poverty. And when what has been offered eventually finishes; the poor come back to their state of being poor. And more importantly, it tends to keep people dependent on material things rather than God, leading to spiritual poverty.

Considering all the four approaches the church has employed in combating the problem of poverty, one notable threat that runs across all the approaches is the tendency for social-spiritual dichotomy. Almost all the approaches are likely to forego or overemphasize either the social or spiritual element of the gospel. If this happens, then a development practice ceases to be holistic. Hence, the next subsection calls the Christian church to work for the proper balance of the two important elements of the gospel.

Christian Evangelism and Social Services

The primary task that Christ gave to the church is to proclaim the good news. He gave this instruction to the disciples when he sent them out to preach, saying, "Go and preach, 'The Kingdom of heaven is near!' Heal the sick, bring the dead back to life, heal those who suffer from dreaded skin diseases, and drive out demons" (Matt 10:7–8, GNT). It is quite evident in the text that evangelism and social actions go together – sharing our faith and demonstrating good works. Churches have made the error of overemphasizing one over the other. According to Maggay, a section of the church is of the opinion that "evangelism is social action," putting emphasis on spiritual enrichment in their dealings with the society; while the other is of the opinion that "social action is evangelism,"[42] putting much emphasis on bringing about sociophysical development as they approach the needs of the society.

Overemphasis on either of these two principal elements of the gospel strips the gospel of its holistic nature. While a spirituality-centred model opens people up to the blessings of kingdom's spiritual benefits, it deprives them of enjoying the sociophysical blessings.[43] The work-centred model deprives people of the fullness of God's blessing in that their hungry soul is not fed by the truth of God's word.

sWhen the nonspiritual components of human aspects of life also have their relevant needs met, this brings much joy to their Creator whose intention is to see his people enjoying all the goodness of life as indicated in Luke 4:18–19. Hence, Nkansah-Obrempong rightly concludes the matter when he submits that these two elements of the gospel – spiritual enrichment and social services – are inseparably one.[44]

The Prosperity Gospel as a Means of Development Intervention

Although the theological correctness of the prosperity gospel has been questioned by many scholars; this study notes that the prosperity gospel is a form of response to the challenge of poverty and other social crises in Africa. As it is noted in the preceding section, the church over the years of its existence has made different forms of attempts to combat the problem of poverty. The prosperity gospel is one of those attempts by the Christian church, although it is particularly prevalent among the Pentecostals. In this section, my task is to affirm this claim and then do a theological appraisal of the teaching of the prosperity gospel in light of its impact on development in Africa. I will begin the section by considering two ways in which the prosperity gospel directly or indirectly attacks the root cause of poverty in Africa.

---

42. Maggay, *Transforming the Kingdom*, 23.
43. Larbi, "Theological Examination of Poverty," 167.
44. Nkansah-Obrempong, "Holistic Gospel," 202–5.

The Prosperity Gospel as Directed against Ignorance

The Bible indicates that lack of knowledge can bring about destruction (Hos 4:6). Isaiah notes that the people of God would go into captivity because they did not have knowledge (Isa 5:13). Proverbs also teaches that the way to gather strength is through knowledge (Prov 24:5). We can therefore deduce from the given scriptural texts that accumulation of relevant knowledge should always culminate in freedom.

It has been the pursuit of many ministers of God, who are known for prosperity preaching, to empower people with knowledge, believing that if people are well informed, they will be liberated. I once personally heard a message of Bishop Oyedepo of Nigeria (president of the Living Faith worldwide) which put much emphasis on why people have to be informed. One of those practices that are encouraged in his church is that members should be ardent consumers of knowledge. He often challenges his church members to buy and read as many books as they can. He wrote a number of books that particularly emphasize the role that knowledge plays in personal productivity. Such books include *Towards Mental Exploits* and *Mental Excellence: Testimonies of Career and Academic Exploits.*

Like Oyedepo of Nigeria, Mensa Otabil of Ghana is also known as an advocate of self-improvement. His book *Four Laws of Productivity: God's Foundation for Living* focuses on this.[45] Otabil is also noted for opening the eyes of his church members to business opportunities. He charges them never to waste their time seeking for government employment, but "teaches that success comes from skills and training."[46]

The prosperity gospel does not only combat sociophysical ignorance but also spiritual ignorance. It calls people to be aware of who they are in Christ and the promises of God for their lives. This is clearly exemplified in a song by Osinachi Kalu (stage name Sinach) titled "I Know Who I Am."[47] Sinach influenced by Chris Oyakhilome, a Nigerian prosperity preacher, reminded people of their heritage in Christ. For prosperity preachers, Satan and spiritual household wickedness is the ultimate cause of poverty.[48] Hence, the prosperity

---

45. Gifford, *African Christianity*, 82.
46. Gifford, 162.
47. Osinachi, "I Know Who I Am," accessed 11 July 2020, https://www.youtube.com/watch?v=frtZ4XfoXxM.
48. Myers, "Progressive Pentecostalism," 116.

gospel calls people to take their spiritual position against Satan and household wickedness, reminding people of the power of God that is able to crush the powers of darkness.

The Prosperity Gospel Teaches Entrepreneurship in the Face of National Sociopolitical and Economic Breakdown

It has been discussed in chapter 1 that the problem of underdevelopment in Africa largely has to do with failed political institutions. A political theology is therefore evolving from, not just within the Pentecostal circle but the Christian communities at large, challenging the church to arise to the political failure in the society. The prosperity gospel therefore yields to Katongoles' call for the church to be "a new *polis*," a political entity of itself that does not wait for the political government to come and solve the societal problem.[49] This gospel fulfils this call by building quality social and educational facilities for their communities. Both Oyedepo and Otabil built leading private universities and social amenities in their respective countries, Nigeria and Ghana.

Likewise, in the spirit of preparing people for opportunities, which is a way of getting them out of poverty, prosperity preachers also emphasize entrepreneurship. This is also the spirit behind Otabil's *Laws of Productivity*, where he puts emphasis on training and acquisition of skills. In Botswana, Sitima is also noted for teaching church members on entrepreneurship.[50]

The prosperity gospel has bridged the gap of unemployment in Africa, an area where most African governments have failed. Churches are going out of their way to train their members in diverse skills so that they can be useful for the society and earn a living without waiting for the government to provide them jobs. During a conversation with a pastor in Winners Chapel, it was made clear that the aim of the church in the area of entrepreneurship is to make people become financially responsible for their lives and not put blame on the government.[51] On this note, Togarasei is right in his conclusion that, "Be that as it may, it is my conviction that the gospel of prosperity is contributing, and has the potential to contribute, to poverty alleviation in Africa."[52]

---

49. Katongole, *Sacrifice of Africa*, location 1392.
50. Togarasei, "Pentecostal Gospel of Prosperity," 345.
51. Pastor Sackor, oral interview at Africa International University, 17 March 2017.
52. Togarasei, "Pentecostal Gospel of Prosperity," 344.

Variation in Pentecostalism and Prosperity Theology

The prosperity gospel is a phenomenon that was born out of Pentecostalism.[53] Therefore, there is no way of delving into the study of the prosperity gospel without referring to the Pentecostal background from which it is said to have emanated. This subsection shall explore the tenets of the prosperity gospel, the problem it seeks to address, its theological validity, and its possible danger and impact on holistic development in Africa.

Ogungbile has noted that different scholars have grouped Pentecostalism into different categories. From his finding, it is realised that many scholars do not agree on their categorization of Pentecostalism.[54] Therefore, we can conclude that Pentecostal churches are not a sort of homogeneous Christian denomination. Likewise, the prosperity gospel has also proven to be complicated. While discussing the nature of its complication, Heuser writes:

> Prosperity Gospel cannot be reduced to a monolithic canon of ideas, ethics, or practices. . . . [It] has neither developed into a consistent theology nor can it be used to label a distinctive single movement within global Christianity. Rather, it is transformative in nature, adapting to contexts and traveling through history; its pathways are winding through local and transnational networks of churches and individuals; its messages are circulating in modern mass media and are meandering through disparate political spheres and cultural spaces. . . . Prosperity Gospel builds up theological sediments and ritual fragments in non-Christian milieus as well.[55]

In Heuser's view, the prosperity gospel does not always have a consistent theological claim among its preachers. It varies from context to context and with individual Pentecostal church. On this note, I submit that the message of the prosperity gospel focuses on its environment and adapts itself to it. Perhaps this could be the reason for the inconsistent nature of its theology.

---

53. Ogungbile, "African Pentecostalism," 133.
54. Ogungbile.
55. Heuser, "Religio-Scapes of Prosperity Gospel," 16.

The Central Focus of Prosperity Theology in Africa

I have noted that the message of the prosperity gospel varies with people's contexts. However, I shall explore the similarity among African social contexts that could have led to the upsurge of the message of this form of gospel. By doing this, we would be able to discover the common themes in the varieties of theologies of the prosperity gospel, particularly in Africa.

Ogungbile, being a Nigerian, views that "the depth and intensity of poverty in contemporary Africa provide a strong context for the theology and practices of the prosperity gospel and its message."[56] In the same vein, Kasera, talking from his Namibian point of view, indicates that following the hopeless economic situation of his country, the prosperity gospel becomes an "attractive intervention, appearing to offer hope and answers to the poverty problem."[57] Similarly, Edwin Zulu, being a Zambian, also believes that the prosperity gospel responds to the issue of poverty in Africa.[58] Having argued for the holistic view of the prosperity gospel, his conclusion is that "a holistic view of prosperity in the Zambian context could help people in the extreme poverty to start to view themselves positively."[59]

The above-mentioned scholars all agree that the prosperity gospel is a response to the challenge of poverty in Africa. Therefore, we can conclude that the common context in Africa within which the prosperity gospel was borne, and to which it is addressed, is poverty. No one needs to be told of the unfavourable socioeconomic situation in Africa. It is a well-known fact.[60] As has been indicated earlier, the prosperity gospel, being preached among the Pentecostals, is largely a means to salvage the situation of poverty in Africa. It is mainly a response to the economic situation of the people of God on the continent.

Theological Evaluation of the Prosperity Gospel's Tenets

According to Zulu, the central tenet of the prosperity gospel states, "being a Christian is a guarantee of good life and material wealth. In addition, there

---

56. Ogungbile, "African Pentecostalism," 136.
57. Kasera, *Biblical and Theological Examination*, 3.
58. Zulu, "'Fipelwa Na BaYahweh,'" 27.
59. Zulu.
60. Magesa, *Christian Ethics in Africa*, 41.

is also the assertion that this life needs to be free from suffering or sickness as this is not the will of God, and by implication, whoever is suffering can be deemed to be living in sin."[61] Speaking from the African American context, Mumford enumerates the central tenet of the prosperity gospel by saying, "the prosperity gospel teaches believers that where the system fails, God succeeds. If believers are faithful to the word, they can be rich and have good health."[62] Paul Gifford prefers to use the term "Faith Gospel" in place of "Prosperity Gospel." According to Gifford, the paramount message of the preachers of this gospel is that, "God has met all the needs of human beings in the suffering and death of Christ, and every Christian should now share the victory of Christ over sin, sickness, and poverty."[63]

Considering the tenets of the prosperity gospel stated above, it is evident that God is put at the centre: (1) God is portrayed as the giver of good things; (2) quality relationship with God always guarantees all good things – material and immaterial. Hence, anyone whose life does not show forth all desired good things has done something wrong in God's eyes, and that is why he/she goes through such experience. These two foregoing points stand out in the teaching of the prosperity gospel. The question now is how congruent are they to the teaching of the word of God about prosperity?

God as the Giver of All Good Things

Deuteronomy 8:18 makes it known that "For it is [the Lord] who gives you the ability to produce wealth" (NIV). In 1 Samuel 2:32, God promises to "pour out prosperity on the people of Israel." The writer of Ecclesiastes tells us in 5:19 that, "It is a good thing to receive wealth from God and the good health to enjoy it" (NLT). In Proverbs 22:10, we learn that "The blessing of the LORD makes a man rich, and he adds no sorrow with it" (NLT). With much consideration on these verses of the Scripture, there is no doubt that God is the one who gives all blessings. There is no doubt that he promises to send prosperity upon his people, those who obey his command. Therefore, the prosperity gospel has served in many ways in emphasizing the benevolent nature of God. If then, the prosperity gospel preachers truly point people to

---

61. Zulu, "'Fipelwa Na BaYahweh,'" 21.
62. Mumford, *Exploring Prosperity Preaching*, 9–10.
63. Gifford, *African Christianity*, 39.

the God of heaven, the Jehovah Jireh (Gen 22:14), as the giver of all blessings, there is no biblical error in their assertion. That is who God really is – the source of all blessings.

However, we also need to consider Christ's statement in Matthew 6:24, "No one can serve two masters. Either you will hate the one and love the other, or you will be devoted to the one and despise the other. You cannot serve both God and money" (NIV). The delicate issue about the emphasis of the prosperity gospel in calling people to the giver of all blessings is that more attention may be given to the "blessings" than the giver himself; hence, the blessings become the symbol of idolatry. People may be attracted to the blessing that God is able to give rather than God himself, and therefore, make it the object of worship. The prosperity gospel poses a dangerous risk of making the blessings of God more appealing than God himself; thus, making people to "be devoted to one [in this case money] and despise the other [God in this case]" (Matt 6:24, NLT).

Calling people to worship or serve the God who is the giver of all blessings does not have any theological inaccuracy in itself. The distortion only comes when the blessing is elevated above God, either in a subtle or obvious manner. It is important to call people to adore the giver of blessings, and not the blessing.

Talking about the excessive emphasis of prosperity gospel, as it calls people's attention to the God of all blessings, Adeleye is of the opinion that, "The danger is not just that the means and methods of evangelism have become cheap and commercialised but the very heart of the gospel is being corrupted."[64] On this note, this study also calls the attention of the prosperity preachers to one pitfall of prosperity gospel: the danger of forging a utilitarian relationship with God.

Does Quality Relationship with God Always Guarantee All Good Things?

Many people in the Bible whose lives are characterised by quality relationship with God are known to be prosperous. We read in the Bible, "Abram was very rich in cattle, in silver and in gold" (Gen 13:2, KJV). Solomon enjoyed a tremendous blessing from God in his time because of his selfless prayer

---

64. Adeleye, *Preachers of a Different Gospel*, 2.

(2 Chr 1:12). Job, who was said to be a man of unbeatable integrity, was the richest person in the entire "East" (Job 1:1–3). Many other people are said to have enjoyed God's blessing because of their relationship with him.

Good people usually enjoy the blessing of God. Meanwhile, it is also true that good people, in fact, all of them in the Bible, have their own share of misery. Therefore, we cannot say, in an absolute sense, that quality relationship with God and good moral life always guarantee all "good" things, at least not all good things in term of our human desires. Meanwhile, it is necessary to mention that sometimes we do not have what we desire and many times we face unfortunate situations neither because of any sin nor any lack in our service to God. The story of Job reminds us of this fact.

In practical terms, human needs will always remain insatiable. However, God will always give us what is good for us, according to his will. There is a place for the will of God and his sovereignty. Christian maturity gives room for this two. It is only a child who wants things at all cost from a parent. In the same vein, maturity in Christian life propels us to say to the sovereign God, "Let your will be done!" Whenever things do not go the way we desire, Christian maturity enables us to sing a song of faith like Habakkuk did:

> Though the fig tree may not blossom,
> Nor fruit be on the vines;
> Though the labor of the olive may fail,
> And the fields yield no food;
> Though the flock may be cut off from the fold,
> And there be no herd in the stalls:
> Yet I will rejoice in the Lord,
> I will joy in the God of my salvation. (Hab 3:17–18, NKJV)

There are human imperfections in the teachings and claims of prosperity gospel. However, it is evident that many, if not all, churches and pastors whose message puts emphasis on prosperity are making a positive impact on the continent of Africa. As Folarin also mentions, the approach that many prosperity preachers take in addressing the issue of poverty may not always be appropriate, but they are well-meaning.[65] The dangers of the prosperity gospel are that: (1) it can overly draw people's attention to physical blessings

---

65. Folarin, "Contemporary State," 81.

rather than God the giver of all blessings; (2) it can be a means by which the message of the gospel can be corrupted, by putting something else at the centre of the message rather than Christ. These dangers raise the question of holistic nature of the development approach by prosperity gospel. This is because the teaching tends to focus more attention on physical needs, even though it is done in the name of the gospel. And in this case the problem of sin, which is a spiritual poverty, can often be overlooked.

Over the centuries of its existence, the church has attempted to involve itself in the care of the poor. It has developed a theological stance on how to respond to politics so that the political decisions and practices are favourable to the masses. The African church, particularly the Pentecostals, has done so much to respond to the problem of poverty and underdevelopment in Africa. Prosperity gospel is one of the remarkable interventions from the Pentecostals. All of these are commendable efforts towards combating underdevelopment and the problem of bad governance in Africa. However, there is still more work to be done.

The Church, Political Theology and Development

One more effort by the church in its quest to address the problem of poverty is political theology. In this section, I seek to call upon the church of God to rethink its mode of involvement in politics and development, and also challenge it to do more. The church has long since embraced social ethics. Nevertheless, the question to be asked is whether the church has been consistent and effective in this social role. Katongole points out one of the weaknesses in the political role of the church by evaluating its social ethics. On this account, he writes, "Christian social ethics embrace the fact that Christianity has social relevance in the prevailing issues in Africa but never explains the reason why war, tribalism, poverty, corruption, and violence have been endemic to Africa's social history."[66]

Considering Katongole's observation, the church deserves applause for being aware of the fact that it can make a significant impact in the society by getting involved socially. Nevertheless, the church still owes its community an explanation for the prevailing sociopolitical predicaments, particularly in

---

66. Katongole, *Sacrifice of Africa*, 1.

Africa. Trying to indicate why the Christian church has failed in this regard, Katongole notes that it is because the church has not given due attention to the political story of the African past.[67]

Christianity has made some specific attempts of salvaging social and developmental issues in Africa by providing strategies for revising, improving, or managing the failed political institution, but has paid "little attention to the story of this institution: *how* it works and *why* it works the way it does."[68]

Here comes a call to the African church to consider critically the history of politics in the continent. If the church gives attention to the details of the sociopolitical events in the past, it will be able to understand the real source of issues in Africa that are linked with political anomaly. The African past is haunting its present. The church needs to examine the events and experiences of the past that have given rise to the present political issues in Africa. This would help to be able to determine how things work and why they work the way they do in the political sphere of the continent.

How the African Political Past Haunts Its Political Present

While interacting with the historical account of African politics, Katongole further notes five prominent problems that haunt African politics:[69]

1. Colonial impact, social memory, and forgetfulness
2. The lies of noble ideals
3. The politics of greed and plunder
4. The wanton sacrificing of Africa
5. The visible, invisibility of Christianity

The first four problems are traced to Africa's political contact with the colonial rulers. The church is particularly blamed for the fifth problem. The colonial leaders have set a bad example for the African political leaders. By virtue of interacting with the colonial rulers, Africa quickly forgot its traditional leadership values. Africans forgot their helpful African ideals and embraced unsuccessful political ideals from the West. Since the time of independence, many African political leaders have not stopped following

---

67. Katongole, location 77.
68. Katongole, 2.
69. Katongole, 10–19.

the brutal example of plunder and greed of the colonial rulers. "The actors changed, but the script seems to be unchanged."[70]

The colonial rulers have been noted to be guilty of being bad examples; the subsequent African leaders who took over from them are guilty of following the bad example of their colonial masters; and the church is guilty of playing a passive role. If the church will take up its divine role, as the light and salt of the world, injustice, selfishness and wickedness will no longer take a prominent place in African politics. Hence, there is still hope for African politics, provided the church will adopt effective ways of engaging the political institution.

It is high time that Africa detaches itself from the example of bad politics it has learned. Apart from Katongole, a number of other scholars also affirm the effect and reflection of the bad political examples set by the colonial masters. Nihinlola notes that the nation of Nigeria in the past was "characterised by decent moral qualities of honesty, sincerity, and commitment to duty and generally was not covetous and greedy."[71] In the same vein, Nkansah-Obrempong while arguing on the negative Western influence on African politics, also writes:

> African political morality was shaped by two important western values: power and materialism. How the west understood power and used it affected political morality of African governments. The conception of power as control, domination, and suppression became a dominant feature in African politics leaving a legacy of authoritarian and undemocratic leaders in many African countries.[72]

Although subject to arguments, it is important for us to admit that African political contact with colonial leaders has caused a profound distortion in African leadership values. The traditional Africa in existence before the arrival of the Europeans was arguably characterised by love, peace, and unity.[73] This is why Africa needs to trace its path back to the past life of political decency. Mugambi also shares the opinion that the African sociopolitical arena has

---

70. Katongole, 15.
71. Nihinlola, "Problem of Corruption," 185.
72. Nkansah-Obrempong, *Foundations for African Theological*, 144.
73. Moi, *Kenya African Nationalism*, 8.

been damaged by the past doings of the colonial leaders, and so he calls for the reconstruction of African political institution.[74]

Revising the African False Political Ideals

Having recognized the fact that African political leaders have followed the bad example of the colonial masters in terms of greed and plunder, it is also worth noting that majority of the political ideologies which the African political leaders have employed are what Katongole calls "the lies of noble ideals."[75] To this end, the church in Africa needs to examine critically the extent of the effectiveness and relevance of these ideologies in the African context.

Koyzis calls our attention to the reason political ideologies have to be revisited from the Christian perspective: the vision borne out of those ideologies can end up becoming illusions.[76] Koyzis affirms that God has been kept out of the centre of the widely proclaimed political ideologies. He reminds us, "Most of the political philosophies, under whatever ideological label they may fall, find their origin in a single religious worldview that sees the cosmos as an essentially closed system without reference to a creator/redeemer."[77] Political leaders and thinkers have given the place of God and the truth of his word to human-crafted ideologies. Therefore, our political intentions are tainted with idolatry. Koyzis puts it very vividly by saying that ideologies are "modern types of that ancient phenomenon idolatry, complete with their own accounts of sin and redemption. . . . Every ideology is based on taking something out of creation's totality, raising it above the creation, and making the latter revolve around and serve it."[78]

The question is, how well has the church done in critically engaging the political ideologies that are adopted by the African political leaders? My intention is not to say that everything about political ideologies is bad, but to stress the fact that the church needs to review and make its own strong input in African political thoughts and ideologies. It needs to combat the "false ideals" and idolatry in the thinking of the African politicians and all

---

74. Mugambi, *From Liberation to Reconstruction*, 1.
75. Katongole, *Sacrifice of Africa*, 13.
76. Koyzis, *Political Visions and Illusions*, 7.
77. Koyzis, 8.
78. Koyzis, 15.

citizens. The church has the word of God that is the ever-true principle with which a nation can be effectively governed.

The Church as the Hope of African Sociopolitical and Economic Liberation

We should commend the fact that the church has made some successes in the past in rising to the challenge of poor governance. For instance, the Malawian Christians were said to have spoken vehemently against Banda's dictatorship. In the midst of bad governance in the country of Malawi, "the church would raise questions about the exercise of power."[79]

Since the church has made some efforts in the right direction in the political history of Africa and was successful, this is an indication that there is hope of transformation in the unfortunate experience of African politics. However, the church will not have to relent. African colonial past is haunting its political present. The church should be aware of this and lead a godly redemption campaign that will save Africa from the pathetic historical leadership anomaly, starting from sound political theology taught in the church.

For a long time, one of the erroneous assumptions among the people of God in Africa is that "the task of ensuring peace, democracy, and development – in a word, the social and material condition of life – properly belongs to the jurisdiction of politics."[80] Perhaps, this assumption is the reason that the church is not doing enough in holding the government accountable for its misdeeds.

The church has the responsibility to give a moral direction to a nation. "Without Christian influence, governments will have no clear moral compass."[81] The political institution of a nation always needs the church to put it on the right course. Therefore, Christianity and politics are not "oil and water, best kept in different containers";[82] hence, the need for a strong political theology in Africa.

---

79. Ross, *God, People and Power*, 18.
80. Katongole, *Sacrifice of Africa*, 1.
81. Grudem, *Politics*, 67.
82. Storkey, *Jesus and Politics*, 9.

The Implication of Political Theology

Political theology is not necessarily a call for Christians to serve in political offices. It mainly charges the Christian church to use its position in God to exert a positive influence on the political situation of their countries. Political theology speaks against the politicians who think public service is just their own show. It stands to oppose the people in power who say, "We're running this show, and we don't want any religious types trying to tell us our business."[83]

In this section, I have argued that the church involvement in the political arena is not yet sufficient. It has been approaching sociopolitical and economic issues from the surface, not giving adequate attention to the main root cause of the problem. The church would need to give attention to the colonial history, African politics, and challenge the political institution to change its course from the bad examples of the colonial leaders. The church would need to revisit the ideologies with which African nations are being governed and get rid of lies and idolatry in the political system. More importantly, it will need to prepare its members pastorally for the political arena.

The church always has to keep in mind its holistic calling to the world. God did not give the church to the world only for the purpose of spiritual enrichment, but also for the totality of the sociophysical wellbeing of humanity. Therefore, the church should not leave the work of national governance to the political leaders. The church should not stand aloof from what is going on in the political realms.

Politics is more than mere formulation of political parties and doing elections, as many of us assume. It is an institution that goes a long way in determining policy and events that are part of our daily human life – rule, law, nationhood, power, justice, taxation, statehood, international relations, war, and economic policy.[84] As Christians, we cannot afford to leave so much into the hands of the politicians.

---

83. Oakley, *Engaging Politics?*, ix.
84. Storkey, 10.

A Call for Contextual Political Theology of Development

Although this study strongly holds the belief of separation of church and state, this section calls the church to see the need to engage the national political system with a prophetic voice. In the Bible (especially Old Testament) times, almost all the times when the nation of Israel found itself in national crises, God usually sent solutions through his prophets (cf. 1 Kgs 20). Among other important roles that the church has to play in ensuring that the political system of its society is suitable for development, it must speak to politics with a voice that resonates with God's intention on politics that fosters development.

The tenet of political theology as I hold in this book is that Christianity must have its voice heard by preparing its members for their political roles. There are various variations in the concept of political theology in human history. According to Pam,

> There are at least three different types of political theology; (1) The theological formulation of the age-old political religion; one God in heaven, one ruler on earth, one empire; (2) The modern conflict between anarchism and political authority, with Bakunin's cry "neither God nor state" on the one side and Carl Schmitts's politics of sovereignty on the other; and (3) The "new political theology" of Christian resistance against political idolatry and Christian engagement for the liberation of the oppressed and the acceptance of the excluded.[85]

This book provides another voice in scholarly discussion concerning the new political theology. Hence, the mention of political theology in this discussion refers to the new political theology. Talking about this form of theology, Moltmann brings to our attention that, "[It] demands the public testimony of Christian faith, a political discipleship of Christ in life and work, and taking sides with the persecuted, humiliated and excluded. This doesn't lead to politicizing the church, as some feared, but to the Christianizing of public life and politics."[86] Also talking about political theology, which apparently

---

85. Pam, "Political Theology," 85.
86. Moltmann, "Political Theology," 670.

refers to new political theology, Cole notes that it "involves both a theology of development and nation-building as well as a theology of liberation."[87]

A critical reflection on Moltmann's view will bring us to the awareness that political theology first has to do with testimony of Christian faith through the lives of the adherents of the faith. This implies that believers conduct themselves in "public" (society) in a manner that those who watch them have good stories to tell about them in relation to their positive contribution to the society. Hence, political theology seeks to prepare followers of Christ to live a life of "salt" and "light" (Matt 5:13, 14). Second, political theology prepares followers of Christ to arise to the cause of the oppressed.

Talking in the similar line of thought with Moltmann, Cole brings to our attention that political theology is a blend of theology of development and theology of liberation. Thus, political theology is said, first, to be an attempt to deal with poverty and work towards national prosperity, and second, to advocate for the oppressed.

The interaction with Moltmann and Cole therefore reveals to us that political theology has more than just one element; one of which is the theology of development. As such, we can conclude that political theology has to it a dimension of development, which is the reason this study advocates a contextual political theology of development.

In his discourse on political theology, Cole appears to have dichotomised between a theology of development and a theology of liberation. Nevertheless, the two are interrelated. A theology of liberation also tends towards development. This is because the aim of liberating the oppressed is so that they can live a life of prosperity. Two scholars strongly affirm this belief.

According to Amatya Sen, development is seen as "a process of expanding the real freedoms that people enjoy. . . . [It] requires the removal of major sources of unfreedom: poverty as well as tyranny, poor economic opportunities as well as systematic social deprivation, neglect of public facilities as well as intolerance or overactivity of repressive states."[88] Virgilio Elizondo also believes that poverty can be material, spiritual, psychological, and existential, and that existential poverty is the worst form of poverty.

---

87. Cole, "Africanising the Faith," 15.
88. Sen, *Development as Freedom*, 3.

It has nothing to do with lack of material possession or meaninglessness but has to do with the very reality of who people are, where they are born, the color of their skin, the shape of their body, the language they speak, the ethnicity that radiates through every fiber of their being.[89]

Liberation theology aims at advocating for people who are experiencing existential poverty, people whose prosperity and dignity are hampered by the virtue of conditions around their lives. Thus, we can argue that even liberation theology is also a quest towards development; and consequently, we can submit that political theology always has something to do with development.

By doing a contextual political theology of development in this book, I call for the necessity of a teaching for African Christian citizens about development-oriented politics based on the Bible and culture. African Christians should be able to live out an authentic Christian life that reflects in the political and socioeconomic situation of their society. And they would not be able to live up to this if the church does not have a particular organised teaching that prepares them to make positive contributions to the political and socioeconomic wellbeing of the society, through their lifestyles.

Contextual political theology of development is necessary in the church; the form of political theology brewed from the African cultural context and with an emphasis on holistic wellbeing of human life. Kwame Bediako has rightly noted that African Christianity is going through a process of self-definition. Meanwhile, self-definition is the basis upon which both second-century and twentieth-century theologians formulated their theologies.[90] It is time the church provided a systematic teaching that answers an ontological question, what it means to be a Christian whose past is rooted in "traditional" political and economic system but presently lives in a "modern" political and economic system. This shall be done through "a process whereby the Scripture and culture are fully engaged."[91]

As was discussed in chapter 1 and will be later discussed in chapter 5, present-day African culture is a hybrid of traditional and modern "cultures." Contextual political theology of development puts into account these two

---

89. Elizondo, "Culture, the Option," 159.
90. Bediako, *Theology and Identity*.
91. Moon, *African Proverbs Reveal Christianity*, 18.

cultures and the Scripture. With this consideration, it therefore uses and proposes a methodology with which a contextual political theology of development can be developed from any given culture.

Conclusion

This chapter has discussed both the characteristics and necessity of contextual political theology of development. Contextual political theology of development seeks to pursue a development agenda from the political point of view, taking into cognizance African traditional practices and thoughts, contemporary theories and biblical teaching about politics and development. It acknowledges the basic needs required by all the human existential components. It gives a prominent place to the human spiritual domain, noting that it is the part of humans which relates directly to God. Human negligence of this domain is the reason for all the chaos in the world. The basic need of the spiritual domain is the opportunity to relate with God. When this is missing, humanity will fail in every other form of relationship.

Sin, a result of lack of relationship with God, is paramount of all factors of bad governance. It is the reason for all political vices perpetuated by political leaders whose tenures of leadership are known for bad governance. Negligence of godly principles, in other words, sin, is one of the crucial factors that leads to almost all indices of underdevelopment and poverty trap, which make it difficult for a nation to experience good governance.

The bulk of Christian developmental practices and thoughts over the years are prone to the danger of dichotomising the human need for the gospel and human need for physical wellbeing (or other nonspiritual needs). Contrary to this danger of dichotomy, this study puts a premium emphasis on teaching about relationship with God, which must be reflected in all our human activities and from where all other human needs are drawn. I shall subsequently discuss more about this in chapters 3 and 4 from the study of Yoruba people.

While prosperity gospel teaches a message that calls people into relationship with God, nevertheless it poses the danger of calling attention to the good things God is able to give, rather than relating with him out of absolute love for him and for who he is. Similar to what this study is about, the church has remarkably engaged in political theology with the intention of making things right in the society; however, not much has been done from the cultural and traditional historical points of view.

The next two chapters take us into the study of Yoruba traditional thoughts and practices on development and politics. These thoughts and practices shall form our bases for a political theology framework that addresses the social systems of African societies.

CHAPTER 3

Àlàáfía Lójù: Yoruba Traditional Developmental-Political Thoughts

Introduction

Ambe Njoh asserts that every culture in the world "has some concept of development and aspires to attain it."[92] In the discussions that unfold in this chapter, I shall explore traditional thoughts upon which Yoruba political practices and thoughts about development are rooted. The discussion shall cut across the Yoruba sociodevelopment variables such as values, structures, and networks, and the poor; all of this in relation to politics and development.

In the sections that make up the chapter, I shall explore Yoruba basic thoughts and beliefs, first, on development and then relate these thoughts and beliefs to political leadership of the society. I shall discuss the Yoruba understanding of development, how it is sustained and how it can be forfeited. I have established the place of human sin in political governance and development in chapter 2, in this chapter I shall develop that further by a theological exploration of the Yoruba concept of sin and how it is traditionally dealt with.

Since education is generally known as an instrument of development and good governance, I shall explore the Yoruba traditional concept and philosophy of education in relation to community wellbeing and the political responsibility of society members.

---

92. Njoh, *Tradition, Culture and Development*, 2.

I shall also discuss the general way by which Yoruba ensure everybody's wellbeing against material poverty. Through this, I shall draw some further conclusion on Yoruba traditional thoughts on wellbeing and political responsibility. The chapter also draws a link between politics and development by doing a linguistic analysis of a relevant Yoruba proverb.

Life and Wellbeing in Yoruba Traditional Thought

A well-lived life among Yoruba implies many things, but first it begins with having breath within oneself, and therefore the proverb, "*B'ẹ̀mìí báwà, iṣe kò tán*" (If there is still breath, there is no limit to actions or achievements). Likewise, in the Yoruba view of wellbeing no one admires a life merely characterised by "breath". There must be something more than just life. Therefore, "when the Yoruba think or speak of life with reference to a person or society the meanings they attach to it embrace good health, prosperity, longevity, peace, and happiness."[93] However, the prerequisite of it all is peace. When a man has breath in him and peace, this is the foundation of all things. This is reflected in the popular saying among Yoruba that "*Àlàáfíà l'ójù*" (Peace is supreme).

The implication we draw from this is that Yoruba concept of wellbeing also holds that, "One's life does not consist in the abundance of things he possesses" (Luke 12:15, NKJV). This is not to say that some people among the Yoruba traditional society did not possess inordinate longing for avarice. Nevertheless, this is not traditionally accepted. One way to console oneself in times of material inadequacies is to remind oneself that *Àlàáfíà l'ójù*" (Peace is supreme), and that "*Bẹ̀mìí báwà, iṣe kò tán*" (as long as there is life, there is no end to achievements).

Therefore, peace "is the sum total of all that is good that man may desire – an undisturbed harmonious life. . . . *Àlàáfíà* as it is being conceived, is very similar to the Hebrew concept of *shalom*." Awolalu, using the words of Alan Richardson, expresses that the Hebrew *shalom* "is a comprehensive word covering the manifold relationships of daily life, and expressing the ideal state of life in Israel . . . The fundamental meaning is totality, well-being, and harmony, with stress on material untouched by violence or misfortune." In

---

93. Awolalu, "Yoruba Philosophy of Life," 21.

the same vein, *àlàáfíà* "is incomplete or disrupted when there is no totality about it."[94] Yoruba concept of *àlàáfíà* is holistic in nature, which is said to be missing when there is any distortion in any area of human life.

Human life is divided into two: life here on earth and life after death, both of them being viewed essentially as a continuous existence. In any case, a good life is characterised by peace in its holistic nature. Elements of a peaceful life include joy and happiness, increase in prosperity, ritual devotion, and observance of moral values, and long life. The idea of peace as wellbeing in Yoruba traditional thoughts therefore does not imply that there is no longing for material prosperity at all. However, so basic is the Yoruba perception of wealth and poverty that it is believed that "*Bí ebi bá kúrò nínú iṣẹ́, iṣẹ́ bùse*" (If hunger is out of one's struggle against poverty, poverty is already conquered).

All the elements of peaceful life as conceived by Yoruba fit somewhat into the discussion of the holistic nature of development in chapter 2. Physically, a human being is said to experience wellbeing when he/she has an increase in prosperity and has long life. Yoruba view of wellbeing also goes as far as the domain of human emotion, holding that a peaceful life is a life of joy and happiness. The wellbeing of a human in the spiritual domain is indicated in the devotion to rituals and observance of moral values.

Many factors can disrupt *àlàáfíà*. Such factors include wrath of the divinities, anger of the ancestors, failure to observe taboo, witchcraft, and sorcery. However, *àlàáfíà* can be restored by consulting oracles, warding off evil, joining secret societies, and joining *aládùúrà* (prayer) group. Looking at the reasons why *àlàáfíà* can be disrupted among Yoruba people, the place of cordial relationship between the divine and fellow humans is very vital. The wrath of the deities and ancestors, which is normally provoked by violations and perversions, can disrupt *àlàáfíà* among Yoruba people. The wicked or immoral acts perpetuated against fellow human beings or the community by breaking taboos, and practice of witchcraft and sorceries are also critical reasons for disruption of *àlàáfíà*.

I have noted earlier in this section that Yoruba *àlàáfíà* is similar to the biblical *shalom*, which in both cases entail totality of human wellbeing. Writing on the nature of the Hebrew *shalom*, Cafferky notes that it begins by obedience to God's commandment. When Israelites fail in any way to obey God's

---

94. Awolalu, 21–22.

law, they live a life that is void of *shalom*.⁹⁵ Summarising the entire Law into the Golden Rule, Jesus puts the summary of all the Law and Prophets as doing unto others what we would wish others do to us (Matt 7:12; Luke 6:31). Jesus would also single out the love for God and neighbours as the greatest commandment.

Therefore, it becomes obvious that loss of *àláàfíà* for the Yoruba, as also in the case of loss of *shalom* for the Hebrews, is primarily because of spiritual and moral failure. Bryant Myers also speaks of the Yoruba community when he concluded that the cause of poverty is fundamentally relational and spiritual.⁹⁶ When there is a relationship breakdown with self, God, community, and, environment, poverty ensues.

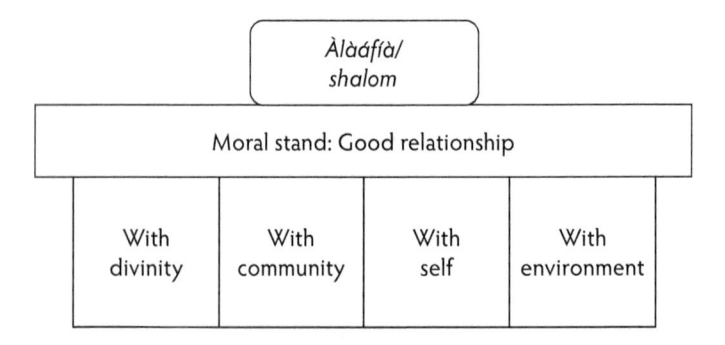

```
                    ┌─────────────┐
                    │   Àláàfíà/  │
                    │   shalom    │
                    └─────────────┘
┌─────────────────────────────────────────────────┐
│       Moral stand: Good relationship            │
└─────────────────────────────────────────────────┘
┌──────────┬──────────┬──────────┬──────────┐
│   With   │   With   │   With   │   With   │
│ divinity │community │   self   │environment│
└──────────┴──────────┴──────────┴──────────┘
```

Figure 2. *Àláàfíà* as based on Good Moral Standing Marked by a Four-Dimensional Relationship

We should also note that as it is the case in the biblical laid-down principle, the Yoruba also have systems that place responsibility on individuals to maintain good relationships with the community and the environment.⁹⁷ When people fail in their obligations to the deities and in their responsibility to fellow humans and care for the environment, what follows is the lack of wellbeing. Human failure in all or any of these dimensions is therefore nothing other than sin, since sin implies any form of lawlessness (1 John 3:4).

---

95. Cafferky, "Ethical-Religious Framework," 1–36.
96. Myers, *Walking with the Poor*, 143–45.
97. Awolalu, "Yoruba Philosophy of Life," 28.

Related Words for Wellbeing and Development in Yoruba Traditional Thought

In Yorubas' discussion of wellbeing, the following words are important for a better understanding of the concept: *ìdàgbàsókè*, *ìlọsíwájú*, and *ìtura*.

Ìdàgbàsókè: This can loosely be translated as growing up. The same word is used to refer to a child who is advancing in age and stature, which implies maturity,[98] meaning that one would also be right to translate *ìdàgbàsókè* as growth.[99] The word *ìdàgbàsókè* is also applicable in farming. Maize should grow upward. Examining the concept of growth everywhere in the world, it occurs with time. Hence, it is expected that the passage of time should bring about a development. Things should not always be the way they are. There must be a progressive positive change. Relating it to child-rearing experience, it is the joy of all parents to see their children growing. This gives us the idea that development is a desirable experience.

Ìlọsíwájú: This can be directly translated as progress. However, *ìlọsíwájú* is one of those Yoruba words whose meaning is clearly reflected in their pronunciation (*ìlọ-sí-iwájú*), that is, as soon as they hear the word mentioned, any Yoruba speaker can easily know its meaning without consulting any dictionary or asking the elders. Translating the word by ear, it means moving/going forward: *ìlọ-* (going/moving, departure[100]) *sí-* (a post-verbal adverbial, which in this use means "to"),[101] *-iwájú* (front/forward). Nevertheless, the deeper meaning of the word, according to Delano, is "*lílọ síwájú nínú ohun rere*"[102] (moving forward in good things).

Ìtura: The meaning of this word also comes out clearly when broken down, *itu-ara* (the comforting of the body). Therefore, it is usually translated as "comfort, ease; the refreshing of a cool breeze."[103] *Ìtura* is therefore the word used to refer to a state of comfort or wellbeing after one's body has gone

---

98. Crowther, "Idagba," 106.
99. "Development," *WordHippo*, n.d., accessed 23 November 2019, https://www.wordhippo.com/what-is/the-meaning-of/yoruba-word-c94d677daa58f930b9e850fffd8a3931cb5f275e.html.
100. Crowther, "ilo," *Vocabulary of Yoruba Language*, 147.
101. Awobuluyi, *Essentials of Yoruba Grammar*, 76.
102. Delano, "ilosiwaju," *Atumo Ede Yoruba*, 106.
103. Crowther, *Vocabulary of Yoruba Language*, 166.

through some unpleasant experience. Just like the timeless hymn, "Showers of Blessings" prays for "seasons refreshing"[104] that follows a moderate rain on a patch of land, this is what *itura* means to Yoruba people. Therefore, the Yoruba rendition of "seasons refreshing" is "*ìtura dídùn*" (sweet refreshing).

With the simple analysis of these words, one also gets the idea that the concept of wellbeing among Yoruba entails growth, progress, and comfort. This implies that the opposite of all these spells lack of wellbeing. It is also an indication that the fact that Yoruba people primarily regard peace as wellbeing does not rule out their longing for progress, comfort, and growth. Meanwhile, no growth, progress, or comfort is possible without peace. Because of the interrelated nature of the meanings of "peace," "wellbeing," and "development" in this study of Yoruba culture, I shall take the liberty of using the three words interchangeably.

The Concept of Sin and Its Implication on Wellbeing in the Yoruba Traditional Thought

Àlàáfià is based on cordial relationships, with God (also deities in Yoruba case), fellow humans, self, and environment. A distortion or perversion of these relationships is said to be sin.[105] As I have briefly noted in chapter 1 and in the preceding section, sin is commonly an enemy of human wellbeing. On this premise, an elaborate discussion on sin is brought into this study. Since the study focuses on Yoruba culture, I shall explore the concept of sin within this context, and emphasize its implication on wellbeing.

As shall be discussed further in the subsections that follow, the implication of sin on development is in the fact that it is the main enemy of individual and communal wellbeing. Among the Yoruba, sin is not limited to individual misdeeds; it also entails communal wrongdoing. Dealing with sin is not just an individual responsibility; it is also a communal responsibility. As we shall see in chapter 4, Yoruba community is politically structured from the head of the larger community – king or chief – to the smallest family unit. Hence, the mention of communal responsibility and actions in the discussion on sin is politically implied.

---

104. Sims, *Baptist Hymnal*, 264.
105. Myers, *Walking with the Poor*, 145.

The Meaning of Sin in Yoruba Traditional Thought

The Yoruba word for sin is *èṣè*. Sinners in Yoruba are called *ẹlẹ́ṣẹ̀, òdaràn, aṣebi, òṣìkà, arúfin, oníláabi,* or *aṣèbàjé*. Examining how Yoruba refer to sinners would give us an idea of their perception about sin. Therefore, we shall take a closer look at each of them.

Ẹlẹ́ṣẹ̀: *Ẹlẹ́ṣẹ̀* can be loosely translated as "he who has transgressed." In other words, this refers to someone who has crossed the normal limit. He/she has gone beyond the extent to which he/she should not go. Therefore, going by this Yoruba nomenclature for a sinner, we can infer that Yoruba people regard sin as going beyond the proper limit of standard set by the society. The word *ẹlẹ́ṣẹ̀* also denotes "he who has done wrong," leaving us with the impression that what the sinner has done is not acceptable or right.

Òdaràn: This can be translated as "he/she who has committed *òràn* (a crime)." *Òràn* is a very grave offence in the land. Therefore, when someone is called *òdaràn,* it implies he/she has committed a very terrible offence that has caused severe pain or discomfort to an individual or the community. It is usually the violation of major judicial laws, for instance if one commits murder or armed robbery.

Aṣebi: The word *aṣebi* can be broken down to *aṣe-ibi. Aṣe* means "He who does. . . ." *Ibi* is translated as evil. Therefore, *aṣebi* is someone who has perpetrated evil. This is pointing us to the fact that committing sin implies doing something evil. The idea of associating evil with sin is borne out of the belief that sin will always bring about an evil repercussion either on an individual or on the community. Since evil is associated with painful experiences,[106] Yoruba people hold that sin always culminates in painful experience in one way or the other.

Òṣìkà/oníláabi: "*Òṣìkà*" and *"oníláabi"* are synonymous words that mean "he who has done wickedness." *Ìkà*, the root word for *òṣìkà,* means "wickedness." By virtue of associating wickedness with a sinner, it would mean that sin is considered an act of wickedness in Yorubaland. Meanwhile, to have done wickedness literally means someone has hurt another person. Hence, we can conclude from this that Yoruba people believe that one commits a sin when one hurts another person.

---

106. Daniel, "Investigation of Sin and Evil," 145.

Arúfin: This translates to mean lawbreaker, a general name that is given to anyone who violates societal laws (*òfin*). This suggests to us that Yoruba people regard sin as violation of the law.

Aṣèbàjẹ́: This is derived from the word "*ibàjẹ́*," which is usually translated as "corrupt," "mess" or "indiscipline." Corrupt practices and indiscipline are called *iwà ìbàjẹ́*. When someone also does something otherwise when he/she should have demonstrated restraint, it is also called *iwà ìbàjẹ́*. Therefore, *aṣèbàjẹ́* refers to a corrupt, indisciplined, or unrestrained person. Someone who defecates somewhere on the road is said to have committed *iwà ìbàjẹ́*. It is also said to be *iwà ìbàjẹ́* when someone receives bribe or indiscriminately cut down trees that should not be cut down.

From the foregoing definitions stating how Yoruba defines a sinner, we would note that they regard sin as violation of law, an act that causes pain and hurt to an individual or the entire community. We would also note that sin could be synonymous with wickedness. All the acts that are said to violate wellbeing in the society are said to be sin. Sin entails crossing some particular boundary, committing grave offenses, perpetrating evil, breaking the law and not being self-restraint.

The Essence of Iwa in Human Wellbeing in the Yoruba Traditional Thoughts

In contrast to *ẹ̀ṣẹ̀* (sin), Yoruba people celebrate and praise *iwà rere* (good character) in the lives of people. To them, rather than giving oneself to sin, one should always maintain *iwà rere*. This is why it is said that, *"Ìwà rere lẹ̀ṣọ́ ọmọ ènìyàn"* (good character is the ornament of human beings). Therefore, everybody in the society is encouraged to guard their behaviour so that they do not sin. When someone commits a sin, it is said of him/her, *"Ó sì'wà hù"* (He/she misbehaves). Therefore, sin is also regarded as misbehaviour. Oladosu explains the prominence of human character in Yorubaland, in Bolaji Idowu's words:

> To the Yorùbá, man's character is of supreme importance and it is this which Olódùmarè judges. Thus the demands which Olódùmarè lays upon man are purely ethical. Man's well-being here on earth depends upon his character . . . therefore; morality

is summed up in Yorùbá by the word *Iwà* which can be translated by the English word "character" . . . It is therefore stressed that good character must be the dominant feature of a person's life. In fact, it is the one thing which distinguishes a person from a brute.[107]

From Idowu's words, one learns that individual wellbeing has much to do with *iwà*. This is why it is essential that one's *iwà* be jealously guarded. It is a profound Yoruba belief that sin can be avoided if every individual is able to control his/her *iwà*. As such, one attains the level of morality through intentional character development.

Those who perpetually stay morally upright are able to do so because they are intentional about their character. In light of this, Yoruba share a contrary belief to that of Christianity that holds that human sinful nature is inherited from Adam.[108] The problem of sin in an individual is because they cannot guard their good behaviour (*iwà*) given by Olodumare, every individual should strive on their own to become *ọmọlúàbí* (an individual whose life is characterised with good character and conduct).[109]

To enhance people's character development, the society has devised some means of imparting moral lessons to community members, right from childhood. Examples of this means of character development are storytelling, proverbs and so on. "This shows that moral values in Yoruba setting provide checks against misdemeanour and they serve as the keeper of the conscience for the members of the society."[110]

Some introspective indices determine people's moral behaviour. People who are well acquainted with these indices are more likely to live above sin. These include *inú* (the psychological, inner self), *ọkàn* (mind), *ogbọ́n* (wisdom), *ọpọlọ* (intellect), *ẹ̀rí ọkàn* (judgement), *ojú inú* (insight), *iyè inú* (self-consciousness), *iwà* (character), and *sùúrù* (patience).[111] The use of the aforementioned elements aids reflective minds, self-consciousness, and

---

107. Oladosu, "Ethics and Judgement," 144 – 45.
108. Grudem, *Systematic Theology*, 494.
109. The concept of "*omoluabi*" is well discussed in works such as: Olanipekun, "Omoluabi," 217–31; and, Adedayo, "Concept of Omoluabi," 1–7.
110. Oladosu, "Ethics and Judgement," 146.
111. Garuba, "Good, Bad, and Beautiful," 61.

decision-making.¹¹² This can be the simple formula through which people can help themselves become *ọmọlúàbí* who live a good moral life and maintain *ìwà rere*.

Sources of Moral Codes in Yoruba Traditional Thoughts

Moral codes are some forms of knowledge that outline what people should do and should not do. Failure to live according to knowledge and direction provided in this code is considered tantamount to sin. Sources of moral code in Yorubaland according to Oladosu are Ifa divination, proverbs, taboos (*èèwọ̀*), customs, stories, folktales, and tradition of the people.¹¹³ In addition to all these, people are expected to follow the dictates of their conscience as they seek to make moral decisions. Likewise, the instruction of someone in a place of authority also forms a moral code. My argument in this subsection is that Yoruba sources of moral code are spiritual in that they have to do with the Yoruba spiritual universe. Each of the codes can be explained as follows:

Ifa Divination: Ifa is known to be the god of wisdom in the Yoruba pantheon.¹¹⁴ He is also said to be the most important deity among the Yoruba gods.¹¹⁵ People within the community consult his oracle from time to time so that they would know what is expected of them. Ifa's recommendations through his oracles usually become a law that everybody must abide by, or as the case may be. His will is usually known through his devout priests, nationally known as *olúáwo* or *ìwòrò*.¹¹⁶ They bring forth Ifa's message and instruction to the community of people, after consulting him.

Òwe (Proverbs): Proverbs can be a means through which moral instructions are given to the community members in the form of wisdom nuggets. They contain values that guide people in whatever they do. An example of such proverbs is *"Ọmọ ẹni kìí dára káfi sʼaya."* (No matter how pretty one's daughter is; one does not take her for a wife). This is an example of a proverb that contains a moral law against incest. Proverbs are known to have originated

---

112. Garuba, 61.
113. Oladosu, "Ethics and Judgement," 91–92.
114. Adelowo, "Rituals, Symbolism," 189.
115. Obayemi, "History, Culture," 83.
116. Adelowo, "Rituals, Symbolism," 163.

from the ancestors. That is why they are said to be *òwe àwọn baba wa* (proverbs of the fathers).

Èèwọ̀ (Taboo): Oladosu quotes Idowu as saying, "What has been named taboo took their origin from the fact that people discerned that there were certain things which were morally approved or disapproved by the Deity."[117] They are usually strict laws within the society because it is believed that those laws are handed down to the society by the ancestors, gods, or the supreme being; and therefore, if they are not obeyed, a communal or personal disaster would always follow.

Ẹ̀rí ọkàn (Conscience): Nkansah-Obrempong quotes Idowu as saying, "God made humans; and he implants in him the sense of right and wrong. This is a fact, the validity of which does not depend upon whether man realizes and acknowledges it or not."[118] With this assertion, Yoruba people are of the opinion that everybody has moral codes written on their heart. Therefore, there are some instances whereby nobody has to give a stipulated law but an individual's conscience will at this point dictate to him/her what to do. In fact, it is believed that a person knows by himself/herself whether an action is right or wrong, without being told. This is an allusion to the operation of human conscience in making moral decisions.

Àṣẹ (A decree or command from a higher authority): "In human relationships there is emphasis on the concept of hierarchy based partly on age and partly on status. In practice, this amounts to a ladder ranging from God to the youngest child."[119] For the fact that Yoruba people, like the other Africans, place emphasis on hierarchy, therefore it could be counted as a sin or taboo for someone of a lower hierarchy to disobey the instruction given by the one in a higher hierarchy. In fact, a decree made by a king in traditional Yorubaland is like a law given by the gods. This is because *oba* (king) is said to be *aláṣẹ ẹkẹ̀jì òrìṣà* (he whose authority is next to the gods).[120] As such, a person becomes an offender by disobeying the instruction given by a higher authority.

---

117. Oladosu, "Ethics and Judgement," 91.
118. Nkansah-Obrempong, *Foundations for African Theological*, 17.
119. Mbiti, *African Religions and Philosophy*, 205.
120. Pemberton III and Afolayan, *Yoruba Sacred Kingship*, 1.

Unlike the Jewish source of moral code that is found singularly in the Scripture, especially as stipulated by the Law of Moses, the Yoruba appear to have more than one source of moral code. However, the line of similarity between the Jewish and Yoruba sources of moral code is in their spiritual characteristic. The spiritual implication of the Jewish source of moral code is rooted in the awareness that it is handed down by God to Moses. Similarly, Yoruba sources of moral code are said to be spiritual in that they have to do with the Yoruba spiritual universe – the world of the ancestors, deity, and Olodumare.

For instance, èèwọ is said to be from the deity,[121] ọba is said to be embodiment of the deities,[122] and òwe is the sayings of the ancestors, which is why it is referred to as òwe àwọn baba wa (proverbs of the fathers). As I shall further discuss in chapter 4, Yoruba spiritual universe is all wrapped up by the supreme being (Olodumare). Therefore, anything that originates from the Yoruba spiritual universe is ultimately believed to have been of Olodumare. Hence, as the Jews trace their source of moral code to Yahweh; Yoruba also trace theirs to Olodumare.

Some Specific Sins among Yoruba People

The aim of this subsection is to show in some specific ways how sin is a breach of the four-dimensional relationship. I shall enumerate and briefly explain some acts that are typically considered sinful among the people:

Sexual immorality: Everybody is expected to be faithful to their marriage partners. Sex before marriage is highly prohibited; and therefore, a young woman who loses her virginity before marriage will be subjected to shame on her wedding night.

Unfriendliness/selfishness: All members of Yoruba society are responsible for the wellbeing of their neighbours. Therefore, hospitality and tolerance are highly regarded. Of course, this is because Yoruba people, like the rest of Africa, cherish a communal life. Yoruba people's expression of hospitality is quite similar to that of Igbo people as described below by Umeasiegbu:

> If a family has a visitor the neighbours will all entertain the visitor in turn. The wife goes to the house where the visitor is

---

121. Adelowo, "Rituals, Symbolism," 163.
122. Pemberton III and Afolayan, *Yoruba Sacred Kingship*, 1.

lodging and asks the host or hostess to bring the visitor to her house. Secretly she will find out what the new-comer likes and prepares that food. When the guests arrive, kola is served and food is brought. It is a sign of disrespect for the visitor to refuse the food. They are expected to leave morsels of it. Otherwise the impression is created that the guest has not had enough food to eat for a long time. As a rule enough is provided.[123]

Dishonesty: Members of the society are expected to be truthful at all times. A story of the olden day Yorubaland was told that sellers of goods used to leave their goods by the roadside and went about with some other business. They would leave a number of pebbles beside the goods to indicate the selling price. The passers-by who wanted to buy such goods would buy the number of items they wanted and put the exact price of the items. No one would dare do otherwise because honesty was held in high esteem. About dishonesty, Yoruba people will say, *"Òtítọ́ kìí sìnà, irọ́ níí forí bọ̀gbẹ́"* (Truthfulness does not miss the road; only dishonesty goes astray).[124]

Stealing: This is another grave offence among Yoruba people. It is a shameful act for the person who steals, and for his family. Theft usually attracts a long-time stigma on both the thief and his family. It is better to be a slave than to be a thief in Yorubaland. This is why it is said that *"Kàkà kí n ja'lè, ma kúkú d'ẹrú"* (Rather than for me to steal, I'll choose to be a slave). It is believed that stealing is often because of laziness. Lazy people are the ones who usually end up stealing. Therefore, the virtue of hard work is highly encouraged.[125]

Covenant breaking: Covenant breaking is the highest level of dishonesty. People are expected to keep their vows and covenant no matter what it costs them.

Injustice: Injustice is regarded as wickedness among the people. Anyone who is in a place to settle dispute should demonstrate fairness. The parties involved in a dispute must be heard before the verdict is pronounced. This is because the society believes that the truth of a matter can only be revealed when people in conflict have an equal opportunity to present their case.

---

123. Umeasiegbu, *Way We Lived*, 39.
124. Oladosu, "Ethics and Judgement," 94.
125. Olurode, "Ifa, the Deity," 137.

Therefore, Yoruba people would say, *"Agbẹjọ́ ẹnìkan dá; àgbà òṣìkà"* (Judging by hearing one side of the story is great wickedness).

Murder: Anyone who kills will also be killed except in a case of accident.

Disrespect: Children and young people must respect adults. It is disrespectful for a younger person to be seated when an older person is standing in a gathering. A younger person must help an older person carry a load. Plural pronouns are used as a sign of respect when addressing an elderly person. A young man or a boy must prostrate before an elderly person when greeting him/her. A younger woman or girl must kneel down while greeting an older person. A child or younger person should not look straight into an elder's eyes during their conversation. A young person should not say a proverb in the presence of the elders unless he has their permission. There should be a high measure of respect for one's in-law. This is why Yoruba people would say: *"Ọba l'àna!"* (An in-law is like a king). Sin of disrespect can attract curse from an elderly person. In fact, it is believed that a person who disrespects an elder is bound to lose his/her honour.

Violation of taboo: Many taboos are instituted to protect some certain sacred objects or nature. An example of this is the destruction of an evil forest.

Committing any of the sins above disrupts someone's peace or that of the society. It breaches the four-dimensional relationship, a violation of one or all-important relationships upon which peace is based. A careful look at all of them shall call the reader's attention to the similarity between Yoruba ethical life and the biblical Ten Commandments upon which *shalom* is based. And so, committing any of the notable sins in the Yoruba culture is also a violation of some portion of the Ten Commandments.

Although the traditional Yoruba moral codes were not directly gleaned from the Bible, it is evident that both sources place similar moral and ethical demands on people. This therefore confirms the nature of God's general revelation to the Yoruba people. They were without the written Scripture, yet they had the knowledge of God's requirement manifest in them (Rom 1:19–20). The Yoruba's focus and advocacy for moral life, like most of African cultures, has an anthropocentric appearance in that it is intended for the people's wellbeing. Nevertheless, the Yorubas' quest for moral life has some spiritual implication in the awareness that God is concerned about human behaviours. According to Idowu, it is believed that God himself is the one who places ethical demands on humans.[126] He is the *Adákẹ́ Dájọ́* (Silent Judge) who judges all human actions. Therefore, a component of human life is sensitive to the fact that Olodumare has some certain expectations of them. Yoruba people are aware of the fact that he will administer his punishment if they violate his demands.

Causes of Sin according to Yoruba Traditional Thought

The purpose of this subsection is to emphasize the immaterial nature of sin, which emanates from the immaterial aspect of human life. I shall achieve this by briefly discussing some of the factors that cause sin.

Evil Desires: Yoruba people acknowledge many other reasons why people can misbehave or commit a sin. However, among all these reasons they believe that evil desire is the root of them all. This is why it is said, *"Ẹni tí a f 'ìkà lọ̀ tó gbà, tinú ẹ̀ lófẹ́ ṣe"* (One who is enticed with sin and consents already has a desire to sin). Therefore, sin is largely seen as the expression of one's evil desire.

Èèdì/ẹ̀sún: Like in many other African cultures, Yoruba people also strongly believe "in forces or powers which affect human behaviour in important ways."[127] It is held that people can be bewitched to misbehave. When someone's misbehaviour is suspected to have a supernatural manifestation, it is called *èèdì*. *Èèdì* is said to be a supernatural spell cast on someone, and it is capable of causing them to misbehave.

On the other hand, it is called *ẹ̀sún* when someone is deceived by someone else so that he/she commits a sin. The word *ẹ̀sún* literally translates to mean "being moved, or pushed." Human beings can move or trick other human beings into sinning through persuasion, seduction, tricks, deceit, and so on. So when someone commits a sin by being lured into committing it, it is called *ẹ̀sún*.

Esu: Apart from being tricked or lured into sin by fellow humans, it is also believed that people can be spiritually tricked to commit a sin by Esu (devil). Mitchell has this to say about Esu:

---

126. Oladosu, "Ethics and Judgement," 91–92.
127. Mitchell, *African Primal Religions*, 53.

> Some African peoples number among their divinities one which is especially associated with misfortune and the uncertainties that mark daily life. The Yoruba god eshu [sic] is such a divinity. Basically eshu is the trickster deity. He has a great deal of power and is highly respected. Some say that he is a messenger of the gods; others say that even the Supreme Being is subordinate to eshu in certain matters. Eshu's character is such that his "hobby" is creating mischief.[128]

Because of the belief that Esu is capable of causing people to misbehave, any person who commits any deed which results in unpleasantness to himself/herself or to others . . . could be asked, "Is it Esu who stirred you?"[129] Asante and Nwandiora also explain this Yoruba belief by saying: "When a human [does] evil, he is called Omo Eshu [sic], and the community members say . . . 'It is eshu who stirred him.'"[130]

Orí: *Orí* is people's prenatal destiny which determines almost everything that happens in their lives. Ray gives a vivid description of the role of *orí* in human life:

> It is a semi-split entity having two complementary aspects. One aspect is located in the person's head and constitutes the essence of his personality or ego. The other is located in the heavens and constitutes the person's alter ego of "guardian" soul. Taken as a whole, the *ori* (sic) represents the partial rebirth and incarnation of a patrilineal ancestor; hence it is sometimes called the person's "guardian ancestors." Before a person is born, the ancestor *ori* in heaven chooses his destiny; it is called the "predestined share" or *ori*'s "lot." It determines a person's character, occupation, success in life, and time of death.[131]

In line with the foregoing discussion, some people are naturally born with some specific moral defect. And that some people are destined to be thieves, troublemakers or womanisers, etc. According to tradition, nothing much

---

128. Mitchell, 65.
129. Ikenga-Metuh, *Comparative Studies*, 154.
130. Asante and Nwadiora, *Spear Masters*, 69.
131. Ray, *African Religions*, 135–36.

may be done to change people who are acting based on the content of their *orí*. However, a little effort can be put in place to appeal to one's *orí*, whereby the Ifa priest would offer some ritual so that a little adjustment can be made about those who chose wrong *orí* as they make their way to the world from the heaven.

Dealing with Sin in the Yoruba Traditional Thoughts and Practices: Kingship Involvement

The Yoruba are aware of the gravity of sin in the society. Therefore, serious measures are put in place to deal with it. The central idea of this subsection is that the Yoruba way of dealing with sin is such that the social and political systems are built to ensure the daily pursuit of morality by all members of this society.

Communal Accountability

The Yoruba culture has a system of accountability that is socially entrenched. This system provides a public eye through which every member of the community is watched, and therefore, helped to live a moral life. It also serves as a chain of information through which the leader of a community, either chief or king, can be fed with information concerning how community members are conducting themselves.

It is the responsibility of every community member to ensure that his/her neighbour complies with the moral law, embedded in moral codes earlier discussed. One holds the right to confront any member of the community who is observed to be violating these laws; otherwise, repercussions will catch up with both the violator and the witness. This is why Yoruba people would say "*Bí ará ilé eni bá ń jẹ aáyán, kí a kìlọ̀ fún un*" (If you find your neighbour eating cockroaches, do not hesitate to warn him/her [because when the repercussion comes, you will also suffer sleepless nights like him/her]). Serious violation of moral laws can attract punishment such as banishment. Likewise, anyone who violates this law would be consciously or unconsciously stigmatised by other members of the society.

When someone is going out of the house, it is expected that the head of the family should know where he/she is going and what he/she is going to do there. The term used for this is *dágbére n'ílé* (informing your household of your whereabouts). It is also important to ask critical questions from one's neighbours when their movement is not understood. Neighbours want to know how someone got his/her wealth, where someone goes at night and so on. As much as this could be done by direct enquiry, people can also learn about the movement and behaviour of a neighbour by silent observation. To this end it is said that "*Àwòdì òkè, kó má rò'pé ará ayé kò rí òhun*" (Let not the eagle in the sky think people walking on the earth do not see her). The implication is that everyone is under public scrutiny.

Since every kind of sin has its consequence, when the consequence comes, both the sinner and the community will suffer from the consequence. Therefore, for any known bad act or sin, the community is obliged to rebuke the sinner collectively; they will call one another and say, "*Ẹ́ jẹ́ ká pa ẹnu pọ̀ ká bá olè wí*" (Let us put our mouths together to rebuke a thief). Of course, this does not apply only to theft but any form of unacceptable acts.

Through community accountability, the head of the community (king or chief) is able to know how everybody is behaving in the society. This is portrayed in the saying, "*Ojú ọba n'ílé, ojú ọba l'óko, èèyàn ní ń jẹ́bẹ́ẹ̀*" (The king's eyes are able to see what happens both in the city and in the village because people are feeding him with information). Through communal accountability, every member of the community serves as the police to one another, sending hints to the king in case of gross misconduct. It therefore becomes everyone's responsibility to call a reported sinner to order or bring him/her to book, when necessary, so that the peace and wellbeing of the community can be preserved.

Atonement Rituals

Sins that have spiritual implication, that is, sins that have to do with offence against the ancestors or gods are usually atoned through "purification rites which seek to cleanse the people"[132] and the land. These rites are usually in the form of burnt offerings and sacrifices. They serve as "propitiatory offerings to turn away the anger of the spirits, or solicit their help."[133] However, "the object for sacrifice may be determined by the custom or by divination, but shedding of blood is an essential element."[134]

---

132. Parrinder, *African Traditional Religion*, 84.
133. Parrinder, 84.
134. Turaki, *Foundations of African Traditional*, 79.

For any sin that is not atoned for or forgiven, it is believed that brutal repercussions would follow, *ẹ̀san á ké* (vengeance would cry out). Such brutal repercussions always imply unfortunate incidents in the community. Meanwhile, as I shall discuss in chapter 4, it is the responsibility of the king to initiate rituals of atonement for sin, although with the help of specialists in the community spiritual matters.

Forgiveness for a Sinner

Yoruba people share the biblical injunction that no one is totally righteous (Rom 3:23). This is why they say that *"Gbogbo ènìyàn l'olè b'ílé bádá"* (Everybody is a thief when no one is watching). This is an allusion to the fact that every human being has the tendency to do something wrong. Thus, there is a place for mercy in dealing with any erring member of the community. When sin is committed against fellow human being(s), a sinner can be forgiven; but when the sin has to do with the ancestors or gods, it is usually atoned for mostly by carrying out rituals, as I earlier noted.

People of the community are proverbially reminded that, *"Bí a kò bá gbàgbé ọ̀rọ̀ àná, a kò ní rí ẹni bárín* (If we do not forget the hurt of the past, we would soon find ourselves without any friend). It is acknowledged that there would always be a sinner in the community. If every act of sin is met with hostility and punishment, the community would never live in peace. Anyone who commits a sin would be asked by the community elders, which is politically constituted, to apologize (*túúbá*). Following the apology, the elders will emphasize the importance and essence of oneness in the community. With this, they would appeal to the offender to offer forgiveness and warn the sinner not to repeat such a sin.

In case of stealing, restitution would be required. Meanwhile, Yoruba people hardly require reparation in their judgement. It is believed that making reparation does not signify brotherhood. To demand reparation is to *"gba ẹ̀san"* (can be translated as "reparation" but with negative connotation). After all, everything in the community, irrespective of the rightful owner, belongs to the entire community. Not demanding reparation has its strong implication on the unity of the Yoruba people.

The kingship role in pardoning a sinner is to facilitate the coming together of involved parties, although in many cases done on his/her behalf by the chiefs. The negotiations between the parties are also facilitated by the king through the chiefs. He also has the responsibility of pronouncing blessings upon the involved parties at the end of the reconciliation process.

From this subsection, we learned that Yoruba have put in place measures both to prevent sin and mitigate its effects. The implication of this is that the people so jealously guard cordial relationships that they do not give room for sin and its effect to disrupt relationships.

Theological Reflection of Yoruba Concept of Sin in Light of Human Wellbeing and Political Responsibility

This study has pointed out that Yoruba consider sin as evil. It is evil in the sense that, it always comes with consequences that bring about pain to an individual or the community at large. It is also a violation of the four-dimensional relationship. Sin is the violation of moral codes that originated from social norms, human conscience, figures of authorities, the ancestors, and the gods. The way to live above sin is to guard one's *ìwà* (behaviour). While sin simply results from an individual's evil desire, at the same time, it is acknowledged that some external factors can make a person to commit a sin; such external factors are *èsun, èèdì, orí,* and Esu. Nobody is above sin; therefore, there are communal provisions for a sinner who acknowledges his or her sin.

The Scripture reveals that the Law is given by God, and it dictates the modality of human relationships with him, the self, environment, and fellow humans. Yoruba people also hold similar beliefs in their understanding that moral codes, although they are known through human instituted sources, are from Olodumare. He will judge all human actions based on his demands on them.

While the Scripture teaches that sin is the enemy of *shalom*, Yoruba people hold a similar belief that sin is the enemy of *àlàáfíà*, which is the Yoruba basic understanding of development. Kwame Gyekye speaks for Yoruba and biblical perspective of development when he contends that "development is essentially a behavioural concept."[135]

According to Yoruba thoughts on development, a community tends to experience development when its people exhibit behaviours that are a requirement for *shalom (àlàáfíà)*. Such behaviour expresses itself in all areas

---

135. Gyekye, *Unexamined Life*, 16.

of human life – political, social, economic, etc.[136] As such, in Yoruba traditional thoughts, like the biblical thought, development is subject to people's behaviour. When their behaviour is favourable to all relationships; that is when there will be development. This is the central message of Deuteronomy 28, whereby God admonishes the Israelites to live a life of obedience to his commandment, as obedience brings blessings, and disobedience, curses.

In Yoruba traditional thoughts, the king has important roles to play in dealing with sin in the society. He has the responsibility of fishing out a sinner to be brought to book. This political responsibility is confirmed in Paul's teaching when he notes that a political leader "is God's minister, an avenger to execute wrath upon him who practices evil" (Rom 13:4, NKJV). Both in biblical and Yoruba beliefs, when a king diligently plays the role of purging the land of evil, the nation will become great and known for peace and prosperity (Prov 14:34). In this way, the role of a king is connected to wellbeing and development.

One important responsibility of a political leader in Yorubaland is to oversee atonement rituals, in order to ward off the evil that comes with the repercussion of a sin. Although this specific assignment was given to the Levites according to the Mosaic law (Lev 16); nevertheless, in 2 Samuel 21, David exemplifies good political leadership when he initiated the "atonement" (v. 3) for Saul's sin in order to ward off the famine caused by it.

Yoruba traditional thoughts hold that a king has a crucial responsibility in pardoning a sinner. This thought has its biblical similarity in the principle of the City of Refuge. In this principle, a sinner who accidentally kills a person finds a means of escape from punishment. If he runs to the city of refuge he would be spared from the death sentence of Mosaic life-for-life law (Exod 21:22–24).

If an individual or a communal sin has the power to cause pain, then sin is capable of violating *àlàáfìà*, which is the true essence of human wellbeing and what development is all about. This has a direct correlation with the scriptural teaching that sin is the destroyer of *shalom*. As such, foundation to human wellbeing, or rather development, is a sin-free life, which is characterised by good relationship between self and God, others and environment. As I have discussed in chapter 2, many antidevelopment phenomena

---

136. Gyekye, 18.

in Africa – corruption, injustice, war, political instability – are largely because of some sin. What if in our world everybody chooses to be an *ọmọlúàbí*?

Although Yoruba sociopolitical system largely has similarity with that of the biblical system, nevertheless they are not without significant pitfalls that make the system fall below God's required standards. As shall be discussed in chapter 4, one of these pitfalls is the involvement of the spiritual intermediaries which comes with its own antidevelopment baggage. The section that follows discusses Yoruba philosophy of education, which prepares community members to be *ọmọlúàbí*.

Yoruba Educational Philosophy and Its Implication for Development

In the previous section, I have talked about the role of sin in human wellbeing. This section shall continue the discussion by highlighting the role played by Yoruba education in ensuring good character in social life and human careers. The aim of this section is to explore Yoruba educational thoughts and practices. Having done that, I shall discuss the basic aim of education in Yorubaland in relation to community wellbeing (which development is all about in Yoruba understanding) and individual political responsibility.

One may say that Yoruba people do not have what is called formal education in Western understanding of education; nevertheless, learning takes place in their traditional setting. This usually takes the form of informal mentorship, apprenticeship, and didactic forms of education such as storytelling, proverbs, etc. In Subari Biobaku's words, we have an idea of the educational tools with which Yoruba pass down knowledge. He writes that Yoruba traditional "learning was essentially oral and remembered and so elaborate traditions of oral literature are built up in praise poems, folklore, proverbs, and wise saying."[137]

The learning begins at home. As a child grows, it is the responsibility of the older family members (parents, aunties, uncles, older siblings, and cousins) to teach the societal norms and values to the younger members. They make use of the educational tools mentioned above. It is believed that a child's good behaviour in the society will depend on how much *ẹ̀kọ́ ilé* (home training)

---

137. Biobaku, "Effect of Urbanization," 452.

he/she received. It would therefore be said about a bad-mannered child that "*Ọmọ tí kò l'ẹ́kọ̀ọ́ ilé*" (A child who lacks home training).

As much as it is the responsibility of every individual family to instill a sense of value into a child, it is also held that a child is raised by a community. This is why it is said that, "*Ojú kan níí bímọ; igba ojú níí bánií wò ó*" (A child belongs to only one eye; but it takes two hundred eyes to raise her). In some instances, young people are taught as a group with the intention of initiating them into a traditional religious cult.[138] Another mode of education is apprenticeship. In this case, a young person acquires knowledge about a trade or vocation under someone else's tutelage.[139]

All the aforementioned Yoruba means of education take place in such a way that meets the universal aims and objectives of education. Education entails seeking knowledge and information and passing them on to others. In Rather's opinion, "Education equips an individual for social, moral, cultural, and spiritual aspects and thus makes life progressive, cultured, and civilized."[140] This implies that education touches all the aspects of human life.

This is also true of Yoruba mode of education. It touches all aspects of human life – social, vocational, intellectual, spiritual, physical, and psychological. Through all the enumerated educational forms and tools among Yoruba people, a child is trained into holistic adulthood. Basic to Yoruba aim of education is that children grow to develop in personal character in order to become *ọmọlúàbí* (well-behaved persons). Having *ìwà rere* is therefore central to Yoruba education. Whatever the mode of education is, whether at home or in the community, the foundational thing is that an individual under training or tutelage grows to become someone who demonstrates good moral standing. *Ìwà rere* must reflect in one's social interaction and career life.

As discussed earlier in the previous section, Yoruba sources of moral code, of which obedience to them leads to *ìwà rere,* are spiritual in nature. In Yoruba education, learners' attention is therefore called to the spiritual universe where all codes that lead to *Ìwà rere* are generated. Dependence on this universe is therefore a necessity. It begins from spiritual dependence.

---

138. Biobaku, 452.
139. Obidi, "Skill Acquisition," 369–84.
140. Rather, *Theory and Principle*, 1.

Yoruba, like all other African people,[141] are people of spirituality. They are people of great devotion to their deities and the supreme being. Therefore, youngsters in the community are taught by their elders the need for revering the spiritual world – the ancestors, deities, and the supreme being. There must be reverence for the divinity (ancestors, deities, and the supreme being) in all day-to-day activities. The younger generations are usually taught to involve the ancestors in whatever they do – in their occupation, marriage, journey, and so forth.

Acquiring knowledge about religious and spiritual matters usually takes place during festivals, ceremonies, and daily events. On such occasions, people offer up prayers to the deities and recite songs and poems that sing their praises and express how they require to be worshipped.

In addition to learning to relate with the spiritual universe through spiritual dependence, another crucial concept whose importance is emphasized as Yoruba young people grow up into adulthood is *ìfura* (spiritual sensitivity).[142] As children grow into their adulthood, they are charged to be spiritually alert and sensitive to whatever is happening around them. The divinity is always communicating to the humanity through some sort of inner feeling. This is what *ìfura* is all about.

This concept is stated as, "*ìfura lòògùn àgbà*" (spiritual sensitivity is the greatest juju possessed by an elder). This may not be taught in any technical form. However, the elders (parents, masters, leaders) often model it to the younger ones, in the way they demonstrate their perception about things. With *ìfura*, people learn from the spiritual universe about how things should be perceived, what decisions need to be made, and what action needs to be taken.

Education towards Social Life, Vocation and Trade in Yoruba Traditional Thoughts

In the social aim of Yoruba education, one important cultural orientation is the role of an individual in the community. Even though there is a place for some personal decision, an individual cannot be detached by any means

---

141. Bediako, *Christianity in Africa*, 97.
142. Olumide Omoboye, an oral interview held at Karen, Nairobi, 29 November 2017. Omoboye, presently in his mid-fifties, is a Yoruba missionary to Kenya.

from the society.¹⁴³ Every individual must learn to think about the community. One is accountable to the community and must think of the good of the community. Individual members of the community must take pride in their community and have their identity rooted in it. One is usually reminded that, *"Odò tó bá gbàgbé orísun rẹ̀ yóó gbẹ"* (A river that forgets its source will dry off). Likewise, the need for one's dependence on the community is highly stressed.¹⁴⁴

Having being reminded of the necessity of one's affinity with the community, an individual must also learn not to do evil things to anyone in the community. In order to register this impression on the mind of everyone, the elders would say, *"A kìí ta ẹ̀kọ rírọ̀ f'árá ilè"* (It is a bad thing to sell spoilt pap to a relative [which generally refers to a community member]). As people are given this impression as they generally prepare for life, it is also a necessary orientation for people in their vocations and trades.

Vocations and trades in Yorubaland, in many cases, are carried out on family basis. Many families are usually known for their family vocation or trade. Family or clan names usually indicate the nature of the careers they are known for. Examples of family names in the Yorubaland are: *ilé alágbèdè* (blacksmith family), *ilé aláyàn* (drummers family), *ilé ọlọ́dẹ* (hunters family), etc.¹⁴⁵

The implication of this is that people entered into the vocations or trades they inherited from their forebears. These kinds of career that are inherited or handed down from one generation to the other are called *iṣẹ́ àjogúnbá* (inherited vocation) or *iṣẹ́ abínibí* (vocation by virtue of birth). Because it is *iṣẹ́ àjogúnbá*, children grow up learning it from their parents. The *iṣẹ́ àjogúnbá* in Yorubaland could be either *iṣẹ́ ọwọ́* (craftwork) or *òwò ṣíṣe* (trade).¹⁴⁶

Aside from having a child automatically towing the family career line, parents also consult the oracle to determine the kind of vocation or trade that befits the destiny of a child.¹⁴⁷ In some cases, the kind of vocations advised by the oracle may not necessarily be a family vocation or trade. In such cases, there is probability that the child will undertake his/her apprenticeship with

---

143. Oyeshile, "Traditional Yoruba," 86.
144. Aladejana, "Axiological Analysis," 21.
145. Omoboye, oral interview.
146. Omoboye.
147. Obidi, "Skill Acquisition," 374.

another person other than his/her parents. The essence of consulting the oracle is to be sure that a child carries out the kind of vocation or trade he/she was sent to do in the world by the gods. This is called *"iṣẹ́ Orí ránni"* (The career entrusted by *Orí*, the god of destiny and fortune).

In any case, there are certain levels of social responsibility placed on people as they undertake their vocations and trades. People are expected to demonstrate a high level of morality in their careers. Upon the completion of a young person's career training, a ceremony is conducted where he/she will be charged to uphold good virtues as he/she pursues his/her vocation or trade. Such virtues include honesty, promise-keeping, reliability, and so forth.

Yoruba believe that some careers, and perhaps all careers, have deities that are associated with them. For instance, all vocations having to do with iron (or metal smelting, blacksmithing, hunting, and so forth) are associated with *Ogún* (the god of iron).[148] *Ogún* is actually said to be the founder of all ferrous vocations. People who are engaged in trade are also greeted as *"Ajé á bugbá jẹ"* (The god *Ajé* would consume your merchandise). Through this greeting, it is probable that *Ajé* is widely associated with trade or the "god of wealth."[149] Associating vocations and trades to deities is an indication of sacredness of work. Human vocations and trades are handed down by the deities and the deities are particular about how they are carried out. People who engage in dubious practices in their work would attract the wrath of the deities.

It is believed that a community is built when everyone carries out their work. It is popularly said that, *"Ọmọdé níṣẹ́ àgbà níṣẹ́, la fi dá'lẹ̀ Ifẹ̀"* (Ife was built by virtue of the work of both young and aged). Apart from the individual fortune that comes to the workers through the profit they make in their businesses or the income from their vocation, work is a way of contributing to the growth and development of the society. The examples of vocational practices in Yorubaland are *àgbẹ̀dẹ* (blacksmith), *ọdẹ* (hunting), *àyàn* (talking drumming) *àdìrẹ* (tie and dye), *ọlọ́nà* (tailoring), *gbẹ́nà-gbẹ́nà* (carpentry), and so on.

---

148. Obidi, 374.

149. Martin Kondwani White, "Salute to Aje, Goddess of Wealth," *Oral Poetry from Africa*, accessed 21 March 2020, https://africanpoems.net/gods-ancestors/salute-to-aje-orisha-of-wealth/.

Theological Reflections on Yoruba Educational Philosophy

As indicated in the foregoing discussion, the concept of education among Yoruba is built on informal interactions – there is no classroom, syllabus, or assessment. Children and young people are taught all the concepts discussed above. This shall be further discussed in chapter 6.

Education brings about changes in human life. It offers knowledge that is capable of bringing about change of perspective and, ultimately, attitude. It creates awareness that leads people into helpful discoveries that enhances their safety, wellbeing, and better life. This is why education is a vital instrument in human development. People perish without knowledge (Hos 4:6).

Moses told the people of Israel that the nation would be seen as a great nation if people follow the Law and commandments which he has *taught* them, as given by the Lord (Deut 4: 5–6). This Law and commandment should therefore be *taught* to the children: "Impress them on your children. Talk about them when you sit at home and when you walk along the road, when you lie down and when you get up" (Deut 6:7, NIV).

In obedience to Moses's instruction in Deuteronomy, the writer of Psalm 78, perhaps on behalf of the people of his generation, made a promise that all the things they have *learnt* from the previous generation would be *taught* to their children (vv. 3–4). What the Israelites are simply instructed to pass down to their children, according to Deuteronomy, is God's commandment given through Moses. This is so that they would always remember to obey it in order to prosper as a nation (chapter 28).

As the prosperity of the nation of Israel is based on obedience to God, so it is believed too among the Yoruba people. Therefore, among other orientations provided by education, of most paramount importance is the knowledge of God that leads to good character (*ìwà rere*), and enables one to make divinely inspired decision. For Yoruba people, education is incomplete without knowledge and practice of spirituality whose ultimate end is *ìwà rere* in their daily lives.

Another important concept as reflected in the discourse on Yoruba choice of career is "*Iṣẹ́ Orí ránni*." This leaves us with the idea that work is God's mission entrusted into human's hand. It brings us to a critical understanding in the theology of work, that work makes us all God-sent (Gen 1:27). It is also a reminder that we are all God-called (2 Pet 1:10). This is a reminder that "everything we are, everything we do, and everything we have is invested with a special devotion and dynamism lived out as a response to his summon and service."[150]

Talking about human career, politics, and community, Aquinas opines that each career is an aspect of human learning, and that it is impossible for a single individual to be an expert in all these areas of learning. This is why it is important that each person in the community devotes himself/herself to one branch of learning, "one to medicine, another to something else, another to something else again."[151] As such, human career becomes a means by which people complement one another in the community (Eccl 4:9). This is therefore a political responsibility of every member of the society. Yoruba therefore uphold the biblical truth in their thoughts concerning education, career, and community wellbeing when they say, *"Ọmọdé n'íṣẹ́ àgbà n'íṣẹ́, la fi dá'lè Ifẹ̀"* (Ife was built by virtue of the work of both young and aged).

In summary, Yoruba philosophy of education in relation to life and career takes seriously the place of character and values, borne out of the awareness of divine requirement of humans. Good character and values must reflect in daily social interaction and that people should go about with their career with the awareness that the divine is involved in it. Yoruba also speak in line with the scriptural belief that human branches of learning and people's careers are the means to make the society a better place. In this way, Yoruba educational concept and philosophy has made a significant contribution to the wellbeing (development) of the society in that it emphasizes the place of good character, made possible by spiritual dependence and sensitivity, and the need to apply one's vocation for the betterment of the society. Meanwhile, the application of one's vocation, in Aquinas's view, is a political responsibility of every member of the society.

The Role of Yoruba Politics in Development

So far, in this chapter, I have discussed the Yoruba concept of development, effect of sin on development and Yoruba educational philosophy in relation to development. This section seeks to discuss the role of political leadership in community wellbeing and development. I shall achieve this aim by doing

---

150. Guinness, *Finding and Fulfilling*, 4.
151. Hoelzl and Ward, *Religion and Political Thought*, 42.

a linguistic analysis of a proverb that relates the kingship role with society's wellbeing and development.

Yoruba political system is monarchical, headed by a king. Kingship is a critical concept in Yorubaland in that almost everything centres on the king. Everybody belongs to the king and the king belongs to everybody. Everything belongs to the king and the king takes charge of everything. The lives of both animals and humans are in his hands. The prosperity and progress of the land are all his responsibility. The prominence of kingship in the wellbeing of a society is revealed in the proverb, "*Ọba tó jẹ tí ìlú rójú, a kò ní gbàgbé rẹ̀*" (The king whose reign is characterised by order will not be forgotten).

The use of this proverb is not limited to a king who rules over a town or city. It is also used to apply to all forms of leaderships, generally to imply that any leader whose leadership is positively remarkable is the real leader. The concept of *ìlú rójú* in the proverb is important in stressing the ultimate expectation of a king or a leader. Breaking the phrase into two words, *ìlú* is usually translated as "town," "city," or "society." However, *ìlú* as used in the proverb refers generally to the community of people, since the proverb applies to all forms of leadership. The word *rójú* (whose complicated translation will soon be discussed) can be summarily translated as "enjoy order" so that the phrase *ìlú rójú* can be loosely translated as "society is in good order." With this loose translation, the reader can grasp the overall idea at first sight. Nevertheless, there is more meaning to the phrase.

Now coming to the details of the translation of the word *rójú*, we can have the deep understanding of the expectation a community has from a leader or king. The root of *rójú* is evidently found in the word *ojú*, which generally means "eyes" or "face."[152] It is a contraction of either or both of these phrases *rí ojú* and *rọ ojú*. Taking *rójú* as a contraction of *rí ojú*, this is well explained with the saying "*Ọkọ kò rójú aya, aya kò rójú ọkọ*" (Husband cannot see the face of his wife, while wife cannot also see the face of her husband). This saying is usually used when people are carried away by an event or there is chaos in the society so that people cannot sit down and have family fun together. Therefore, the connotation of *rójú* in this sense is peace and order.

To consider *rójú* as a contraction of *rọ ojú*, the phrase will be better defined when we consider it in relation of its opposite, *le ojú*. The phrase *rọ*

---

152. Delano, "Oju", *Atumo Ede Yoruba: Yoruba*, 150.

ojú can be loosely translated as "to have soft face." The opposite of *"rọ ojú"* is *"le ojú"* (to have a hard face). These two opposite terms are usually used in two cases: (1) when people have a frown on their faces (also said in Yoruba as *"le ojú"*) rather than a friendly look (also said in Yoruba as *rọ ojú*); (2) in case of a boil at the time when it is still hard to press (*le ojú*) and when it is now soft to press (*rọ ojú*) and the sufferer begins to feel some comfort. The connotations of *rọ ojú* as seen in this explanation are "smile," "friendliness," "peace," and "comfort," whereby the first three connotations can be subsumed into the word "peace." We can therefore say that the term *r'ójú* partly implies peace and comfort in the society.

Quite metonymically, *ojú* is also used to mean "a point of entry or a point where something is done or begun." For example, *ojúlé* means the point of entry into a house or doorway; *ojúbo* means the point where a god is worshipped; *ojútùú* means the point where to begin disentanglement of a tangled rope or twine.

It is more probable that the word *r'ójú* in the proverb of discussion also has to do with the phrase *rí ojútùú* (to find a point where to begin disentanglement), which is literally used relating to a tangled rope. When the *ojútùú* (the point of disentangling) is found in a tangled rope, it comes with a feeling of peace for the one trying to disentangle the rope, knowing that solution to the problem has been reached. Hence, *rí ojútùú* (or *r'ójútùú*) in Yoruba language is figuratively used to mean "solution to a problem."

Yoruba language being a language that uses much contraction could then have shortened or contracted the word *r'ójútùú* into *r'ojú*, so that the implication of the proverb *Ọba tó jẹ tí ìlú r'ójú, a kò ní gbàgbé rẹ̀* is that "the king whose reigns brings solution to the society's problem will always remain in people's memory."

The term *r'ójú* also can denote "chance or opportunity." For example, people pray that *"Ọlọ́run jẹ́ n r'ójú r'áyè setèmi"* (God, give me the opportunity and room to do all that concern me). Meanwhile, *r'ójú* as in *"Ọlọ́run jẹ́ n r'ójú r'áyè setèmi"* usually could be translated as "opportunity" or "chance." It is essentially referring to ability to be able to do a thing, which is obtained from good health, peace, and favourable chance. Therefore, when Yoruba pray *"Ọlọ́run jẹ́ n r'ójú r'áyè setèmi,"* they are begging God to give them all it requires for them to do all they are required to do.

Substituting this into the main proverb of analysis, *"Ọba tó jẹ tí ìlú r'ójú, a kò ní gbàgbé rẹ̀,"* we can infer that people also mean to say that "the king who reigns and the society is able to do all that concern them during his reign shall always be remembered." And as it has been indicated in the foregoing analysis, being able to do all that concerns them is a matter of good health, peace in the society, and favourable chances. With this, we come to the awareness that in the Yorubaland the good health of the people in the society, their peace, and good luck is attributed to the political terms of the ruling king.

Putting all these analyses together, we can infer that when people say *"Ọba tó jẹ tí ìlú r'ójú, a kò ní gbàgbé rẹ̀,"* they are relaying their expectation of a king to ensure peace, order, prosperity, comfort and solutions to problems in his time. It is always believed that solutions to all problems in the society should come from the palace. The success of the reign of a king is measured by the amount of *ojútùú*, peace, and cosmic order, which prepares the ground for all indices of wellbeing – progress, comfort, growth, etc.

The importance of peace and cosmic order is also depicted in the saying, *"Kí eku máa ké bíi eku, kí ẹyẹ máa ké bíi ẹyẹ"* (That the rat squeaks like a rat, and that the bird chirps like a bird). The folktale below vividly communicates the belief that it is the role of the king to find solutions to all threats against peace and cosmic order of the society.

> Once upon a time, there was a woman, *Ìyá Alàkàrà,* who sells *àkàrà* (bean cake) for her daily business. Tortoise (*ìjàpá*) employed the service of giant rat (*òkété*) in digging an underground hole from his house to *Ìyá Alàkàrà's* business joint. He dressed himself in masquerade regalia and used the underground hole to access the joint. On getting there, he changed his voice like that of a masquerade and scared *Ìyá Alàkàrà,* who took to her heels and left her *àkàrà* behind. Tortoise packed and ate all the *àkàrà*. He did this repeatedly.
>
> The first time this incident happened, *Ìyá Alàkàrà* brought it to the notice of her husband who attempted to do something about the predicament. He did not succeed; therefore, he took the matter to the village head (*Baálẹ̀*), who in turn reported the matter to a chief in the king's court, who finally reported the

matter to the king. This is when the king reported the matter to the ancestor, the Ifa oracle.

Then, the ancestors instructed them to make use of *àròni* (a handicapped man with one hand and one leg) to fight the battle against the mischievous "masquerade." The *àròni* set a net trap for the Tortoise-turned-masquerade and was captured, and killed. And thus, the predicament came to an end.[153]

This folktale portrays the role of a king in the society – the centre of all solutions to the societal problems.

Since events in people's lives are dated in relation to the reign of a king, it makes it tenable that a king's reign is not just remembered because of the peace and prosperity enjoyed by the people, it is also remembered because of the misfortunes. This is why it is also true that *Ọba tó jẹ tí ilú dàrú, a kò ní gbàgbé rẹ̀* (the king whose reign is characterised with chaos will also not be forgotten). The implication of the proverb under study is, therefore, that it is the fundamental responsibility of a king to make sure that everything needed for community wellbeing is in place. He exists solely for the state's wellbeing.

This Yoruba developmental-political thought is similar to the Bible's use of "shepherd" as a kingship connotation (Isa 40:11; Jer 23:4; Ezek 34:23; 37:24). The role of a shepherd is to ensure the wellbeing of the sheep (Ps 23; John 10:11–16), just as the Yoruba king must ensure the wellbeing of his people.

Conclusion

This chapter began by discussing the Yoruba understanding of development, which fundamentally implies living in peace (*àlàáfíà*). A line of correlation was drawn between this belief and *shalom*, the biblical belief of wellbeing. The peace (which implies development in Yoruba traditional thought) of a community is said to be founded on cordial relationships between individuals and divinity, community, self and environment. *Ẹ̀ṣẹ̀* (sin) is said to be the paramount inhibitor of *àlàáfíà*. Violation of any of the relationships stated above implies sin. With this in mind, it is therefore noted that development

---

153. Agbaje, *Alo Ninu Asa Yoruba*, 61–62.

in Yorubaland has a behavioural concept. Development ensues when people exhibit behaviours that are favourable to relationships.

In traditional Yoruba means of dealing with sin, which are communal accountability, atonement, and forgiveness, the king plays a prominent role. This implies that the king has a crucial responsibility of ensuring the behavioural requirement, *ìwà rere,* of the community.

Yoruba philosophy of education emphasizes *ìwà rere,* which must be reflected in people's social interactions, careers, and everyday life. Talking about people's obligation to one another in times of need, *ìwà rere* propels them into social responsibility of taking care of the ones who are in need. As it is the responsibility of all community members to maintain *ìwà rere,* it is also the responsibility of the king to do everything within his capacity to ensure good governance and good character of the people so that there is *àlàáfíà* (Yoruba foundation for development) in the society. This is his primary responsibility as a political leader, if the community must experience wellbeing.

The chapter that follows shall discuss some specific practices in Yorubaland common to political leadership. As it has been stressed in this chapter that the king, in his political role, only exists to ensure the wellbeing of the society, all his political endeavours, which naturally take on other dimensions – social, spiritual, military, etc. – are all development initiatives. Everything the king does, according to the expectations placed on him, is geared towards ensuring the wellbeing of the society.

CHAPTER 4

Kábíyèsí, Aláṣẹ Èkejì Òrìṣà: Yoruba Traditional Developmental-Political Practices

Introduction

In his discussion relating politics with development, Gyekye notes:

> Even though political development, as a species of development, cannot logically be equated with genus of development as such, nonetheless political development, inasmuch as it creates conditions for other kinds of development, appears to hold a prominent position in the whole process of development. This point seems to be rationally non-negotiable.[1]

Although politics is not everything when it comes to the discourse on development, it plays a significant role in influencing all other elements of development in the society. It influences the economy, culture, judiciary, commerce, education, and so forth, in that all of them, naturally, operate within a social system under a political leadership.

In Ayittey's *Indigenous African Institutions* and Njoh's *Tradition, Culture and Development in Africa*, both of which I have earlier cited in this book, traditional Africa is portrayed as a community with institutions that were

---

1. Gyekye, *Unexamined Life*, 19.

favourable for development. Both Ayittey and Njoh made a noteworthy reference to the fact that the distortion of the African political system has led to distortion in all other traditional development institutions in Africa.

This chapter, therefore, shall examine some vital Yoruba traditional political practices and their theological implications for development. As a way of preparing the ground, I shall first do a brief historical sketch that will help better understand Yoruba political practices and then go on to paint a picture of how Yoruba traditional political system operated in order to ensure development.

Meanwhile, in accordance with my conclusion in chapter 3 that the king only exists for the wellbeing of the society, all the political activities and beliefs discussed in this chapter are in themselves taken for development initiatives. All political actions, as gravitated around the king, are all in place to ensure the wellbeing of the society.

The Political History of Yoruba

There are two popular versions of Yoruba origin. One is found in their creation myth passed down by oral tradition, while the other relates to the migration story of the Yoruba progenitor; usually regarded as the academic version.[2] Yoruba creation myth ascertains that the creation of the earth began from Ile Ife.[3] Olodumare (also called Olorun), the supreme being, co-existed with many *òrìṣà* (gods). In the beginning, there only existed the *ọ̀run* (sky) and *ayé* (the world). The world had no solid ground since everywhere was filled with water. One day God had an idea to create human beings and have them live in the world.

Therefore, he summoned all the *òrìṣà* led by the one called Obatala (also called *Òrìṣà Ńlá*) and discussed this idea with them. However, Olodumare left the responsibility to Obatala to carry out the idea. Obatala descended from heaven through a strand of rope. On getting to the earth, there was water everywhere so that he did not find any place where he could land. He had travelled down with a chicken and a snail shell filled with sand. He poured

---

2. Samuel Ajuwon, WhatsApp interview, 5 October 2019. Ajuwon is a senior lecturer of Yoruba Language at Federal College of Education, Obudu, River State, Nigeria.

3. Trieber, "Creation," 114–18.

the soil on the surface of the water at a particular spot in Ile Ife and released the chicken to scatter the soil with its feet so that any place that the grains of the soil landed became a habitable solid ground.

Through this story, the Yoruba people believe that the earth started extending from the spot where Obatala poured the soil and left the chicken to spread it all over. Upon the completion of the creation of the earth, Olorun again instructed Obatala to mould human beings. He did this and Olorun breathed into the images that Obatala had moulded and they became human beings.

Among other gods that accompanied Obatala was Oduduwa, known to be the favourite of Olorun. Some version of the creation myth credited the creation work to Oduduwa. He later became the first king of Ile Ife. As such, Oduduwa became the central figure in Yoruba history. In fact, the migration story of Yoruba people centres mainly around him.

The migration history reveals that the founding father of Yoruba people, "Oduduwa, son of a Meccan king, rebelled against his father and Islam, and fled to Ile Ife, where he founded Yoruba kingship."[4]

On getting to Ile Ife, he met Obatala and Agboniregun, the leaders of the indigenous people. The community of the indigenous people was helpless in the face of a neighbouring community who frequently attacked them. Following Oduduwa's arrival, his spiritual valour put an end to the frequent savage attacks and battles. Upon achieving this feat, Oduduwa was crowned king of the community.[5]

Each of the popular versions of the Yoruba origin is not without criticism. The Yoruba creation story is considered a myth since no one can ascertain its scientific validity. These creation stories are metaphysical in nature and are not subjected to scientific proofs. The critics of the story wonder about the size of the snail shell carried by Obatala such that it packed such a quantity of sand that was sufficient to fill the entire earth. They also wonder how long it would take a chicken to scatter such a quantity of sand throughout the earth.[6]

On the other hand, some historians also discredit the validity of the migration story of Oduduwa from Mecca, noting that "no such accounts as the above are to be found in the records of Arabian writers of any kings of

---

4. Apter, *Black Critics and Kings*, 15.
5. Andy, *Oduduwa*.
6. Ajuwon, interview.

Mecca; an event of such importance could hardly have passed unnoticed by their historians."[7] Because of this, another account of the origin of Yoruba people, particularly by Samuel Johnson whose work is said to be the "principal glory of Yoruba historiography,"[8] holds that Yoruba actually originated and migrated from the East, but not necessarily from Mecca. This is where the mix–up came:

> With them the East is Mecca and Mecca is the East. Having strong affinities with the East, and Mecca in the East looming so largely in their imagination, everything that comes from the East, with them, comes from Mecca, and hence it is natural to represent themselves as having hailed originally from that city.[9]

Considering the two narratives concerning the origin of Yoruba people, this study holds the migration story to be more probable. Although there are different arguments and versions of the story about where Oduduwa migrated from, many scholars and historians concur that he was not originally from Ile Ife.

In addition to the concerns raised above, regarding the validity of Yoruba creation myth, I question its authenticity because of the claim that Ile Ife is the origin of all human races, where the work of creation began. Tracing the dating of Yoruba history, the earliest reliable date of Oduduwa's kingship is AD 782.[10] Meanwhile, all available indications show that the earth had already existed long before.

At Ile Ife, Oduduwa married Olokun and gave birth to only one son, Okanbi, from whom all the tribes of Yoruba descended. Okanbi had seven children, five males, and two females. The first two children were princesses who married men of their choices. Olowu of Owu and Oniketu of Ketu were respective sons of the princesses. The sons also became kings alongside their uncles: Oba of Benin; Orangun of Ila; Onisabe of Sabe; Onipopo of Popo; and Oranmiyan who ascended the throne of his grandfather Oduduwa.

Oranmiyan, having taken over the throne of his grandfather, became militarily powerful. Some traditions hold that at the peak of his power, he deemed

---

7. Johnson, *History of the Yorubas*, 4.
8. Law, "Early Yoruba Historiography," 72.
9. Johnson, *History of the Yorubas*, 5.
10. Ojo, "Brochure: Oranyan Festival 2017," 19.

it fit to go to Mecca and avenge his father who was chased out of there. As he set out on this mission, he appointed one of his servants (some accounts hold that he was his son) to watch over the affairs of the state.[11] Oranmiyan could not go beyond the River Niger for some reasons that are strongly debated among scholars. He settled down at Oyo Ile (also known as Eyoe, or Old Oyo by contemporary historians) to avoid the shame of going back to Ile Ife.

Oyo Ile became the political headquarters of the Yoruba people while Ile Ife remains the spiritual headquarters since it still holds the physical presence of the places of worship of the deities. Likewise, all the royal treasures remained in Ile Ife. However, they were usually brought to Oyo when the need arose. For instance, upon the death of Oranmiyan, *idà* Oranmiyan (the sword of Oranmiyan), a symbol of power for the Yoruba king, was always brought from Ile Ife when a new king was to be crowned.

The descendants of Oranmiyan known as Yoruba proper began to spread across many parts of the country. During this time when Oranmiyan's descendants were at the height of their military prowess in the eighteenth century, "they spread from Eyeo (Old Oyo) to as far west as Ketu, Idassa, Shabe and Kilibo and beyond into Dahomey and Togoland; to as far as the banks of the Niger; and their influence reached as far east as Benin."[12]

In order to provide a more vivid description of how Yoruba people scattered across the country, Parrinder's account, as quoted by Ojo, is worthwhile:

> The kingdom of Yoruba extends from Puka on the South, which is within five miles of the sea, to Lagos and Whydah in that line, to the north about 10th degree of north latitude. It is surrounded by Dahomey to the north-west, which is reckoned a tributary province: Ketto and Maha countries on the north, Borgoo on the north-east, five days distant; Jaboo to the south and west. Its tributaries are Dahomey, Alladah, Badagry and Maha.[13]

The picture painted of the geography of Yoruba nation in the excerpt above shows the vast geographical spread of the people, such a spread that can be said to be approximate size of the present-day Sierra Leone or Gambia. As

---

11. Ogunmefu, *Yoruba Legends*, 446–55; Crowther, *Brief History of the Yoruba*, 29.
12. Ojo, *Yoruba Culture*, 18.
13. Ojo, 18.

the Yoruba proper, the descendants of Oranmiyan began to spread, so also their other Yoruba relatives from Oduduwa stock – the Benin, the Ijebu, to mention a few.

In the long run, the spread of the people, as they were separated by distance, resulted in creating subgroups among Yoruba people. During the course of time, some Yoruba subgroups metamorphosed into kingdoms such as Egba kingdom, Ijebu kingdom, Ekiti kingdom, and so forth.

The Yoruba settlements are categorised into six: *ìlú aládé* or *olú ìlú* (crown town or capital town), *ìlú eréko* (outlying or secondary towns or settlements located, literally, on the fringe of farmland), *ìlú ọlọ́jà* (market town), *ìletò* (village), *abúlé* (hamlet), and *agọ́* or *abà* (camp settlement). Each of these categories of settlements has their political life. While some settlements pay tributes to the heads of other communities, some independently exist on their own. All the settlements founded by the direct descendants of Oduduwa are always capital towns and therefore pay no tributes to other community heads. This is because they are all headed by crowned kings. It is important to note that only community heads of *ìlú aládé* hold the right to wear crowns; heads of other categories of settlements do not.

The Political Administration of Oyo Empire

In the Oyo Empire, the political system was conically structured. All the stakeholders in the society were organised in a way that there was vertical flow of order and authority from the palace to the smallest political entity. Ajayi and Buhari indicate the order of the political units as follows:

> The smallest unit called *Idile* (Nuclear family) is headed by a *Bale*. The next unit is the *Ebi*, (extended family headed by *Mogaji* who is the most influential or usually the eldest person in the *Ebi*. Extended family includes all people who have blood ties. The last tier of the units is the quarter, which comprizes of several family compounds headed by a *Baale*, (the chief-of-ward/quarter).[14]

---

14. Ajayi and Buhari, "Methods of Conflict Resolution," 143–44.

However, there were some other political headships in between the *Baálè* and the king depending on the category of the settlement. For instance, if the settlement was a hamlet, it would be headed by a *Baálè* (pronounced differently from *Baálé*, the head of a family compound), who would be reporting to a chief in the king's court, who in turn reported to the king.

The Alaafin being the head of Oyo Empire had the responsibility both to govern the royal city as well as the tributary settlements. How did he go about ruling the vast empire? I posed this question to the Alaafin of Oyo's palace, during a focus group discussion with a team of elderly princes led by Chief Hazzan Adeyemi, the Mogaji of the kingdom.[15]

There were three notable aristocratic groups associated with kingdom matters in the Oyo Empire. These were the *Òyó Mèsì*, *Ìwèfà* and *Èṣó*. The *Òyó Mèsì* consisted of seven most notable and honourable councillors of the state,"[16] namely, (1) *Basòrun* (2) *Àgbàakin* (3) *Sàmù* (4) *Alápini* (5) *Lágùnà* (6) *Akinikú* and, (7) *Aṣípa*. The council was constituted as the representatives of the people in the kingdom, who spoke on behalf of the people in the king's court. They were also in the position to serve as kingmakers (*afobaje*).

Basòrun who was the head of the council is next in command to the king. While the role of many of the members of the council remains unclear, members such as *Alápini* were said to be in charge of *Egúngún* worship, and perhaps in charge of all religious matters. *Lágùnà* served as "the state ambassador in critical times." *Aṣípa* was the one who "distributes whatever presents are given to the *Òyó Mèsì*.[17] The enormity of the power accrued to the leader of *Òyó Mèsì*, *Basòrun*, is reflected in how, in history, he dealt with some kings, as narrated by Falola and Heaton:

---

15. This focus group discussion took place at Alaafin of Oyo's palace on 13 June 2019, with a group of five elderly princes, of which only Chief Hazzan Adeyemi, the official head of the prince (*mogaji*), agreed to be identified. It is culturally unacceptable in Yoruba culture for a younger person to ask the age of an elder (I was in my mid-thirties at the time of the interview); we could only guess the age of the princes as follows: while Chief Hazzan appeared to be in his early to mid-seventies, other princes, who appeared younger and addressed him with respect according to Yoruba culture, could be in their mid-sixties. However, the discussion in this subsection is based on the outcome of the focused group discussion and the literature materials that are referenced.

16. Johnson, *History of the Yorubas*, 69.

17. Johnson, 72.

Such powers made it possible for the Oyo Mesi to exert significant, sometimes even disruptive, control over the office of alafin [sic]. The most famous example is the case of Gaha, who, as the basorun, or leader, of the Oyo Mesi from 1754 to 1774, secured the suicides of two alafins, Labisi and Awonbioju. Gaha then forced Awonbioju's successor, Agboluaje, to accede to Gaha's authority, over which issue Agboluaje eventually committed suicide. It is speculated that Gaha may also have been responsible for the death of Agboluaje's successor, Majeogbe, supposedly through magic or poisoning. Gaha was eventually overthrown by Alafin Abiodun, who called upon aid from the provinces of Oyo to end Gaha's tyrannical rule.[18]

Reinforcing Falola and Heaton's narrative of the extent of the power of the Ọ̀yọ́ Mèsì, Lloyd also notes that among Yoruba people, the king was made answerable to the chiefs to the extent that he could rarely do anything "except with the advice of the chiefs." He describes the rivalry between the king and the chiefs by saying, "King and chief . . . vied for power. Since the king had no direct control over the army and no substantial personal bodyguard of the palace slaves, he was in a weak position to coerce the chiefs, who in the last resort could depose him, often by asking him to commit suicide."[19] It therefore holds to be true that, "The alaafin was, in theory, an autocrat or absolute ruler of the empire's government. . . . [But] in practice, his authority was limited; he was subject to powerful non-royal chiefs . . . the Oyo Mesi."[20]

The ìwẹ̀fà, the second aristocratic group in Oyo Empire, were upgraded slaves. In a discussion related to this, Apter notes only three members of this group,[21] whereas I gathered from the focus group discussion that this aristocratic group had at least nine members, who were also referred to as ẹmẹ̀wà. Apter mentions only Ọ̀tún Ìwẹ̀fà, Ọnà Ìwẹ̀fà, and Òsì Ìwẹ̀fà in his writing, whereas the remaining ones were: Ilú Sìnmí, Kúdẹ̀fù, Ọbágborí, Mápèńpa, Ilú gbànńkà, and Ọbákáyéjá.

---

18. Falola and Heaton, *History of Nigeria*, 50.
19. Lloyd, *Africa in Social Change*, 39.
20. Usman and Falola, *Yoruba from Prehistory*, 121.
21. Apter, *Black Critics and Kings*, 24.

The term *ẹmẹ̀wà* meant entourage. This implies that this aristocratic group usually accompanied the king on his official outings. Meanwhile, among the aristocratic group, *Ọ̀tún Ìwẹ̀fà, Ọnà Ìwẹ̀fà,* and *Òsì Ìwẹ̀fà* were noted to be the most senior ones.[22] *Ọ̀tún Ìwẹ̀fà* (which can be translated as "the eunuch of the right") was officially in charge of Sango cult. In accomplishing his responsibility, his office was connected with the *ìlàrí* and *ajelè*.[23] *Ìlàrí* were the king's personal messengers and servants. "Some of the *ìlàrí* were exclusive representatives of the king in territories outside the capital, or they performed religious functions in the palace and collected taxes at the city gates."[24]

Meanwhile, the *ajẹlẹ̀* were known to be the king's resident overlord whose roles were similar to that of the *ìlàrí*.[25] With the similarity between the roles of the *ajẹlẹ̀* and *ìlàrí*, it is therefore difficult to differentiate the two groups. However, they were both saddled with the responsibility of serving as a link between the capital town and the tributary ones. One of the prominent missions they accomplished with the official linkage responsibility, under the supervision of *Ọ̀tún Ìwẹ̀fà,* was to unify the constituent towns by passing down religious ideology, especially concerning Sango the deity with which the office of the Alaafin was mystified. Apter narrates the story this way: "The Shango [sic] cult was . . . fused with Oyo's imperial administration to distribute the Alaafin's ritual power and political authority."[26]

The third aristocratic class of the Alaafin's administration was the *ẹ̀sọ́* (the group of war chiefs). According to Johnson, the *ẹ̀sọ́* were the military group of chiefs that served as the guardians of the kingdom. Whereas the title of *ẹ̀sọ́* was a prestigious one, it was not hereditary. It was earned by one's own military prowess. The group was headed by *ààrẹ ọnà kakañfò*, who was a respected officer in the Alaafin's administration. He did not live in the capital city and was usually appointed from outside the capital city. His role was to mobilize all the war chiefs for battles.[27] Talking about warfare in the Oyo Empire, Robin Law writes:

---

22. Falola and Heaton, *History of Nigeria*, 50.
23. Apter, *Black Critics and Kings*, 24.
24. Usman and Falola, *Yoruba from Prehistory*, 123.
25. Usman and Falola, 123; Apter, *Black Critics and Kings*, 24.
26. Apter, *Black Critics and Kings*, 24.
27. Johnson, *History of the Yorubas*, 72–75.

> Warfare was normally the business of small group of specialists the war chiefs and their trained warriors recruited largely from the slaves and junior relatives of their households. . . . The military force consists of the caboceers [chiefs] and their own immediate retainers. . . . It appears however that the principal military force in the capital consisted of seventy war chiefs called the *eso* who lived in the non-royal wards of the city and came under the authority of the Oyo mesi.²⁸

One should not confuse the *ẹ̀ṣọ́* with the king's bodyguards and messengers. The king's bodyguards and messengers were a group of low-ranking people.²⁹ Aside from the *ẹ̀ṣọ́* who provided security service to the society, the hunters, in addition to their job of killing games for food, also played the role of police and night guard in the community.³⁰

Apart from the three aristocratic groups discussed above, which were quite peculiar to the Oyo Empire, other political structures also surrounded a king in Yorubaland. These included "council of chiefs (*Ijoye* which consisted of *Iyalode, Otun, Osi, Iyaloja*, etc.), the kingmakers (*afọbajẹ*, part of whom might be the chiefs), the Baale . . . and the religious cult."³¹ One paramount religious cult across Yoruba kingdoms was *ògbóni*. Although the roles of the cult varied from one Yoruba kingdom to the other; nevertheless, in Oyo Empire, their role was to administer justice when an innocent blood is shed and to sanction some decisions of the *Ọ̀yọ́ Mèsì*.³²

Theological Reflection on the Political Administration of Oyo Empire

Reflecting on the development implication of the Yoruba political administration, one thing that expressly comes to mind is the nonexistence of anarchy in the political system. We learn from the biblical book of Judges that the

---

28. Law, "Making Sense," 397.
29. Law, 397.
30. Lloyd, "Craft Organization," 35.
31. "Yoruba Pre-Colonial Political Administration | Pre-Colonial Political Systems," *Nigerian Scholars*, accessed 28 March 2020, https://nigerianscholars.com/tutorials/pre-colonial-political-systems/yoruba-pre-colonial-political-administration/.
32. Morton-Williams, "Yoruba Ogboni Cult," 363.

state of anarchy in a land got people into distress rather than enjoying *shalom* (2:15; 10:9; 11:7). The book talks about the sporadic state of anarchy in the nation of Israel. There were times when the nation was without a king and everyone did what was right in their own eyes (Judg 17:6; 21:25).

A historical view of the Yoruba traditional political practices proves to us that people were not doing whatever they liked in the land. There was order and definite structures through which people could channel their concerns. The political head could reach down to everyone in the society through a pattern. And so, for the Yoruba people, the fact that the society enjoys order, *ìlú rójú*, as discussed in chapter 3, entails development.

Another development implication of the political pattern of the Yoruba society is the measure put in place for checks and balances. Although the king is supreme, systems have been put in place so that there is no abuse of power. Political tyranny is one of the elements that impaired development in Africa.[33] Yoruba method of checks and balances offers a commendable model to address the problem of tyranny in Africa.

In the Bible times, the office of the prophet appears to be the office that provided checks and balances to the king's use of power and authority. God always sent his stern rebukes to oppressive leaders who used their political power to take advantage of people. A typical example of a king who used his power to take advantage of a citizen is King Ahab. When he grabbed Naboth's vineyard, God sent Elijah to rebuke him (1 Kgs 21). Another example is David when he slept with Uriah's wife and murdered him for cover-up. Having done this, God sent Nathan to pronounce judgement against him (2 Sam 12:1–23).

Finally, Yoruba order of political units ranging from the family to the state has a correlation with the Israelites' concept of leadership as fatherhood. The Israelite community is said to have had a three-tier political hierarchy. First was the home headed by the father of the house. The second tier was the nation, headed by the king. The third tier was the level of divine kingship. The first tier of the political unit depicts the prototype of what it means to be a king, the father of the nation. It also captures the meaning of God's divine kingship, God as the Father of all.[34]

---

33. Ayittey, *Indigenous African Institutions*, 469.
34. King and Stager, *Life in Biblical Israel*, 4.

As we shall see in the section that follows, a king is next in command to God who is the Father of all. The way *baálé* (father who is the owner of house) serves as the father figure to an extended family, and *baálẹ̀* (father who is the owner land) to the village, the king is the father of all – *ọba ni bàbá* (king is the father). It is observed that in all the five palaces I visited during my field trip, the king is referred to as *Bàbá* (father).

Everything belongs to the king including all human beings ("*ọbá ba lórí ohun gbogbo*, the king is the guardian of all, like the hen and the chicks"). The overall idea of the political hierarchy is that *baálé* and *baálẹ̀* represent the king (who is installed for the wellbeing of all), in all political units of the society. Every head of all political units takes care of the people on behalf of the king. Political administration is therefore for the sake of individual wellbeing. As portrayed in the story of Iyá Alákàrà in chapter 3, solutions to all ill-beings are always close by because the king has his agents at all levels of political units.

"*Kábíyèsí, Aláṣẹ Èkejì Òrìṣà*": The Sacred Kingship in Yorubaland

One prominent concept of kingship in Yorubaland is its sacredness, as portrayed in how kings are praised, "*Kábíyèsí, Aláṣẹ èkejì òrìṣà*," which can loosely be translated as "king, the one whose authority is next to that of the gods." Another appropriate way to translate this is according to Pemberton III and Afolayan, "The power of Oba is like that of the gods."[35] We can say that the authority of a king is both next to that of the gods in hierarchy and that his power is like that of the gods. This is because sometimes kings are said to be gods themselves, and another time considered next in command to the gods.

In Yorubaland, the king is a figure of authority next to the gods. In hierarchy, the husband as the head of the house submits to the authority of the *baálé* of the compound, the *baálé* of the compound submits to the *baálẹ̀* of the village whose authority in turn should be in submission to the king's. The king's authority submits to that of no living human. That is why it is said, "*Oun tí ọba bá sọ l'abẹ́ gé*" (The decree of the king is final).

---

35. Pemberton III and Afolayan, *Yoruba Sacred Kingship*, 1.

Nevertheless, the Yoruba believe that there is another realm of life where all the authority lies – the spiritual realm, the realm where all the power of the universe lies. The people who reside in the realm see and know what is obscure to the living humans. The spiritual realm belongs to the ancestors, gods, and Olodumare. Those are the only ones whose order the king must obey. Therefore, in this regard, a king is said to be next in command to the gods.

On the other hand, kings are also said to be embodiment of the deities. For instance, describing the reverence that was shown to the Awujaale, the paramount ruler of Ijebuland, Ayandele points out:

> So sacred was his name, that it was believed by his subjects that to mention it would mean instant death. Regarded by his people as the vicegerent of God on earth, the Awujale was seen in Ijebu-Ode once in a year, during *agemo* festival, when the sixteen priests brought ritual material and he said blessings for all his subjects.[36]

In an interview with the Alaafin of Oyo, while explaining the processes that are involved in ascendancy to the throne of the Alaafin, he noted that,

> Through the process, one was inducted into the mysteries of the various gods, like the Ifa mysteries, and the Sango mysteries. One also has to undergo these inductions in order to be the direct representative of these deities on earth.[37]

These instances about the Awujaale and Alaafin form an indication that a king in Yorubaland is not just an ordinary human being. He has a kind of life different from that of the people. There is a divine implication regarding the life of a king. He has a more direct access to the spiritual realm and knows the mysteries that many people do not know. Kingship is therefore sacred, and saintly in nature. It commands honour and worship. It is highly important and valued. The kingship sacredness is traditionally rooted in the following: (1) the belief that all kings are descendants of Oduduwa who was from Olodumare;[38] (2) the kind of processes that are involved in the prepara-

---

36. Ayandele, "Ijebuland," 94.
37. Adeyemi, "Civilization," 35.
38. Lloyd, "Sacred Kingship," 221–37; Parrinder, "Divine Kingship," 115.

tion of a king;[39] and (2) the nature of rituals[40] and taboos that surround the life of a king.

Relationship with Oduduwa

In the Yoruba traditional belief, Oduduwa, the progenitor of the race, was not a mere human, he was (and is still) a god, with his temple standing at Ile Ife in which people of different calibres pay homage.[41] As indicated in the Yoruba creation myth, Oduduwa was one of the *òrìṣà* sent by Olodumare for the creation of the earth. His grandchildren became the primary founders of all Yoruba nations, who in turn founded other crown Yoruba towns. However, some scholars doubt if this chain of succession is intact as it is traditionally claimed.[42] For instance, discussing the succession of the *Oòni* throne, Falola and Heaton note:

> The political system of Ife was monarchical, headed by the ooni. Although lines of succession for the ooniship did exist, occasionally wealthy people within the community were able to succeed to the throne, indicating that the monarchy was not strictly hereditary.[43]

Whether a king has royalty in his blood or not, people believe that all Yoruba are descendants of Oduduwa. And as a matter of fact, there are a number of ritualistic objects and symbols that connect a king to his predecessors, something they all share in common as inheritor of the throne, which could be in one way or the other traced to Oduduwa. For example in most of Yorubaland, the new *ọba* is made to eat the heart of the former king.[44] "It is in eating the heart and thus entering into direct contact with his predecessor that he actually becomes king."[45] "To become king" in Yoruba language is expressed as "*jẹ ọba*" which translates in English to mean, "to eat king."

---

39. Pemberton III and Afolayan, *Yoruba Sacred Kingship*, 73.
40. Apter, *Black Critics and Kings*, 97–116.
41. Parrinder, "Divine Kingship," 114.
42. Parrinder, 115; Falola and Heaton, *History of Nigeria*, 23.
43. Falola and Heaton, 23.
44. Johnson, *History of the Yorubas*, 43; Parrinder, "Divine Kingship," 115; Lloyd, "Sacred Kingship," 227.
45. Parrinder, 115.

Hence, in this case, what the successive kings have in common is the literal eating of heart, which can symbolically imply that they all share the same heart. Another thing that is passed down among kings, particularly among the Yoruba proper, is the sword of justice from Ile Ife, which is said to have belonged to Oranmiyan, the grandson of Oduduwa. In a Yoruba town like Ila Orangun, one of the shared symbols among successive kings is "the *ogbo* (cutlass) of the Orangun."[46] In all these, we can infer that all successive kings in Yorubaland share something sacred in common, which serves as a symbolic link connecting them to their ancestor-gods, and consequently turning them into human-gods.

More essentially in Yoruba kingship, the crown won by the king is another sacred symbol that sets a king apart as a saintly being who is linked to Oduduwa. Pemberton III and Afolayan report that,

> The Oba's crown remains the principal symbol of political authority and cultural identity as a particular people . . . The authority (*àse*) of an Oba is inextricably linked with a people's sense of identity as a particular people – as Ife or Oyo or Owu or Ijebu or Igbomina Yoruba – which is to say that the political memory of a people is intimately linked to the crown and those who wear it.[47]

Robert Thompson also informs that,

> according to tradition, it was none other than Oduduwa himself, awesome maker of land upon water and the father of the Yoruba, who initiated the wearing of the beaded crown with veil as the essential sign of kingship. He placed a crown on the head of each of his sixteen sons. These journeyed from the site where traditional Yorubas believe Oduduwa lived, Ile-Ife, in the forests of what is now southwest Nigeria, and established separate kingdoms. In time these kingdoms became the modern Yoruba states. The rulers of these ancient provinces all claim

---

46. Pemberton III and Afolayan, *Yoruba Sacred Kingship*, 79.
47. Pemberton III and Afolayan, 2.

descent from Oduduwa. They are honored as seconds of the gods (*ekeji orisa*).⁴⁸

Therefore, a king's crown is seen as a symbol of political authority and people's identity. This is because it gives the people a visual connection with the sources – Oduduwa and Ile Ife.

Choice by God

Another factor that makes kingship a unique one is the fact that a king is chosen by the gods, according to the nature of the person's destiny *orí* (destiny, literally head). *Orí* in Yoruba worldview "is the element which symbolizes human destiny and the whole of a person's personality."⁴⁹ The gods will never choose a person who is not destined to be king, and any case of manipulation would cause an adverse effect during the reign of the king.⁵⁰

The process of choosing a king is highly competitive. In Ila Orangun, the process of choosing king is expressed thus:

> With the end of the mourning period [over a deceased king], the Kingmakers meet in Obaale's House [house of prominence]. Their deliberations begin the process of selecting a new Oba. A message is sent to the Alasan, the head of the *omoba* (princes), asking that he nominate a candidate for the throne. The Alasan, who has been discussing the succession claims with the elders of the three royal houses, requests nominations from the royal house whose turn it is to provide candidates. . . . Theoretically, every prince can present himself as a candidate for the throne. . . . Competition among lineages and candidates is usually intense and bitter.⁵¹

The proverb "*Orí l'oyè, èdá l'àyànmọ́*" (becoming a ruler is determined by head [or destiny], every human is a product of their destiny), suggests that whoever emerges a king among many candidates to the throne has a preferred *orí* that makes him a suitable king for the time. It is important to note

---

48. Thompson, "Sign of the Divine," 8.
49. Balogun, "Concepts of Ori," 119.
50. Quadri, *Opa Oranmiyan*.
51. Pemberton III and Afolayan, *Yoruba Sacred Kingship*, 76–77.

that someone's *orí* is connected with his *ìwà* (essential character).[52] Hence, the sacredness of a king is also rooted in the knowledge that he came to the world with a kingly "head" that engenders kingly character and authority.

Process of Coronation

In addition to the fact that Yoruba kings are connected to the ancestor-gods by some ritualistic and symbolic link, as noted earlier, the kind of process that is involved in their coronation also turns them to sacred beings. The summary of the process can be elicited thus:

> The rituals of enthronement are long and vary from place to place. They usually involve a recapitulation of the circumstances of the foundation of the kingdom and of the migration of its rulers from the sacred city of Ife. The principal rite is a visit to the royal mausoleum, and in some towns the king is crowned here. A horse, a cow and a ram were offered at the tombs of the principal ancestors, the meat being cooked and consumed on the spot by the accompanying noblemen.[53]

The essence of the entire process is for the sake of orientation,[54] so that a new king is able to know deep things pertaining to the kingdom. The process is also done in order to consecrate and empower him so that he would be "able to withstand the magic potency of the charms incorporated within the royal regalia."[55] The rituals in the coronation process also provide the king with extraordinary power of wisdom so that his reign can be a good reign.[56]

The kingship rituals do not end with coronation. Throughout the lifetime of a king, he ought to, from time to time, involve himself to such rituals particularly to the ancestor-gods of the land. Talking about this Olupona notes that,

> In every Yoruba city, there is a major Orisa whose myth, story, ritual, and symbols are intricately linked to both ancient and

---

52. Pemberton III, "Art and Rituals," 101.
53. Parrinder, "Divine Kingship," 115.
54. Adeyemi, "Civilization."
55. Lloyd, "Sacred Kingship," 227–28.
56. Lloyd, 228.

modern-day core values, as well as to the political and cultural lives of the Yoruba people of that particular city. In the same vogue, the ideology and rituals of sacred kingship derive from this particular tradition honoring this same Orisa. The Oba (king), on his ascent to the throne, adopts this Orisa as his own. Political kingship exists by the very presence of the Orisa religious tradition.[57]

The ancestor gods (òrìṣà) vary from one Yoruba town to another. For the Awujaale of Ijebuland, the ancestor-god is *Agẹmọ*;[58] for Alaafin of Oyo, it is Sango;[59] and for *Àtaójẹ* of Oṣogbo, it is *Ọ̀sun*.[60] And in addition to the worship of these gods, the kings have many taboos around their lives, which also is an indication of their sacred humanity. For instance, *Ọ̀ràngún* of Ila Orangun must not set his eyes on his mother again upon his ascent to the throne.[61]

The Essence of Yoruba Sacred Kingship

The place of the sacredness of a king in a Yoruba community cannot be overemphasized. The sacredness of the king ultimately earns him the *àṣẹ* (authority) like that of gods, to which everyone must submit. This is the source of order in a Yoruba society, in that a king without authority will rule over the people who can choose to do whatever they like. When everyone in the society begins to do whatever they like, it spells chaos and lack of peace. Meanwhile, no society can enjoy development in the face of disorder and chaos. Therefore, there must be *ọba aláṣẹ* (a figure of authority) who commands respect and can put things right in the society.

The sacredness of a king as rooted in its supernatural humanness is so important because without it a king lacks wisdom to rule the community and make it prosper. The wisdom of a leader emanating from proper preparation for the office and the supernatural ability from the spirit universe always culminates in a forward-moving society.

---

57. Olupona, "Orisa Osun," 75.
58. Ayandele, "Ijebuland," 94.
59. Parrinder, "Divine Kingship," 120.
60. Olupona, "Orisa Osun."
61. Pemberton III and Afolayan, *Yoruba Sacred Kingship*, 80.

Theological Reflection on Yoruba Sacred Kingship

The nation of Israel enjoyed a remarkable prosperity in the time of Solomon. The prosperity was so remarkable that it was recorded that "the king made silver as common in Jerusalem as stones, and he made cedar trees as abundant as the sycamores which are in the lowland" (1 Kgs 10:27, NKJV).

Such prosperity in the land was not just a random occurrence. The "sacredness" of the kingship of Solomon paid off. It all began with the sacred anointing that was poured on him by Zadok the priest (1 Kgs 1:39). It was God himself who chose Solomon by name (1 Chr 28:5–6), unlike many leaders who force their way to the throne. First Kings 2 and 1 Chronicles 28 reveal the quality of orientation given to Solomon by David at his coronation. Also, God himself appeared to Solomon twice to give him guidance regarding how to lead his people (1 Kgs 1:1–15; 9:1–9; 2 Chr 1:1–12; 7:11–22; cf. 1 Kgs 11:9b). Both human counsel and divine guidance play important roles in the remarkable prosperity in Solomon's reign.

Solomon demonstrated so much wisdom that people held him in awe. This is an important aspect of kingship (and all other forms of leadership) – that a king's subjects hold him in high regard. The antithesis of this is found in the life of Rehoboam who demonstrated folly and therefore had his kingdom divided.

One important leadership lesson from Leighton Ford's book *Transforming Leadership* is that leaders are required to stay "a bit beyond mortals."[62] Quoting what Richard Nixon, former president of the US, once told his former Counsel, Charles Colson, he said: "The people really want a leader a little bigger than themselves. . . . There's certain aloofness, a power that's exuded by great men that people feel and want to follow."[63] People are naturally attracted to leaders who seem to have an appearance that is beyond ordinary, someone whose presence and authority produces something divine.

For Yoruba people, this is what sacred kingship is about: a king whose origin and choice is traced to God himself, who is adequately prepared for leadership, and keeps to the taboos that set his lifestyle above immorality. Such kings are respected and obeyed. As it has been pointed out above, the Yoruba concept of sacred kingship is familiar to the Bible readers. Leaders

---

62. Ford, *Transforming Leadership*, 70.
63. Ford, 70.

(i.e. judges or kings) whose reigns were characterised by remarkable peace in the Bible times were said to be called and set apart by God, prepared by him and who lived up to certain principles laid down by God. They were God-anointed and carried *charisma*.

Religion, Rituals, and Community Wellbeing

Central to the Yoruba religion is Olodumare (translates as he who has everything in bulk), who is also called Olorun (the owner of the heaven) or *Olúwa* (Lord). Olodumare is the supreme being. He works through many agents who form a link between the terrestrial and divine beings, deities that are called *òrìṣà*. Laitin notes that "the religion claims 401 deities in its pantheon."[64] These deities are not regarded as the supreme being but only a means to him. Apter provides a good summary on *òrìṣà*:

> An orisha [sic] is a person who lived on earth when it was created, and from whom present day folk are descended. When these orishas disappeared or "turned to stone," their children began to sacrifice to them and continue whatever ceremonies they themselves performed when they were on earth. This worship was passed from one generation to the next, and today an individual considers orisha who he worships to be an ancestor from whom he descended.[65]

Òrìṣà were originally human beings. It is said among the Yoruba people that "*Ènìyàn níí d'òrìṣà*" (It is human beings who become *òrìṣà*).[66] Their ascent to deity status is because of their heroic deeds during their life on earth. They grew strong and popular among the people in their lifetime such that they are deified after their death. However, scholars debate as to whether the *òrìṣà* were born like other human beings, or were created by God the way the Bible described the creation of Adam.[67]

---

64. Laitin, *Hegemony and Culture*, 34.
65. Apter, *Black Critics and Kings*, 150.
66. Oduyoye, *Vocabulary of Yoruba*, 22.
67. Apter, *Black Critics and Kings*, 151.

The òrìṣà are not without symbols of worship. These symbols of worship range from stones to wood and metal carving, plants, animals,[68] stones, rocks, mountains and hills, thunder, lightning stormwinds, whirlwind, sun, moon, and stars.[69] Although many people have erroneously believed that these symbols are the real object of worship in òrìṣà worship, Adelowo however sheds light on this confusion, noting that these "symbols are not ends in themselves but means to certain ends."[70] Talking about òrìṣà's rituals and rites, Adelowo writes:

> Rituals and rites are a means of bringing into the limelight the religious experience of a group of people; rituals and rites thus constitute some kind of religious expression. They are a means of concretising one's belief system. They are a means of expressing one's experience of the supersensible world and the supernatural beings. In short and simple terms, they are acts of forms of worship or communion and communication between one and one's objects of worship.[71]

In any case, the òrìṣà are known to be objects of worship and honour.[72] Though objects of worship, they are not by any means equated with the supreme being. They are only means through which human beings can reach him.[73] Some examples of these òrìṣà are Sòpònná (deity of small-pox), Sango (deity of thunder), Esu, Ifa (deity of wisdom) and so forth,[74] each of whom requires rituals, rites, and worship from his living human adherents.[75] The forms of rituals, rites, and worship of the òrìṣà are clearly specified. Each of the òrìṣà has some specified ways by which they are approached by people. These specifications are well known to the individual priests in charge of the òrìṣà, who are otherwise known as àwòrò.

---

68. Adelowo, "Rituals, Symbolism," 168.
69. McKenzie, *Hail Orisha!*, 23–51.
70. Adelowo, "Rituals, Symbolism," 168.
71. Adelowo, 168.
72. Oduyoye, *Vocabulary of Yoruba Discourse*, 24.
73. Adelowo, "Rituals, Symbolism," 162.
74. Obayemi, "History, Culture," 82.
75. Apter, *Black Critics and Kings*, 150.

Òrìṣà's ritual specifications have to do with the presentation of the worshipper and sacrifice. The worshippers must appear in certain ways as required by the òrìṣà. In some cases, some òrìṣà have the kinds of items that must be present in their worship. For instance, Obatala requires that his worshippers put on white apparel and specifically offer "white (or bitter) kola instead of the red one."[76] The òrìṣà hold the rights to accept or reject the sacrifice being offered to them, usually based on whether the worshippers adhere to the ritual prescriptions. As such, during the course of òrìṣà worship, worshippers would charge one another: "Ẹ jẹ́ ká seé bí wọ́n tíí ṣeé, kó lè baà rí bíí seé rí" (Let us do it the way it is usually done, so that we may have the usual result).[77]

The worship of òrìṣà is very important not only because they serve as intermediaries between Olodumare and human beings, but also because of the good things that they can do for the society. In fact, failure to offer them sacrifices would bring about some form of lack of peace in the society. The study of òrìṣà provides an insight that each of them has their areas of specification. Ifa is the god of wisdom whom people approach for knowledge about the future. Obatala is the god in charge of civic guardianship who protects the town gates. Sango is the god of thunder; *Ogún*, the god of iron; *Òrìṣàoko*, the god of agriculture; *Ṣọ̀npọ̀ná*, the god of chicken pox, and so on.[78]

In order for people to secure the intervention of an òrìṣà in accordance to his area of specialization, propitiatory or appeasement sacrifices are made. Tokunboh Adeyemo puts it succinctly:

> The Yoruba call this category *Ebo Etutu*. According to the oral tradition this sacrifice is usually prescribed by the oracle or the priest in reply to an enquiry as to what can be done to save the situation during a crisis like epidemic, famine, drought, or serious illness. If the whole community is involved the sacrifice may be expensive. . . . In the ancient times, a human offering used to be the main feature of the sacrifice.[79]

---

76. Farrow, *Faith, Fancies and Fetich*, 43.
77. Adelowo, "Rituals, Symbolism," 165.
78. Farrow, *Faith, Fancies and Fetich*, 34–59.
79. Adeyemo, *Salvation in African Tradition*, 34.

In addition to the good that they do to the society by virtue of their areas of specialization, they also serve as protection against *ajogún*, the evil spirit at work within the society.[80] By implication, there are two types of spiritual forces in Yoruba cosmology – the *òrìṣà* and the *ajogún*; the *òrìṣà* are good deities while the *ajogún* are the negative spiritual forces whose sole intention is to cause misfortune in the society.

The discussion on *òrìṣà* and *ajogún* gives a clear hint that there are spiritual powers at work whose disposition can determine the state of wellbeing of the society. The favour of the *òrìṣà* must be sought if peace must reign in the society. The power of the *ajogún* must be put at bay for people to enjoy wellbeing.

King's Role in Religion, Ritual, and Wellbeing

The king plays a prominent role in all the Yoruba religious practices. This is because it is his sacred responsibility to ensure that there is peace in the society. No other thing a king does will receive as much praise as ensuring peace. Adelowo states the prominence of the king's responsibility in spiritual search of the society's wellbeing, when he writes:

> The king's existence as a political figure or military leader is a secondary thing. Over and beyond those secular functions, a Yoruba Oba has to maintain harmony and concord between society and its natural environment by means of ritual action of a regular kind which he alone could take. His functions in this realm are three-fold: to perform the daily rites for which he is uniquely qualified by office; to provide for and direct the activities of the cults; and to sustain and control his own spiritual potency.[81]

Although Adelowo employs the use of the word "secular" to describe the secondary role of the king, all these "secular" roles are approached from a sacred point of view as consultation with the divinity is involved in all of them. This will soon be further discussed before the end of this section.

---

80. Abimbola, "Ifa: A West African," 106.
81. Adelowo, "Rituals, Symbolism," 164.

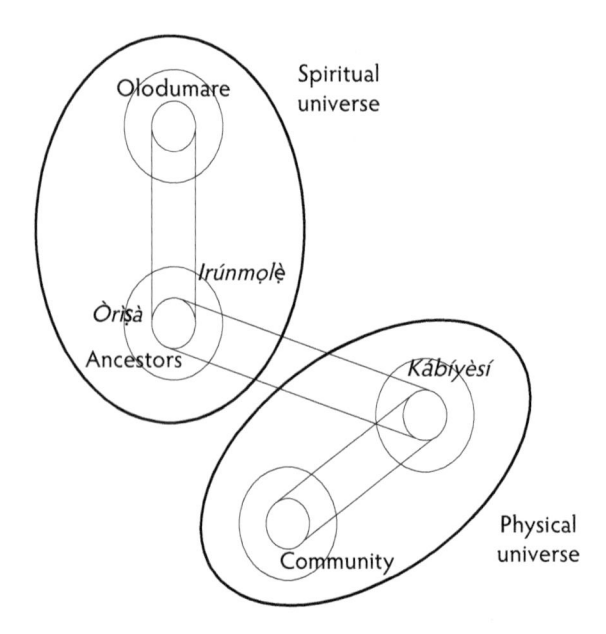

Figure 3. Yoruba Political Involvement of the Divinity for the Sake of Wellbeing

During my interview of His Royal Highness Oba Samuel Awoyemi Oroja of Meiranland, he noted that the vital reason why Nigeria as a nation experiences all manners of incidents that spell its backwardness is due to failure of political leaders to give the *irúnmọlẹ̀* (a variant name for *òrìṣà*) what belongs to them. He lamented that Christianity and Islam have brought some strange teachings that have made us undermine the *irúnmọlẹ̀* and therefore the nation is suffering the consequences.[82]

As I interact further with Oba Oroja's point of view, I infer that all Yoruba societies have some *irúnmọlẹ̀* to whom they pay their allegiance. This revelation is clearly portrayed in a film made by Mike Bamiloye, the founder of Mount Zion Ministry, a leading Christian movie ministry in Nigeria, titled *Esin Ajoji* (The Strange Religion).[83] The setting was Agbayun Town. During the reign of the founding king, Oba Arinadegbo, the community was recurrently being ravaged by wars waged against it by a neighbouring Yoruba community, Elegbeta Town. When the attacks became so prevalent to the extent

---

82. HRH Oba Samuel Ismaila Adisa Adewale Oroja, "Oral Interview," Palace of Onimeiran of Meiranland, Meiran, Lagos, 9 July 2019.

83. Bamiloye, *Esin Ajoji*.

that Agbayun Town was almost going into decimation, the king, Arinadegbo, set out on a critical journey far away in *Igbó Irúnmọlẹ̀* (the sacred forest).

In the *Igbó Irúnmọlẹ̀*, Arinadegbo had a seemingly face-to-face conversation with the *alálẹ̀ ilẹ̀* (gods of the land), where he solicited their spiritual support against the king of Elegbeta Town. The *alálẹ̀ ilẹ̀* having agreed to come to Arinadegbo's aid received his thirty-year-old heir to the throne as their sacrifice. In addition to this crucial sacrifice, the *alálẹ̀ ilẹ̀* also gave a condition and the implication of the covenant, which all the generations of the succeeding kings of Agbayun Town must adhere to. The condition is that no strange religion must be allowed in Agbayun; and the spiritual implication, which is the side effect of the covenant, is that, although Agbayun would never be conquered in any battle again, it will nevertheless remain a little town forever.

The *alálẹ̀ ilẹ̀* kept their promise. Agbayun began to live in peace. However, Agbayun remained a little town hundreds of years after the pioneer king made the covenant, without any significant physical development. Some indigenes of the town became materially wealthy enough to found large companies. Meanwhile, they would rather found their companies in another town and not in Agbayun. This is the trend that keeps Agbayun a town with minimal socioeconomic development. It also happened that all the heirs of the successive kings of Agbayun would die at/before the age of thirty, the age of Arinadegbo's heir when he was offered to the *alálẹ̀ ilẹ̀*.

The modern-day Agbayun, where the plot of the play was set, was preparing for one of the major rituals called *ẹbọ Òféfé Mosálà* (sacrifice to *Òféfé Mosálà*). The present-day king is Oladunjoye, whose heir Olabosipo just arrived from abroad with his family, after being away for several years. Olabosipo has become a Christian. Sacrifice to *Òféfé Mosálà* began in the midnight. The ritual song awakened Olabosipo and his wife who began to pray against all the activities of the gods in Agbayun. The chief priest and all the palace chiefs were out at the *Òféfé Mosálà*'s shrine but the sacrifice was not accepted. It was found out that Olabosipo and wife had brought in the strange religion to the land. The *alálẹ̀ ilẹ̀* were angry.

The story of Agbayun is a typical example of Yoruba communities in relation to the spiritual world. In order to get what they want, people often resort to the deities to tap into their power by striking a covenant. In appreciation or compensation for the assistance that they offer, the deities demand sacrifice and continual worship. In addition to this, they give certain conditions that their supplicants must adhere to or must fulfil at a certain interval of time. When the supplicants fail on their part to fulfil this condition, they face brutal consequences.

As deity-supplicant covenant applies at communal level so it also applies at individual level. People who have special needs, and because of that, cry and offer a sacrifice to a god who receives their supplication must commit themselves to periodic worship of the gods. Moreover, for anything received from the gods there are usually side effects. A testimony is given of a young woman who experienced misfortune as she seeks to get a husband. Rarely would any man ask for her hand in marriage and if at all this happened, she would end up being disappointed.

During an encounter with a spirit-filled man of God, whose ministry gifting is similar to that of a biblical seer, the woman was instructed by the leading of the Holy Spirit to go and destroy the pawpaw tree at the backyard of her mother's house. During the course of this demolition, the young woman found a freshly used bathing sponge. Through a special revelation from the prophet, she was made to know that the sponge she discovered was the sponge that was used to bathe her on the day she was born. Her mother had asked a god to grant her a daughter. In addition to other sacrifices, the sponge was dedicated to the god perhaps as a symbol of the covenant between the mother and the god. The side effect of the covenant is that the child would not be able to get married.[84]

Considering this story and that of Agbayun Town, it becomes clear that there are available powers that people, either individually or as a group, can tap into in their own favour, for personal or communal wellbeing. This then affirms the reality of the mystical power in Africa. Talking about this, Richard Gehman writes:

> The belief in mystical power filling the universe is common throughout Africa. It is experienced daily in every village and city. Endless stories of the effects of this unseen force are told by young and old. In the words of John Mbiti, "The whole psychic atmosphere of African village life is filled with belief in this mystical power. African peoples know that the universe has a

---

84. This is one of the many similar stories told during revival meetings in Nigeria. There are also many other narrated stories which have the same pattern.

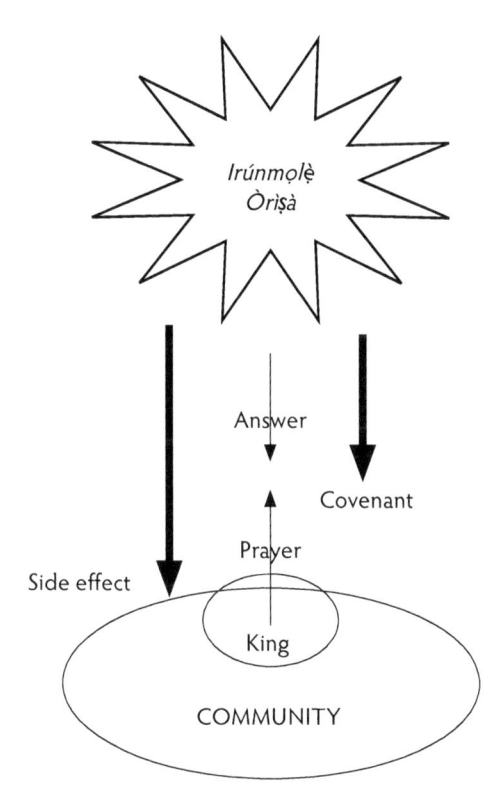

Figure 4. Yoruba Petitions to the Traditional Deities on Development

power, or force or whatever else one may call it, in addition . . ." to the living dead, spirits and the Supreme Being. Mystical powers such as magic sorcery and witchcraft affect everyone for better or for worse.[85]

The mind of modernity and secularization has the tendency to discard the talk on spiritual consultation as a fairy tale or figment of imagination. However, the story and testimony of Yoruba people, which is reinforced by Gehman's research among the Kamba people of Kenya,[86] attests to the fact. Although our mind may not be able to make sense of it, there are all indications that African traditional deities, spirit beings, ancestors, and other elements of the spirit world operate in a realm of potent powers. In Turaki's

---

85. Gehman, *Africa Traditional Religion*, 67.
86. Gehman, 80–97.

words, "The spirit world or the realm of the supernatural is, in a sense, a battleground of spirits and powers that use their mystical and spiritual powers to influence the course of human life."[87]

Theological Reflection on King's Role in Religion, Ritual, and Wellbeing

The religio-political practices of the Yoruba people are commendable because they acknowledge the place of the supreme being, in their search for wellbeing. Nevertheless, in the biblical teaching, the involvement of ancestors and deities as a means to God is rejected. There are many arguments among scholars as to whether deities and ancestors are agents of worship or veneration.[88] Nevertheless, it is obvious that people resort to these deities and ancestors in the time of need, in a way that depicts something more than mere veneration. People seek to connect with them in order to receive help. Seeking help from someone is more than mere veneration, since to venerate someone means to show deep respect and honour.

The Bible clearly speaks against any form of practices that seek to connect the spirit world through mediums.

> Give no regard to mediums and familiar spirits. Do not seek after them to be defiled by them: I am the Lord. (Lev 19:31, NKJV)

> There shall not be found among you . . . one who practices witchcraft, or a soothsayer, or one who interprets omens or a sorcerer, or one who conjures up spells, or a medium, or a spiritist, or one who calls up the dead. (Deut 18:10–11, NKJV)

As earlier discussed in this study, Yoruba deities are gods who once lived on earth and gained the status of deity after their death because of their heroic deeds during their lifetime. The Yoruba saying *"Ènìyàn níí d'òrìṣà"* (It is human beings who become deities) brings to the limelight that Yoruba gods were former humans. Therefore, to consult an *òrìṣà* is to consult the dead. As such, although done out of ignorance, the Yoruba involvement of *òrìṣà* in their supplication is a form of necromancy. This is what Adeyemo candidly

---

87. Turaki, *Foundations of African Traditional*, 45.
88. Turaki, 26.

termed "traditional idolatry" when he calls Christians to stick to the New Testament "separateness."[89]

Although òrìṣà are said not to be Olodumare but his agents, the study of their operations raise them to the level of other gods talked about in the Bible, to whom people presented their supplications and offerings, such as Baal, Ashtoreth, and so on. Judging from the biblical knowledge, it is an unacceptable practice to receive something "from God" through other deities.

In the Old Testament times, people related to YHWH without any spiritual person(s) in between, though prophets who were also fellow humans interceded for them. In the New Testament times, Jesus came to us as the only way to the Father. The Yoruba way of relating with God is unlike any of these. This gives us a hint that there is something unbiblical about the idea of having any spiritual intermediaries, which is found in Yoruba people's mode of seeking God.

The Yoruba Political Structure of Maintaining Peace, Justice, and Conflict Resolution

In any society, peace is at the core of wellbeing. As I have discussed in chapter 3 about the concept of wellbeing among the Yoruba people, without peace there is no wellbeing. One of the factors that threaten the peace of a society and consequently its wellbeing is conflict. In any form of human interaction, conflict is inevitable. Because of this, it is important for all societies to have a viable means of conflict resolution in place.

Yoruba greatly cherish peaceful co-existence among its people. As noted in chapter 1, Yoruba community is said to be the most peaceful community of the Nigerian communities with religious diversity. This is not to say that Yoruba people are also not without conflicts. Pages of history reveal their many wars and conflicts, the more recent and memorable one being Ife-Modakeke land dispute, which lingered for almost thirty years. Nevertheless, in the midst of disputes, Yoruba has taught its people to always remember that "*Bí a kò bá gbàgbé ọ̀rọ̀ àná, a kò ní r'ẹ́ni bárin*" (If we do not forget the offence of the past, we would soon find ourselves without friends).

---

89. Adeyemo, *Salvation in African Tradition*, 14.

The Yoruba political hierarchy, among other reasons, serves as a mechanism for maintaining peace, justice, and conflict resolution. The king's court, which is the highest place of political authority in any Yoruba community, is also the highest court of law. This also applies to the corresponding lower level of political authorities. The level of conflict in the land determines the level of leadership at which it would be resolved. Here again, Ajayi and Buhari's writing gives a good explanation of the level of conflicts as being handled by corresponding levels of leadership.

> There were levels or phases of conflict resolution, there were dispute resolutions at the inter-personal or family level, the extended family level and village or town level (chief in council). These tiers represent the political units making up the community. The smallest unit called *Idile* (Nuclear family) is headed by a *Bale*. The next unit is the *Ebi*, (extended family) headed by *Mogaji* who is the most influential or usually the eldest person in the *Ebi*. Extended family includes all people who have blood ties. The last tier of the units is the quarter which comprizes of several family compounds headed by a *Baale* (the chief-of-ward/quarter).[90]

In addition to the political system in place for settling disputes, the Yoruba religious leaders also play important roles in conflict resolution; when a conflict gets so knotty that it requires the intervention of the gods who can fathom what mere humans do not know. In such complicated issues, Ifa, the god of wisdom is consulted so that he gives clear direction and exposes the secret knowledge that underlies such conflicts.[91]

Yoruba Concept of Justice

Justice in Yoruba is said to be *ìdájọ́ òdodo,* which literally means righteous judgement or judgement based on truth. This implies that judgement must be based on and must be free of partiality. In order to determine the truth, both disputing parties must be heard and eyewitnesses must confirm their claims.

---

90. Ajayi and Buhari, "Methods of Conflict Resolution," 143–44.
91. Gbenda, "Age-Long Land Conflicts."

It is believed that justice must be what it is – *ìdájọ́ òdodo* (righteous judgement or judgement based on truth). Anyone in the community occupying the judgement seat must uphold justice for the fear of the ancestors. With the same fear, people in the community must maintain fairness in their dealings with one another; otherwise, the gods and ancestors would strike.

Yoruba people also have the god of peacemaking in their pantheon. This god is called *Ẹ̀là*. Whenever there is dispute and chaos in the community, *Ẹ̀là* would be consulted to restore peace and harmony that have been missing in the community because of a conflict. Ultimately, it is believed that Olodumare is the Supreme Judge, who can be contacted through the *òrìṣà* (deities).[92] Therefore, the traditional priests who consult with *òrìṣà* on people's behalf are also held in high esteem in Yorubaland as far as conflict resolutions are concerned.[93]

Yoruba Reconciliation: Process of Upholding Justice and Maintaining Peace

While justice must be dispensed, Yoruba also believe that the relationship between disputing parties must be restored after judgement. In order to maintain true justice and at the same time ensure true conflict resolution that is void of subsequent bitterness, the disputing parties go through the following processes: mediation, adjudication, reconciliation, and negotiation.[94]

Mediation

This is a timely intervention of a third party. The mediator takes the time to listen to the parties involved in dispute and brings them to a particular conclusion that the involved parties would by themselves find difficult to arrive at. Mediation usually does not have a touch of coercion. The parties respectfully submit to the mediator, usually by virtue of his leadership placement. It is traditionally wrong in Yorubaland for a mediator to come to his conclusion based on the story of the conflict as being narrated by one party, without also hearing the other. This is why it is said, "*Agbẹ́jọ́ ẹnìkan dá, àgbà*

---

92. Alokan, "Impact of Religion," 10.
93. Gbenda, "Age-Long Land Conflicts."
94. Ajayi and Buhari, "Methods of Conflict Resolution," 149–51.

òṣìkà" (He who bases his judgement on a single story displays the wickedness of the highest order).

It is the role of a mediator to open the eyes of the parties in dispute to the moral laws that guide the behaviours and conduct of the members of the society. Anyone from either side of the dispute who has done anything contrary to the laws is pronounced guilty, and therefore will be required to tender his/her apologies to the other party. However, the party who receives apology would also be reprimanded for putting up an attitude that provoked his/her neighbour to do whatever he/she has done. This is because Yoruba people believe that, *"Bí a bá b'ẹran wí, ká b'ẹ̀ràn wí"* (If we scold a person who commits an offence, we should also scold the person whose attitude provoked the offensive action).

Adjudication

Adjudication in Yorubaland implies the verdict of a traditional official. The conflicts that reach this level are usually serious ones. The highest form of verdict that would be passed to a guilty party is payment of fines. This fine may be cola nut or drinks, which at the end of the day would be shared by everyone. Reparation is not done in Yorubaland. It is considered equivalent to taking revenge, which, on its own, is a grave sin. What is done in the place of reparation is to appeal to the concerned person.

Both parties would narrate the story of their conflict to the topmost official and his subordinates who would be available to give him counsel over the matter. Their counsel would largely determine his verdict. The royal officials around *oba* are called *ìjòyè*. In Oyo Empire, the king's advisers are called *Ọ̀yọ́ Mèsì*. When the case proves too tough that the minds of mortal men would not be sufficient to make a sound judgement, the Ifa priest would be consulted, who will divine and get wisdom from Ifa (god of wisdom) over the matter.

The consultation of Ifa becomes very necessary in some judicial cases that are very murky for any human to judge. And Yoruba believe that *"Oun tó sápamọ́ l'ójú ènìyàn, kedere ni l'ójú Ọlọ́run"* (God sees clearly what is difficult for the mortal man to discern). Without divine intervention, it may be hard or impossible to get to the root of some cases in order to know the truth. Ifa is God's oracle in helping humanity to discern such issues.

Reconciliation

Yoruba people believe two conflicting parties who have been to the court of law cannot truly maintain true friendship thereafter, irrespective of who won or lost the case. Their way of saying this is *"A kìí re'lé ẹjọ́ kábọ̀, k'ád'ọ̀rẹ́"* (Two parties do not hold a case against each other in court and have their friendship retained thereafter). Therefore, reconciliation becomes a vital step of action after adjudication. This is an attempt to ensure true friendship among the conflicting parties. Reconciliation aims at diverting people's attention from dispute to relationship. The Yoruba words for reconciliation drive home the intention behind it: *ìbálàjà* or *ipẹ̀tù*. *Ìbálàjà* means to put an end to quarrels; while *ipẹ̀tù* means to pacify people's anger. The elders in the community are usually the ones being saddled with the responsibility of reconciliation, since they are highly respected, experienced, and wise enough to touch the hearts of the individuals in dispute in a way that will pacify them. They are aware that conflicts are followed by bitterness; hence, they make use of soft speech, like it is stated in Proverb 15:1, to turn away wrath.

Negotiation

It was mentioned earlier that reparation is not done in Yorubaland. Another way to ensure peace in case of damage or loss during the time of conflict is negotiation. Ajayi and Buhari put it this way:

> The secret is to harmonize the interests of the parties concerned. Thus, even when the conflict involves a member against his or her society, there is an emphasis on recuperation and reinsertion of errant member back into its place in society. The recovery of a dissident member can just as well be seen as the restoration of the harmony and integrity of the community, as the assertion of value consensus and social cohesion, so that the management of the conflict favours the concerns of both parties. In traditional Yoruba society, peace was negotiated. Apology for wrongs done to individuals and the entire community was a feature of negotiation. Such apology was channelled through Yoruba elders, compound heads and chiefs of high calibre in the society. It is done on the representative level or quasi-representation. The

Babaogun (patron) played the role of a representative in the sense of conflict resolution.[95]

The foregoing discussion stresses the importance Yoruba people place on dialogue. It takes place in the process of conflict resolution and thereafter, believing that every major dispute creates a wound that takes time to heal.

Assessing the Approaches of Ensuring Peace, Justice, and Reconciliation

This section has pointed out the role of dialogue in the manner in which the Yoruba people ensure peace and reconciliation in their community. This helps get to the root of the matter before it erupts into violence. Peter Dixon would also commend this approach by commenting that "policy dialogue is one of several elements of comprehensive peace-building."[96] Conflict resolution in Yorubaland gives room to talk to the other party; therefore it is in line with Stassen's recommendation to someone who is hurt, "Talk to your enemy!"[97] He sees negotiation as having applications to families, churches, and interpersonal conflicts as well as to international peacemaking."[98] In the light of Christ's message of peace, Yoruba people have done well in that there is always a peacemaker close to any place where conflict may occur. Matthew 5:9 reflects Christ's position on ensuring peace; he gives them a blessing of being children of God. Therefore, the Yoruba people are qualified as children of God, by virtue of their traditional system that puts peace mechanisms in place.

The area of major contradiction of Yoruba conflict resolution with the scriptural injunction is its idolatrous aspect, whereby traditional priests go into divination in order to get to the root of the matter. A Christian leader among Yoruba people would do well in following the traditional approach of peacemaking except he would only turn to the word of God and depend on the Holy Spirit, where human wisdom is not applicable.

Peace in a community should not be sought in a way that violates justice. At the same time, justice must not be sought at the expense of peace in the society. True reconciliation is the only way out to solving this paradox. It has

---

95. Ajayi and Buhari, 149–51.
96. Dixon, *Peacemakers: Building Stability*, 112.
97. Stanssen, *Just Peacemaking*, 102.
98. Stanssen, 102.

been learned from Yoruba people that after justice has been ensured in the court of law, there should be a provision for genuine reconciliation, which restores a smooth relationship among the conflicting parties. This takes time but it is an effective way of ensuring peace and justice, such that one is not done at the expense of the other.

In chapter 1 of this book, Yoruba people are introduced as reputable for having a peaceful society. This is not to say that there had never been any record of lack of peace in their land. Their historical record is also dotted with series of both external and civil wars.[99] Nevertheless, one of the most admirable qualities of the Yoruba community even until the present daytime is peaceful coexistence among the people.[100] This section has served as a revelation on how their society is politically instituted in a way that brings about effective peace and reconciliatory measures.

Drawing a link that connects politics, conflict, and poverty, Collier notes that many poor countries are held in poverty and underdevelopment because of endless conflict.

> Some of them are stuck in a pattern of violent internal challenges to government. Sometimes the violence is prolonged, a civil war; sometimes it is all over swiftly, a coup d'état. These two forms of political conflict both are costly and repetitive. They can trap a country in poverty.[101]

The insight gleaned from Collier's observation is that any community or nation plagued with conflict is bound for poverty and underdevelopment. Conflict in the society (absence of peace) will always culminate in underdevelopment because there will be no favourable atmosphere for profitable enterprizes. One of the significant practices in Yoruba society is the way in which conflict resolution is politically embedded. All political office holders have the responsibility of seeking peace among the people.

---

99. Odebode, "Naming Systems," 209–18; Law, "Chronology of Yoruba Wars," 211–22.
100. Laitin, *Hegemony and Culture*; Akinade, "Enduring Legacy."
101. Collier, *Bottom Billion*, 17.

Conclusion

This chapter discuss in detail the significant Yoruba traditional practices on development and politics, a discussion that I began in chapter 3. Wellbeing of the society is the primary responsibility of political leadership. Therefore, all political endeavours are always targeted towards development, because the king exists primarily for the state's wellbeing.

This chapter has shown that the political structure of the Yoruba society is something far from a state of anarchy. There is order. Order is a significant determinant of peace in the society, without which we cannot talk about development. The political system is also structured in such a way that it is hard for a king to become tyrannical. This is because the political system has a pattern that ensures checks and balances. As such, the right of everyone in the community is secured.

I also discussed the sacredness of Yoruba kingship in this chapter. The development implication of the sacredness of Yoruba kingship is in the fact that a charismatic king, sent by God and operating under divine instruction, is the kind of a political leader who will bring about the true wellbeing of the people.

Although the role of a king is primarily to ensure the wellbeing of the people, he cannot achieve this without divine involvement. All the secular means of securing peace, wellbeing, and development in the society are secondary to the spiritual means. When a king fails in his spiritual responsibility, the society will suffer for it. The way to true community wellbeing is when the divinity is involved in the affair of humanity. Without divine intervention when a community is going through a crisis, no solution will come from any angle. The king, by virtue of office, has the right to speak for the people before the deities.

In order to maintain and keep peace in human daily relationships and interactions, Yoruba traditional political institutions factor in peace and reconciliatory measures into the system. This ranges from the palace, the highest political structure, to the household, the lowest political structure. In seeking for peace, both justice and reconciliation are pursued, so that "loser" and "winner" in a case can still keep a cordial relationship at the end of a judicial process.

At the centre of all Yoruba political practices and thoughts, as indicated in this chapter, is the place for spirituality which shall be developed further in chapter 6. All the practices and thoughts discussed in this chapter have something in relation to divinity. In fact, it was clearly noted that all "secular" efforts by political leadership to secure peace and wellbeing in the community are secondary to the spiritual attempts of involving the help of the divinity.

In chapter 3, I have discussed the fundamental traditional thoughts upon which Yoruba political practices and thoughts about development are based. In this chapter, some traditional political practices and thoughts and their theological implications for development have been discussed. In the following chapter, I shall discuss the implications of modernization theory, which undergirds nation-state politics, on development in Africa.

CHAPTER 5

Modernization Theory of Development and its Implications for African Nation-State Politics

Introduction

In chapter 1, I argued that inauthentic political thoughts and practices in Africa are responsible for the underdevelopment of the continent. In this chapter, I set out to discuss how this happened. In order to achieve this, I will explore modernization theory, which is an important development theory that underlies nation-state politics in Africa. Development practices are driven by many other theories such as dependency theory, neo-liberalism theory, and human development theory. However, the discussion in this book is limited to modernization theory because of the more direct link that it has with the nation-state politics in Africa.

As I discuss modernization theory in relation to African political distortion, I shall highlight some of its beneficial aspects, and also highlight its relationship to colonialism and globalization. The term "modernization" refers to a practice. "Modernization theory" refers to a body of thoughts that led to the practice of modernization, like a blueprint is related to an actual design. Since it is almost impossible to separate a blueprint (theory) from an actual design (practice), I use the term "modernization" interchangeably with "modernization theory" in this chapter and the subsequent ones.

Modernization Theory and Development

Prior to World War II, Western nations had experienced a remarkable economic growth. The beginning of this growth dated back to the period between the mid and late nineteenth centuries. After World War II, the concern of Western world leaned towards the development of the underdeveloped nations, in the non-Western world. The West believed that Africa was underdeveloped and hence needed to be helped to develop. According to the West, for Africa to walk the path of development, it must do the same things that the Western nations did to attain their level of development. This was when the idea of modernization began to germinate. Essentially, the basic tenet of modernization theory calls the non-Western nations to follow the example of the development path of the Western nations.[1] And what was the path to the Western development? As we explore the pathway that took Western nations to development, let us first examine the prevailing viewpoints on modernization.

According to his review of *A Thesis on Modernisation* (Xiandaihua xin lun), Yuan Peng states four categories of scholarly viewpoints on the meaning of modernization theory of development.

1. Modernization is a historical process by which economically backward countries catch up with the world's advanced countries economically and technologically through a revolution under the framework of specific international relations, following the development of modern capitalism.
2. Modernization in essence is industrialization. Put more accurately, it is the development process of industrialization by an economically backward country.
3. Modernization is the process and the generalised categorization of the sudden and abrupt changes of humankind since the revolution in the natural sciences.
4. Modernization is basically the changing process of psychological attitudes, social values, and lifestyles.[2]

---

1. Peng, "Modernization Theory," 39.
2. Peng, 38.

While these four views give different definitions of modernization, they also provide an insight to the practices embedded in modernization: industrialization, capitalism, revolutions in natural sciences and psychology. These practices were the pathway that led the Western states to development;[3] they are the crucial elements of modernization which, according to the West, Africa must follow to attain development.

Modernization is characterised by high mobility, sophisticated agriculture and commerce, advanced technology, secular society, monetary economy, open market, high incomes, literacy, and urbanization.[4] The societies with these characteristics are said to be modern. These characteristics (in the exact same Western form) were not found in the traditional African societies. Rather, traditional Africa was known for subsistence agriculture, sacred society, simple technology, education by apprenticeship, and mostly rural life. Modernization requires that these characteristics be substituted with their direct or indirect opposites.

Hence, modernization entails "the transition from traditional to modern forms of society."[5] Modernization theory is therefore a process or practice that is geared towards attaining that height of socioeconomic advancement. However, modernization is not a stand-alone phenomenon. It is intricately linked with other practices. Therefore, in the following subsections, I trace modernization's link to colonialism and globalization.

Modernization and Colonialism in Africa

One cannot talk about the effect of modernization theory in Africa without the mention of colonialism. Speaking about colonialism in Africa, Kiwanuka writes that colonialism unleashed "its cause by speeding up changes which were already in existence and by introducing new ones: such changes took different forms. They were economic, social, and political. Their combined effect led to modernization."[6] Colonialism was the wagon that brought the application of modernization theory to Africa. It was the Western instrument of tutelage. Almost everything that Africa learned about modernization was

---

3. Berman, "Modernisation in Historical Perspective," 431.
4. Muia, "Concept and Theories of Development," 7.
5. Muia, 7.
6. Kiwanuka, "Three Traditional Foundations," 45.

through colonialism. On this note, I use "colonialism" in relation to modernization (theory) in this section.

Modernization theory, through colonialism, gave rise to nation-state politics. In this case, nation-state politics implies the coexistence of people of diverse tribes and languages. This coexistence was brought about when the colonial rulers combined people groups who individually existed within a close geographical range. An example of this is the Nigerian amalgamation that took place in 1914. The amalgamated tribes in Nigeria and other places in Africa that became a nation-state political entity, later threw off the rule of the foreign leaders and continued to exist as one national entity.

The transition from primeval to modern political practice in Africa underwent a certain sequence that left the nations of Africa far much different from how they used to be. For instance, in Nigeria, this political transition took a period of seventy years (1890–1960).[7] During 1890 – 1945, the colonial rulers were able to succeed in bringing together the existing people groups in Africa who operated in different autonomous states across the continent.

It was around this time that "the white settlers brutally crushed the rebellion of the indigenous peoples"[8] in Rhodesia. During this era, many Africans had received Western education that gave them enlightenment and skill that enabled them to rise to religious leadership and attain other forms of social status among their people.[9]

Between the period of the mid-1940s and early 1960s, African leaders were fully determined to overturn the rule of colonialism. The colonial states of Africa were at the threshold of a new era that marked their independence from the European rule. Considering the journey that took African states that far, one would note a series of evolution that has taken place in African social, economic, religious, and political lives.

Modernization Theory, Globalization, and Colonialism

In the previous section, I indicated modernization's relationship with colonialism. In this section, I shall highlight its relationship with globalization. I have, in this study, taken the perspective of globalization as a phenomenon that

---

7. Balogun, *Public Administration in Nigeria*, 66–67.
8. Phiri, *Proclaiming Political Pluralism*, 56.
9. Lloyd, *Africa in Social Change*, 56.

brings about interrelationships between nations of the world. Globalization has many areas of focus. One can study it from the perspectives of trade, politics, culture, religion, technology, and so forth.

In his discussion on globalization, Nayan Chanda has highlighted the categories of people and human endeavours that led to globalization. According to him, globalization was brought about by traders, preachers, adventurers, and warriors. It is a phenomenon that dated back to the early stage of human history, whereby people from different parts of the world interrelated with one another based on factors such as trade, politics, religion, and adventure.[10] Hence, as we seek to highlight the relationship between globalization and modernization, it is important to note that the former predates the latter. But at what point did the two phenomena cross paths on the continent of Africa?

Considering all the agents of globalization in view of Chanda's categorization – traders, warriors, preachers, and adventurers – one could trace all these endeavours having one thing or the other to do with how Europeans came to Africa. Europeans came as traders of human slaves and mineral resources that were found in Africa. Their coming was also with the intention of Christian mission work. Works of adventurers such as Mungo Park were also remarkable means through which the Europeans encountered Africa. They also came to Africa with much military power that served them well in conquering the traditional political powers in Africa upon their arrival.[11]

Hence, colonialism, which entailed African contact with Europeans, was an offshoot of globalization. Colonialism rode on globalization. And during the process of colonization, "the people of Africa and other parts of colonised world . . . accepted at least partially the European versions of doing things."[12] Meanwhile, as I discussed earlier, the process by which Africa accepted the Western way of doing things was what modernization entailed. As such, modernization and globalization are related in this way: globalization uses the available tools to facilitate modernization in Africa.

In the past, globalization used colonialism as a tool to promote modernization. Another tool it has used up to the present time is the transnational organizations such as United Nations and its agencies. The formation and

---

10. Chanda, *Bound Together*.
11. Falola and Heaton, *History of Nigeria*; Chamberlain, *Scramble for Africa*.
12. Rodney, *How Europe Underdeveloped Africa*, 30.

operations of the (or at least the globally prominent) transnational organizations are said to have begun after World War II.

> During the twenty-five years after World War II . . . transnational organizations: (a) proliferated in number far beyond anything remotely existing in the past; (b) individually grew in size far beyond anything existing in the past; (c) performed functions which they never performed in the past; and (d) operated on a truly global scale such as was never possible. The increase in the number, size, scope, and variety of transnational organisations after World War II makes it possible, useful and sensible to speak of a *transnational organizational revolution* in world politics.[13]

Politics in the mid-nineteenth century seemed to have witnessed a drastic change with the coming of transnational organizations to the scene. These organizations are in a multilayered form covering both areas of global politics and economics.

> The economic forums include the International Monetary Fund (IMF), the World Bank, The World Trade Organisation (WTO), the regional banks and so on. [The] political forums include the Trilateral Commission, the group of 7 (G-7) . . . United Nations (UN), Organisation of Economic Cooperation and Development (OECD) . . . and so on.[14]

Since the inception of the massive formation of the transnational organizations, the political practices of the nation-state have been largely influenced by the dictates of these organizations. One important case in point is the Bretton Woods conference where political and economic decisions binding nations of the world were made. The United Nations' Conference on Sustainable Development at Rio in 2012 is another case in point. The objective of the Rio conference "was to produce a set of universal goals that meet the urgent environmental, political, and economic challenges facing our world." This led to the formulation of the Sustainable Development Goals.[15]

---

13. Huntington, "Transnational Organizations in World Politics," 333.
14. Mentan, *State in Africa*, 65.
15. "Sustainable Development Goals," *UNDP*, accessed 14 April 2020, https://www.undp.org/sustainable-development-goals.

Discussing the effect of transnational organizations (which he prefers to call supranational organizations) on the nation-state, Mentan writes:

> These [transnational] planning institutes are gradually supplanting the national institutions in policy development and global management and administration of global economy. The function of the nation-state is shifting from formulation of national policies to the administration of policies formulated through [transnational] institutions.[16]

Considering the two instances cited above, Bretton Woods and Rio conferences, it becomes clear that Mentan's observation about the role of transnational organizations is correct. Much of the decisions made by the nation-state political leaders are influenced by the resolutions of the transnational organizations.

Considering the activities of the transnational organizations in the global sphere, one would notice that they tend to advance the course of modernization, whose aim is to replace the traditional with the modern.[17] They are established for no other reason than to promote the modernization agenda of industrialization, Western education, capitalism, privatization, and so forth.

The Positive Aspects of Modernization Theory

One objective of this chapter is to spell out how modernization hampers development in Africa. However, this section seems to contradict the arguments in this book in that it speaks well of modernization. I do not mean to be illogical or a vacillating writer. I do this as a matter of respect to the Yoruba wisdom of which I am writing in this book. The Yoruba wisely hold that "*Ọgbọ́n, ò pin síbì kan* (wisdom is not limited to one place), and that "*Ọmọdé gbọ́n, àgbà gbọ́n lafi dá'lẹ̀ Ifẹ̀*" (Ile Ife, the ancestral origin of Yoruba people, was built by the wisdom of the young and the old). As much as Africans have their developmental-political wisdom, wisdom also implies that they learn something good from other people. It is wisdom to share from the wisdom

---

16. Mentan, *State in Africa*, 65–66.
17. d'Orville, "New Humanism."

of other people. Hence, as Africans, what are the wisdoms we can emulate from Western practices and thoughts on modernization?

Having applied the modernization theory of development for a number of decades, we can say that there is something about the theory and its practices that brought some remarkable experience to Africa. Although many of the ways of life proposed to Africans by modernization are not novel in themselves, some of them have remarkable peculiarities. An example of this is education. I have noted earlier that the Yoruba form of education is largely spontaneous, based on mentorship and apprenticeship. In the Yoruba forms of education, there was no reading and writing. There were no specific ways of measuring the progress of the learner. There were no systematic ways of carrying out "scientific" investigations. As much as this may have worked out for the people who lived in those ages, the weaknesses of this practice are obvious.

One should wonder the extent to which the human mind can retain knowledge over a period, without reading and writing it down. One should wonder how teaching effectiveness could be determined without a viable means of assessment. One should wonder how much scientific and technological innovation could be attained without a systematic mode of research.

Against this backdrop, it is evident that by virtue of Western education, which applies science and philosophy, social problems that touch on issues of health and technological development are being effectively addressed. For instance, health science, something not remarkably present in traditional Africa, has brought about medical solutions to diseases, such as malaria, that killed people in early Africa.

It is a clear fact, with historical evidence, that modernization theory (or rather the preceding theories and practices that gave rise to it), as it stands against traditional ways of life, has achieved remarkable results in human history.[18] It applies the use of science and human reason in bringing about significant changes in the areas of medicine, agriculture, science, water development, and technology.

Exposure to Western ways of life and education has liberated many Africans from difficult socioeconomic backgrounds. "Indeed, many of West Africa's scientists, university lecturers, doctors, and surgeons were

---

18. Myers, *Walking with the Poor*, 23–25.

born to poor, illiterate parents practicing a near-subsistence agriculture."[19] Modernization certainly brought about changes in African socioeconomic and technological experiences.[20] If modernization was able to achieve these beneficial experiences, it therefore means there is some wisdom behind the theory. What is some of this wisdom?

One needs to note that the pillars of modernization, particularly industrialization, capitalism, and scientific revolution are rooted in Protestantism,[21] with its work ethics that places emphasis on "hard work, thrift, and efficiency in one's worldly calling."[22] Some of these basic emphases of modernization theory rooted in Protestantism are biblical principles and if applied anywhere, development would follow. As such, modernization should be commended in this regard, leaving critical lessons for African nations to be hardworking, thrifty, and efficient in what they do.

The work ethics of modernization, which was gleaned from Protestantism, values hard work, which particularly speaks to the issue of how civil service is handled lightly in Africa. Among contemporary Yoruba people, it is said that *"A kíí ṣiṣẹ́ ọba, ká làágùn"* (We do not work for government and sweat). The notion behind this saying is that government work is not worth too much diligence. That is why many government workers give less commitment to their work.

The value of thrift upheld by modernization is also a good thing for contemporary African political leaders to learn, many of whom are known for mismanagement of resources. They should also cultivate the value of efficiency, as opposed to shoddy implementation of policy and actualization of projects, which are common unacceptable practices of the present-day political leadership in Africa.

---

19. Lloyd, *Africa in Social Change*, 11.
20. Lloyd, 11; Kiwanuka, "Three Traditional Foundations," 45.
21. Buck, "Protestantism and Industrialization," 210–24.
22. "Protestant Ethic," *Encyclopaedia Britannica*, accessed 26 January 2020, https://www.britannica.com/topic/Protestant-ethic.

Negative Effects of Modernization on African Developmental-Political Life

In the earlier part of this chapter, I noted that modernization brought notable blessings to Africa. In this section, I want to highlight its notable bane. While the advancement of socioeconomic and technological experience that modernization brought to Africa is praiseworthy, nevertheless its influence on African developmental-political life has brought about remarkable distortion. It is as if the Western states have set a trap of nation-state for Africa, a nation-state whose politics is undergirded by foreign development theory of modernization. The transition of the political systems in Africa from the tribal system to coexisting with the nation-state has led to a form of political practice that is alien to the African experience.

Deviation from Divinity

An African traditional political jurisdiction was comprised of several villages whose people shared a common ancestry. It was governed by African political practice of sacred kingship whereby the success of a leader is identified with "fertility of the crop and of women." Political activities in traditional Africa were carried out within a spiritual circle.[23] All political activities were spiritually linked. They entailed rituals and involvement of divinities. This is unlike the modernization-driven politics inherited from the white man, which made a distinction between the sacred and the secular. Therefore, present-day politics in most African states is considered purely secular. This is not to say that political leaders no longer practice religion but that, unlike the Africa of olden-days, interventions of the spiritual higher power are no longer evident. Political decisions are now solely made by human rational thinking.

Therefore, the first notable deficiency of modernization theory is in its deviation from divinity. Somewhere along the line, it subscribes to the Enlightenment theory that dichotomizes secular from the spiritual.[24] The eventual effect of this is that in the long run, modernization downplays the spiritual aspect of humanity and ignores God's provision in dealing with the evil component of the human system.

---

23. Lloyd, *Africa in Social Change*, 38.
24. Myers, *Walking with the Poor*, 5.

Modernization does not absolutely tolerate the evil component of the human system, but rather than dealing with it by abiding to the spiritual laws, modernization resorts to humanism, which is also linked to the Enlightenment.[25] Humanism in its relationship with the Enlightenment is an attempt to pursue morality without God in the equation.

Considering how colonialism and globalization in relation to modernization generate so much power, we can also note that, "the generation of wealth and power in the process was accompanied by costs and sacrifices at level hitherto unimagined." The spurious prosperity brought about by modernization theory is achieved at the expense of other things that are necessary for human survival and wellbeing, such as people's culture and environmental wellbeing.[26] For example, common to the globalization phenomenon is the idea that powerful nations or people take undue advantage of the weak. Hence, modernization poses numerous ethical issues. In order to salvage the situation, this led to the revival of the talk on humanism, which would serve as a means to "sharpen [human] conscience with regard to the potential of a world based on peace, democracy, justice, mutual respect, and human rights."[27]

"Although the exact definition of humanism has historically fluctuated in accordance with successive and diverse strands of intellectual thought, the underlying concept rests on the universal ideas of human emancipation, independence, and social justice."[28] In the same vein, it is noteworthy that humanism is a significant basis for secular ethics – humanistic ethics. Modernization theory has therefore employed humanistic ethics in agitating for a sense of morality that would ensure cordial relationships in some areas of human dealings: relationship with self, fellow humans, and environment, for the sake of human good.[29]

Just as the Enlightenment sought to take the centrality of God away from human affairs, so does the new humanism. To drive this fact home, Sanjay Seth quotes Edward Saïd as saying, "the 'core' of humanism is the secular notion that the historical world is made by men and women, and not by

---

25. Seth, "Where Is Humanism Going?," 6.
26. d'Orville, "New Humanism," 93.
27. d'Orville, 96.
28. d'Orville, 91.
29. Schweiker, "Theological Ethics," 540.

God, and it can be understood rationally. At the core of humanism, then, is a philosophical anthropology, which in according centrality to man diminishes (though it does not necessarily eliminate) the role accorded to god(s)."[30]

The fact that modernization solely seeks to pursue morality through humanism clearly highlights its tendency to separate God from daily human activities. The implication is that it places low premium on the spiritual domain of humanity. We can therefore conclude that modernization, as a theory of development, is not holistic in nature. The nature of holistic development is that it entails a developmental agenda that cuts across all the physical and immaterial aspects of humanity, believing that both the physical and immaterial aspects of human life are inseparable.

Daniel Groody's observation is noteworthy as I seek to address the issue of the immaterial aspect of humanity. He notes that the "inner space" of humanity, which is regarded as the immaterial part of humanity in this study, is the prominent source of human practices that hamper development in our world. He notes that, "The current disorders of the society begin with the disorders of human heart, from which flow destructive choices that unravel relationships."[31] Modernization has ignored the core of all that take place in human actions and relationships, the inner being which needs transformation.

Overgeneralised Idea of Prosperity

Another distortion of African developmental-political thoughts and practices by modernization has to do with an overgeneralised idea of prosperity. The development agendas promoted by transnational organizations (i.e. crucial agents of globalization) are based on Western tastes.[32] Let us take the activities of modernization-driven transnational organizations as a case in point. They are overgeneralised in the sense that the policy makers of transnational organizations believe that African nations must have the same Western perspective of prosperity. Njoh is right when he says that

> Eurocentric culture, in which capitalist ideology and protestant ethic are rooted, places much premium on capital accumulation, entrepreneurial attitudes, and material wealth *inter*

---

30. Seth, "Where Is Humanism Going?, 6.
31. Groody, *Globalization, Spirituality, and Justice*, 11.
32. Kalu, "Globalization and Its Impact," 30.

alia. . . . While these attributes are not completely absent, they are certainly not at the top of the priority ladder, in the context of traditional Africa.[33]

As far as my study in Yoruba traditional thoughts and practices on politics and development is concerned, the most critical missing link in modernization theory that has a negative impact on contemporary African nation-state politics and development, is the belief that *àlàáfíà* is the true definition of development. A typical Yoruba person perceives peace in one's heart, family, and community as the most important need, and all other things are secondary to this. The infiltration of modernization theory has completely overturned this perspective.

Because modernization misses out on the idea that development is about peace (*àlàáfíà*), consequently, there is less emphasis on the only effective way of ensuring good character (*ìwà rere*) in humans. According to Yoruba, *àlàáfíà* is based on the four-dimensional relationship demonstrated by *ìwà rere*. Meanwhile, this distortion (overgeneralised idea of prosperity) is related to the first one (deviation from divinity).

African relational life, a reflection of *ìwà rere* and *ọmọlúàbí* (in Yoruba context), has a significant relation with divinity. Concerning moral life, a Yoruba person believes that "If I misbehave, the ancestors, deities, and Olodumare will punish me." Likewise, because a king knows that the success of his reign is measured by the extent of *àlàáfíà* that the society experiences, he does everything possible to make it happen. This is the reason behind having a political structure in Yorubaland that ensures members of the society conduct themselves properly. It is also the reason for frequent appeasement of the divinity, as discussed in chapter 4. And all of this is done from the perspective that peace is supreme, it is prosperity, and must be ensured at all costs, by having *ìwà rere* which is demonstrated in the fear of the divinity. This African perspective has been distorted by modernization theory.

Crisis of Identity

The third notable distortion of African developmental-political life has to do with identity. Modernization brought about a distortion in African

---

33. Njoh, *Tradition, Culture and Development*, 2.

developmental-political identity. Africa's developmental-political strength lies in its identity. People's identity has to do with who they are, what they know and do best. They are naturally familiar with what constitutes their identity. If it is in our identity, it will always be familiar to us. There are more advantages in the familiar than the unfamiliar, like a Zulu boy hunting for games in a Zulu forest. The boy is identified with Zululand. That is a familiar territory for him. Hunting game in the Zulu forest gives him a better advantage than hunting in the London forest. Meanwhile, modernization has placed the Zulu boy inside a London forest for a hunting expedition. The Zulu boy will hardly find it easy.

Modernization took away the original identity (which is familiar) of Africa and replaced it with a borrowed identity (which is unfamiliar). Interestingly, the original identity never left Africa. This therefore resulted in two forms of identity clashing with each other. Mbiti also affirms this when he says about Africa, "it is wrong to imagine that everything traditional has been changed or forgotten."[34] This is an indication that in today's Africa, there is a contention between traditional and modern Africas, with African culture in a face-to-face conflict with modernization theory, and causing a crisis of identity.

Thinking in the same line of thought, Ayittey writes:

> There are two Africas that are constantly clashing. The first is traditional or indigenous Africa that historically has been castigated as backward and primitive. . . . The second Africa is the modern one, which is lost. Most of Africa's problem emanate from its modern sector.[35]

First, the influence of modernization imposed by colonialism exposed Africa to the unfamiliar. Then, the promotion of transnational policies added to the challenge of doing the unfamiliar. As a result, contention developed between the familiar and the unfamiliar, as two forms of identity collided.

---

34. Mbiti, *African Religions and Philosophy*, xii.
35. Ayittey, *Africa in Chaos*, 14.

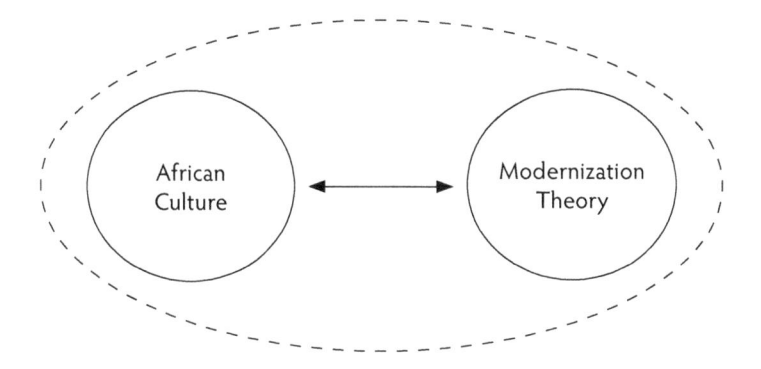

Figure 5. The Clash between Traditional and Modern Africas

Meanwhile, much of the problem faced by contemporary Africa is not in the traditional Africa but in the alien modern Africa. Ayittey affirms this in the quotation above. Njoh also adds his voice when he writes: "Africa's contemporary problems of underdevelopment are not a product of flaws in Africa's culture and/tradition. Rather, the . . . European colonial/imperial époque and the contemporary new colonial era."[36]

Psychological and Evolutionary Implication of Modern-day African Politics

The sequence of events that took place in the nineteenth and twentieth centuries brought about many changes in the lives of the African people. In fact, experiences rarely leave people the same. It is psychologically proven that people's current situation is not just biologically occasioned but also a result of the society with which they are in contact.[37]

Africa has transitioned from traditional tribal system of government into nation-state politics. Even before this phenomenon manifested itself as a political transition, it was first psychologically implied. The experiences that the people of Africa gathered in their interaction and contact with the Europeans (both colonial rulers and missionaries) posed some challenges against their ontological being. The result is an unconscious transformation from who they were to who they are.

---

36. Njoh, *Tradition, Culture and Development*, 16.
37. Lahey, *Psychology*, 20–22.

The situation of Africa under the colonial power can be likened to a person or animal that is confined under a condition for a reasonable period. This condition is naturally passing across a message that consciously or unconsciously registers in the mind of the person or animal. A typical example of this is an experience I had in my childhood days with a caged dove. It had been caged for some time and one day it found a means of escape from the cage. Interestingly, the bird flew just a little distance, perched on a nearby shrub and stayed there for a long time.

Even though the bird later flew away like a normal dove, its first reaction was not the my expectation. My expectation was that the bird would fly as fast and as far as possible by virtue of the excitement of the new-gained freedom. I also thought that the bird should instinctively know that delay in its flight could imply being caught again by its previous "owner."

Nevertheless, I got an insight from the explanation given by an elderly friend who witnessed the same scene with me. First, the physical ability of the bird had been hampered by being encaged for a period. It had not been able to use its wings to fly for some time, hence, the wings could not flap as they used to do before it was caged. Second, having been in the cage for a while, its psychology had been tampered with. It came to possess a new psychology that no longer saw flying as a normal thing.

Since colonialism put some restriction on the people of Africa during the colonial era, we should naturally expect that some ability must have been deterred and psychologically altered. Africa must have possessed a certain mental condition different from the one it had before it got confined under the rule of colonialism. This is the reason people like A. M. Babu, former minister in the Tanzanian government, hold that what Africa needs in times like this, when its situations seem to be getting chaotic by virtue of political decisions and actions, "appears to be the process of mental de-colonization."[38] In its developmental-political thoughts and practices, it is important that Africa boosts itself psychologically by arming itself with familiar ammunition in the battle against underdevelopment.

---

38. Babu, "Postscript," 313.

Conclusion

In this chapter, I enumerated the implications of modernization theory on African nation-state politics. Modernization is an attempt to replace the old with the new in Africa. The process of replacing the old with the new is enabled by colonialism and globalization. Considering its root in Protestantism, modernization theory operates based on some important values, which contemporary African political leaders should emulate: hard work, thrift, and efficiency in areas of one's calling.

Modernization brought both blessings and bane to Africa. Through it, Africa has experienced remarkable advancement in many areas of its socioeconomic life. Nevertheless, it also has had some negative effects that are rooted in (1) deviation from divinity, (2) overgeneralised idea of prosperity, and (3) crisis of identity. In the next chapter, I will discuss the development implications of African political thoughts and practices, in respect to modernization theory and the holy Scripture.

CHAPTER 6

Politics that Fosters Development: Lessons from Yoruba Traditional Developmental-Political Thoughts and Practices

Introduction

This chapter brings the Scripture, modernization theory of development, and Yoruba traditional developmental-political thoughts and practices into conversation with one another. Its goal is to draw the implications of Yoruba traditional political thoughts and practices for development in the contemporary nation-state politics. Scripture is taken as the overall authority as I consider the developmental-political thoughts and practices within these three contexts. The chapter calls for biblical restoration of Yoruba traditional developmental-political thoughts and practices that were favourable to development but were distorted by modernization theory of development.

Biblical Order of Developmental-Politics

The aim of this section is to explore God's development plan for human society, using the story of the nation of Israel in the Bible as a case study. I shall also discuss how this plan relates to politics and development. Other developmental-political thoughts and practices would be assessed with this standard.

God's Agenda for the Wellbeing of the Nations

God's original intention for humanity is depicted in the life in Eden: a life with all provision without toil, a life of cordial relationship with God in the cool of the day, and a life in a well-watered garden. In the garden of Eden, all was well until Adam and Eve disobeyed God. As a result, they had to leave the garden of Eden. Because of their disobedience, the relationship between God and humanity was thwarted. The story that followed is the story of Cain killing his brother Abel, and then the waywardness of the descendants of Cain, up to the time of Noah when the sin of humanity seemed to have reached its apex.

> Now the Lord observed the extent of the people's wickedness, and he saw that all their thoughts were consistently and totally evil. So the Lord was sorry that he had ever made them. It broke his heart. (Gen 6:5, 6, NLT)

The intensity of human wickedness in Noah's time made God destroy everything with water. Noah found favour with God, his family was rescued together with selected animals, and there was a new beginning. Again, in Genesis 11, there was human rebellion against God in their attempt to build the tower of Babel. The narrative of wickedness of humanity did not stop till Revelation. Jeremiah describes the heart of a typical human being: it is desperately wicked (Jer 17:9).

God's care for the sinful state of the human race is evident in his effort to restore them to him. Because of this, he initiated the story of redemption, pivoted in the story of the call of Abraham (Gen 12).[1] The call and obedience of Abraham was followed with God's promise to bless all the nations of the earth through Abraham's descendants (Gen 22:18). With this, we realize that it is God's ultimate desire to bless all the nations of the earth.

The desire of God to bless the world has a great implication. God sets out to act in favour of humanity. His blessing is "a divine utterance expressing [his] will to confer future favour."[2] The blessing of God, when received by humanity, offers a solution to their predicaments. "When God brings [his blessing] it means he will destroy all that is evil and wrong in the world

---

1. Wright, *Mission of God*, 194.
2. Hastings, "Blessing," 307.

and restore all that is right and good and that leads to human flourishing. [Blessing] means all things are made new."[3]

When God struck the blessing deal with the Israelites on the verge of their entering the promised land, the condition for tapping into it was obedience to the commands he had given them (Deut 28). God himself is the initiator of the idea of wellbeing to Israel, in fulfilment of his covenant to Abraham, Isaac, and Jacob (Deut 9:5). He heard their cry when they were in Egyptian bondage and sent Moses to deliver them. He made them a special nation to himself (Exod 19), sealed by a covenant given to Moses on Mount Sinai.

The promised blessing of God to the Israelites is tied to *shalom*. This is the principal end of God's blessings. Perhaps this is why he instructed the Israelite priests to bless the people in this manner:

> The LORD bless you and keep you;
> The LORD make His face shine upon you,
> And be gracious to you;
> The LORD lift up His countenance upon you,
> And give you peace. (Num 6:24–26, NKJV)

The Spiritual and Sociophysical Dimensions of God's Commandments

God's covenant with the Israelites regulates "a social order that is to be maintained through a right relation to God. . . . The vertical axis of God/people covenant facilitates a horizontal axis in which the people bind themselves legally and morally to one another."[4] God's covenant to bless his people is linked to his commandments. If these commandments are obeyed, the people of God will enjoy his true blessings. In fact, God's commandment with a call for obedience on the part of the Israelites is a relational decree – relationship with him, which results in good relationship with others. It has both spiritual and sociophysical dimensions, as reflected in Jesus's summary of the Law:

> Jesus replied, "The most important commandment is this: 'Listen O Israel! The Lord our God is the one and only Lord. And you must love the Lord your God with all your heart, all

---

3. Shaw, *Work, Play, Love*, 100.
4. Hoelzl and Ward, *Religion and Political Thought*, 7.

your soul, and all your mind, and all your strength. The second is equally important: 'Love your neighbor as yourself.'" (Mark 12:29–31, NLT)

The spiritual dimension to God's commandment entails relationship with God, who portrays himself as a jealous God "who will not tolerate your affection for any other gods!" He will punish those who choose not to love him and serve other gods, by punishing their children up to the third and fourth generations (Exod 20:5, NLT). The spiritual dimension of God's law is simply to love him fully, committing to nobody else besides him. The biblical concept of love for God implies faithfully following him and keeping his commandments (Eph 6:24; Jas 1:12; Exod 20:6).

The sociophysical dimension of God's commandment entails his expectation of people to relate to one another with the wellbeing of others in mind. When people live up to the sociophysical dimension of God's commandment, this is what happens: people are so mindful of one another that they do not do what will hurt someone else around them (Prov 3:29).

The sociophysical dimension of God's law has to do with daily ethics, making decisions and taking actions that are considered right before God. Most of our daily actions and activities have some implications on the life of other people. Therefore, God has given necessary guiding principles that will make life better, not just for us as individuals but also for other people around us. The sociophysical dimension of God's law is therefore directed towards our daily lifestyles.

For instance, the Scripture commands that "Let every soul be subject to the governing authorities" (Rom 13:1, NKJV). What if the road users chose to violate highway law and overloaded their vehicles? What will happen if the taxpayers chose to avoid tax payments? What if people chose to violate town planning order and built houses wherever they please?

All of these have negative implications on some other individuals. Overloading would spoil the road and create potholes that may claim the life of an individual. Evading taxes reduces government financial pool from which money could be taken to provide amenities. Building houses anywhere may imply that the road access to someone else's house would be blocked.

Now talking about moral laws, largely spelt out by the Ten Commandments, what if people begin to steal one another's properties? What will happen if people begin to kill other people's family members? Again, these also rob some people of their wellbeing. The sociophysical dimension of God's law is therefore responsible relationship with fellow humans and nature around us for the sake of the wellbeing of all.

The dimensions of God's commandment are ordered both vertically and horizontally. Adhering to the two dimensions of the commandment is the way of *shalom* (Figure 6A). Meanwhile, the vertical axis facilitates the horizontal one. No one can genuinely maintain the horizontal axis without giving heed to the vertical one. Hence, everything about God's blessings finds its source in relationship with God, who is delighted in blessing his people.

A
True spirituality:
Relationship with God demonstrated in lifestyle

B
Pharisaic hypocrisy:
Religion that does not reflect in lifestyle

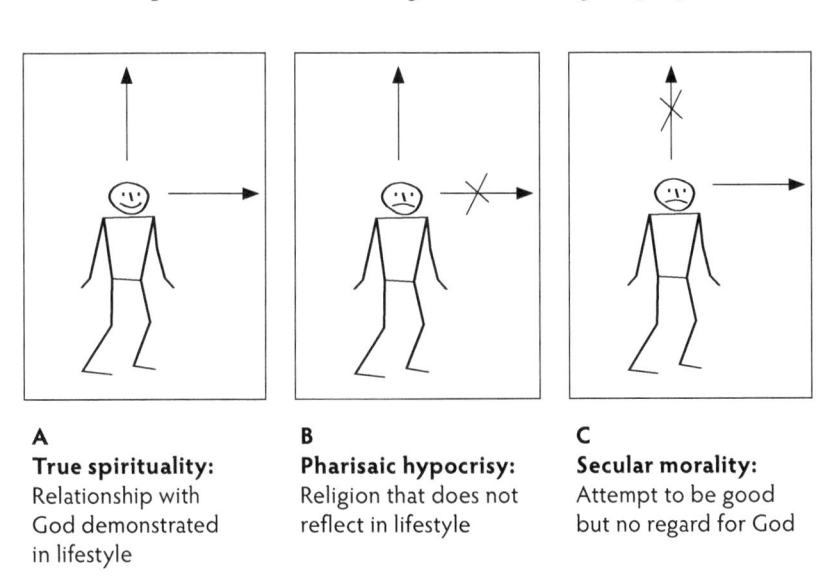

C
Secular morality:
Attempt to be good but no regard for God

Figure 6. The Two Dimensions of God's Law

Some OT prophets such as Isaiah (1:11–17), Hosea (6:6), Amos (5:21–24), and Micah (6:7–8) attributed the ill-being of the Israelites in their times to spirituality that does not reflect in lifestyle. During his time on earth, Jesus also condemned the Pharisees for demonstrating spirituality without a corresponding lifestyle. To this end, he called them hypocrites (Matt 23:23, illustrated in Figure 6B). As such, spirituality that does not reflect in a lifestyle of love, mercy, righteousness, justice, etc., is no spirituality at all.

On the other hand, in the modern world, aided by the Enlightenment, it has been widely held that human beings can make good ethical decisions and actions through their willpower (Figure 6C).[5] Paul stresses the impotency of human willpower in Romans 7:14–24, when he noted his personal failure to overcome sin through the willpower. Therefore, God-required lifestyle is impossible without a relationship with him. The inability to live out the lifestyle that God requires us to live is the reason for sin in the society.

As I have noted earlier in this study, sin is the ultimate inhibitor of wellbeing. However, God has made a provision for victory over sin through the work of redemption. Turning back to God is the only way through which we can daily live out the principles that ensure true wellbeing and development.

Redemption brings us back to God and gives us victory over sin. This is the Christian message for the nations of the world in their search for holistic development and wellbeing. I shall seek to communicate this message in this chapter by drawing biblical correlations and antitheses from Yoruba traditional political practices and thoughts; and contemporary political-development theory rooted in modernization theory.

The Kingship Role in Israelites' Political Setting

As noted earlier, the blessing of God, when received by humans as they obey his commandment, usually results in *shalom,* the peace of God that passes human understanding, which is the biblical term for development. The connection between God's covenant, blessing, and *shalom* is well expressed in Cafferky's words:

> The principles contained in the Decalogue have a direct relationship to the realization of promised blessings of Shalom as experienced in the community as a whole. The Commandments are not merely a random, arbitrary list of ethical "dos and don'ts" for individuals. They form the prescription for how the community as a whole can experience Shalom through individual and collective behaviors.[6]

---

5. Nkansah-Obrempong, "Lecture Notes: Christian Ethics," 3.
6. Cafferky, "Ethical-Religious Framework," 1.

To talk about Israelites as a community of people, beginning from their life in the wilderness, is to talk about a political entity. One of the acceptable definitions of politics is that politics is "the complex or aggregate of relationships of people in society, especially those relationships involving authority and power."[7] The word "politics" originated from the Greek word *polis*, meaning city, with the allusion to the community of people living in the city, according to Plato, "a community of souls."[8]

No human being exists without a relationship with a state – a politically structured society. In fact, it has been argued that "the state and human beings are made for each other: the good human life is simply not possible without the state."[9] Through a study of Aristotle's *Politics*, Book I and II, Rosen and Wolff conclude, "the state . . . exists by nature, and that man is by nature an animal for the state. Anyone who by his nature and not by ill-luck has no state is either a wretch or superhuman; he is . . . like a man condemned . . . as having 'no brotherhood, no law, no hearth.'"[10] According to them, "A state is a human community that (successfully) claims the monopoly of the legitimate use of physical force within a given territory."[11] By this, they are alluding to the sovereign nature of the state, its vested ability to make things happen in a geographical space.

The general administration of a state and election of a leader are said to be critical aspects of politics. Therefore, politics is part of human life. It affects our daily lives.[12] This is also true of the Israelites. Their society, like any other society, is a political entity. God himself organised the people politically by appointing a leader over them and giving them a law.

> Israel was a nation founded in fulfilment of God's promise on the twin pillars of *divine rescue* and *divine law*, and Moses, as the divinely appointed leader, played a vital role in both the

---

7. Hanks, "Politics," 1186.
8. Hoelzl and Ward, *Religion and Political Thought*, 2, 9.
9. Rosen and Wolff, *Political Thought*, 7.
10. Rosen and Wolff, 11.
11. Rosen and Wolff, 55.
12. Storkey, *Jesus and Politics*, 10; Eagles, *Politics*, 19.

rescue and the giving of the law. He became the paradigm of the divinely instituted governor or ruler.[13]

Like the other nations of the earth, God founded the nation of Israel (Acts 17:26). After rescuing them from Egyptian oppression, he gave the Israelites the promise of a land flowing with milk and honey, and organised them into a nation by giving them a Law (Torah). The Law organised the Israelites into a nation, and God set a ruler over them. Even though he set a ruler over them, he remained their King (Isa 33:22; 44:6; Zeph 3:15). He ruled over the Israelites through his Law. Obedience to his Law was the critical parameter for their wellbeing. Due to this fact, God, who is their ultimate king, placed a human king over the Israelites[14] as an individual whose responsibility is to ensure that his will be done among the people (Jer 3:15).

The Israelites' king was a co-regent, while God was primarily their king. The human king as God's co-regent was to rule according to God's law and be a model of righteousness (Deut 17:18–20). He must seek justice and righteousness (Isa 32:2; Jer 23:5). These special qualities of a (human) king bring us to the understanding that living according to God's Law is an essential requirement in a political system.

Although the instruction regarding the worship of Yahweh was largely directed to the priests and Levites (Lev 16), one of the fundamental duties carried out by good kings was to facilitate the worship of Yahweh. Solomon in his early days built a temple for God. In his prayer for the people, he expressed his wish, prayerfully, for them to be able "to walk in all his [God's] ways, and to keep his commandments and his statutes and his judgements, which he commanded our fathers" (1 Kgs 8:58, KJV). After this prayer, he led the people to worship (vv. 62–66).

Asa (1 Kgs 15:11–13), Jehoshaphat (1 Kgs 22:41–50), Hezekiah (2 Kgs 18:1–12), and Josiah (2 Kgs 22:1–23:27) were all said to be good kings because of their obedience to God, which they demonstrated in their personal lives, in their facilitation of Yahweh's worship, and in their opposition to idolatry. If the Israelite kings followed the Law given by God and influenced the nation to serve him, their reigns were remarkable for national wellbeing. Therefore,

---

13. Hughes, *Power and Poverty*, 45.
14. King and Stager, *Life in Biblical Israel*, 4.

in biblical terms, the role of a political leader towards wellbeing is to live according to God's way and influence the nation to do the same.

The biblical order for developmental politics entails that the society embraces God and his principles. This should be demonstrated in the day-to-day life of every individual in the society, and in all forms of human transactions and interactions, and more importantly, the political leader should influence people to embrace these principles.

Although many nations of the earth may not truly acknowledge God as their king but that is who he is and wants to be. God's desire to be King of all the nations is not a matter of imposition; it is a matter of love. "God created the nations. He loves them and longs to bless them. There are more than two thousand references to "nations" in Scripture, and many concern God's desire to bless and heal them."[15]

God intends that humans experience wellbeing in all aspects–socially, materially, spiritually, mentally, and psychologically. However, hardly is there a political society that enjoys this fullness of wellbeing. While some societies enjoy some aspects of wellbeing, they suffer in other aspects of wellbeing.

For instance, Africa socially experiences the joy of relationship in their communal life; but then the continent is ravaged with material poverty. On the contrary, the global North enjoys material wealth while the epidemic of individualism makes many of their citizens experience social loneliness. Human society has failed to enjoy the fullness of wellbeing because they have rejected God and his ways.

Human Wellbeing Is Intrinsic to Kingdom Lifestyle

The Israelite society is a typical political society like any other society. According to the Scripture, as discussed above, the wellbeing of the society was directly linked with people's obedience to God's Law – the Torah. When members of the society lived according to the Torah, it would be well with them and vice versa.

When Jesus came to the political scene in the New Testament, he made an important declaration that indicated his stance about the Law: He had not come to abolish the requirements of the Law but to fulfil them (Matt 5:17). The message of repentance and call for a new lifestyle dominated his

---

15. Miller, Moffitt, and Allen, *God's Remarkable Plan*, 10.

teaching (cf. Mark 1:14–15). Many things he taught touched on the concept of the kingdom of God (Matt 6:33; 12:28; 19:24; Mark 4:11; 9:47; Luke 17:20, to cite a few passages).

The concept of the kingdom of God (or heaven) draws so much theological debate that is beyond the scope of this study. Nevertheless, considering all the parables that Jesus used to teach the concept, God is at the centre of this kingdom. The parable of the sower indicates, "God is at the centre, sowing the seed."[16] The parables of the lost sheep, lost coin, and the lost son, paint the picture of God making radical attempts to bring humanity to him (Luke 15).

As such, Christ's teaching about the kingdom of God has to do with the rule of God, which in human language depicts a political situation. Through his teaching on the kingdom of God, "Jesus shows the significance of the rule of God in relation to work, status, friendship, marriage, time, food, clothing, healing, money, anxiety, and rest."[17] His sermon on the mountain demands radical lifestyles from people contrary to what they initially held – going the extra mile, turning the other cheek, controlling anger, saying the truth without having to swear and so forth (Matt 5–7).

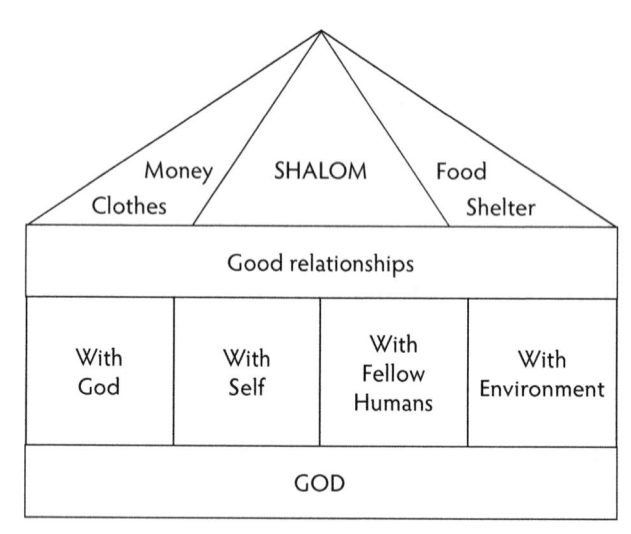

	Money / SHALOM \ Food	
	Clothes / \ Shelter	
Good relationships		
With God	With Self	With Fellow Humans	With Environment
GOD			

Figure 7. Biblical Order for Development

---

16. Storkey, *Jesus and Politics*, 111.
17. Storkey, 112.

Thus, the teaching of Christ about the rule of God is a call to right attitude and lifestyle. Answering this call is the first step in the pursuit of genuine wellbeing. Above all material and emotional needs, Christ commanded his disciples to "seek . . . first the kingdom of God and his righteousness; and all these things shall be added unto you" (Matt 6:33, KJV). Meanwhile, "the Hebrew word "righteousness" cannot be privatised and is best rendered as "justice-with-right-living."[18]

The summary of the biblical order of developmental politics is that God is the ultimate king in the human society. He gives the principle according to which the people of the society must conduct themselves. The wellbeing of the society depends on how much the people in it adhere to the God-given principles. When they live out the principles, they enjoy the *shalom* of God, which attracts the blessing of God in all aspects–material wealth, physical health, and so forth. One significant role of the human king, appointed by God the ultimate king, is to ensure that the will of God is done among his people so that they enjoy *shalom*. This was a primary responsibility of the Yoruba king. He was concerned about the wellbeing of the people and he had to ensure they experience *shalom*.

Central to the argument of this book is the need for biblical restoration of African traditional identity. The story of modernization has also become part of African identity. It is a phenomenon that has existed in Africa for many years. As such, the formulation of the contextual political theology of development, which is the task of this study, is achieved by beaming the light of God's word on the two clashing Africas (Figure 8). I glean the biblical developmental-political teachings from both sides but with special focus on Africa (case of Yoruba culture).

---

18. Storkey, 130.

```
                    ┌─────────────────┐
                    │  The Scripture  │
                    └─────────────────┘
           ╱                                ╲
      ╔═════════╗                      ╔══════════════╗
      ║ Yoruba  ║ ◄──────────────────► ║ Modernization║
      ║ Culture ║                      ║   Theory     ║
      ╚═════════╝                      ╚══════════════╝
                    ┌──────────────────────────────┐
                    │ Contextual Political Theology of │
                    │         Development          │
                    └──────────────────────────────┘
```

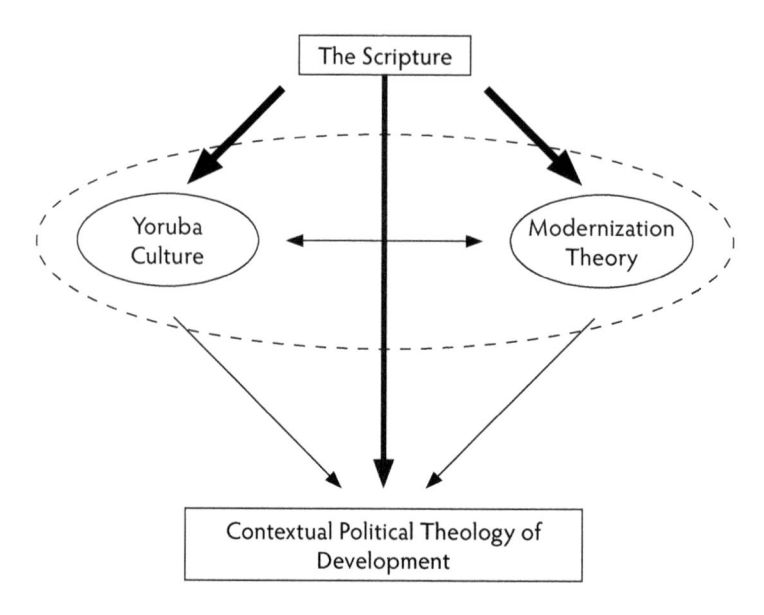

Figure 8. The Contextual Framework for Contextual Political Theology of Development

Review of Modernization Theory and Its Implications for Development in Africa

The aim of this section is to do a review of modernization theory of development. The section is strategically placed here in preparation for the discussion on the implications of Yoruba traditional political thoughts and practices on development, which is the focus of the subsequent section.

Operations, Benefits, and Biblical Correlations

In the previous chapter, I have discussed contemporary order for development as embedded in modernization theory. The discussion reveals that modernization theory is operationally related to colonialism and globalization. Historically, colonialism powered the modernization agenda by imposing nation-state politics on Africa. Globalization, through the operations of transnational organizations, promotes modernization agenda. The ultimate aim of modernization theory is to supplant the old system in "developing" nations with practices that culminate into Western prosperity – industrialization, sophisticated agriculture, commerce, etc.

The discussion in the previous chapter also reveals that modernization is characterised by high mobility, sophisticated economy and technology, secular society, high incomes, literacy, and urbanization. These characteristics then opened up the world for material prosperity, incredibly improved health services, and many other remarkable achievements the world had not known in centuries before Christ and the eighteen centuries that followed his ascension.[19] Rooted in Protestantism (built on biblical principles), modernization theory places emphasis on hard work, thrift, and efficiency in one's worldly calling. This is its significant biblical correlation.

Negative Effects and Biblical Antitheses

In my estimation of modernization theory in the previous chapter, I noted three foundational problems about the theory as they are being applied in Africa. The first problem of modernization theory, the problem of deviation from divinity, resulted in lack of spirituality in Africa. African spirituality is said to be a significant basis for the African people's moral and ethical stance. And as we shall see in the section that follows, loss of African spirituality culminated in downplaying of moral and ethical values. Both biblical- and secular-based development theories acknowledge the moral and ethical need for human wellbeing and development. Hence, I shall discuss in the following section how the downplaying of moral and ethical values in Africa led to corruption of all forms, among both followers and political leaders in African states.

Deviation from divinity is one way by which modernization theory fails to speak in line with God's word. While for Yoruba (and African people in general), divinity is at the centre of all their actions and beliefs, modernization theory has humans at the centre of everything. While Yoruba tradition holds ethical and moral practices that are both anthropocentric and spiritual, modernization theory appeals to moral and ethical practices through anthropocentric humanism.

The second problem is an overgeneralised idea of prosperity. The problem of overgeneralization imposed Western materialism on Africa. African perception about wellbeing and development places a premium on peace, and the cosmic order based on cordial relationships, rather than on material

---

19. Myers, *Walking with the Poor*, 23–26.

prosperity. Western materialistic perception of human wellbeing and development stands in stark contrast to the biblical order of development, whereby *shalom* is the ultimate measure of human wellbeing. Meanwhile, in this regard, the Yoruba traditional beliefs correlate with God's word. Yoruba political system is commended for being structured to enhance *shalom* (*àlàáfíà*). Although Yoruba people are not averse to materialism, it is a secondary index in their talk on wellbeing, as it also is in the teaching of Christ on wellbeing.

The third problem of modernization theory, crisis of identity, causes tension in the minds of African people. Africa is left off-balance juggling between traditional and modern Africa. This study joins a host of thinkers, such as Ayitteh and Njoh, holding that the problem of underdevelopment in Africa is a doing of the "modern Africa."

Implications from Yoruba Traditional Developmental-Political Thoughts and Practices

This section is a review of the discussion on Yoruba traditional political thoughts and practices with the aim of highlighting their implications for development. In chapters 3 and 4, I noted that Yoruba political practices and thoughts are built on the idea that *àlàáfíà* is the primary index for wellbeing, an idea which strongly correlates with the Scripture. I also noted that the political system is structured in such a way to ensure acceptable moral and ethical practices from all members of the society. I also noted the role of traditional educational system in fostering spirituality and acceptable moral practices in the community. Finally, I discussed the implications of the sacredness of kingship in Yorubaland. In this section, I draw some biblical development lessons from Yoruba traditional political thoughts and practices. I also present some biblical antitheses.

Political Society Built on the Idea of *Àlàáfíà*

One of the realizations in the study of the foundations for Yoruba developmental-political thoughts is that Yoruba understanding of wellbeing has some resemblance to biblical worldview. I noted that for Yoruba, the basis for wellbeing is *àlàáfíà* (peace), and in the biblical orientation, the basis for wellbeing is *shalom*. Yoruba believe that peace is supreme, "*àlàáfíà lójù*"; an idea that suggests that there are other things more important than material things. This similarity therefore offers one of the important traditional developmental-political thoughts from Yoruba culture, which can serve as a critical concept in Christian teaching on politics and development.

Earlier in this chapter, citing an Old Testament instance, I have noted that God's ultimate blessing to his people is peace. With the coming of Jesus Christ to the New Testament stage, the emphasis on peace as the ultimate human need is further reinforced. Jesus instructed his disciples, on the evangelistic journey, to give them the blessing (greetings) of peace (Matt 10:13; Luke 10:5–6). More essentially, when he was leaving earth, one of his final statements to the disciples was: "Peace I leave with you; My peace I give to you; not as the world gives do I give to you" (John 14:27, NASB). Likewise, in the apostolic teaching, the gospel of Jesus Christ is a message that brings peace to humanity (Acts 10:36; Rom 5:1). Philippians 4:7 describes the nature of the peace of God as an experience that is beyond human understanding.

The reality about peace, according to both the Old and New Testaments, is that God is the giver of peace. This also applies to the Yoruba belief in *àlàáfíà*. It is only earned by someone to whom Olodumare is favourably disposed. It is a wish. It is a prayer. It is for the lucky ones, an experience that happens by chance. In relation to this, it is believed that *"Àlàáfíà kò sé f'owó rà"* (peace cannot be bought with money). Since peace is a divine-made experience, Yoruba people consult Olodumare through the gods so that peace can be given, either in the life of an individual or community.

Although Yoruba concept of peace as the basis of wellbeing has a biblical similitude, it does not imply that it is the exact replica of biblical teaching on the same. Yoruba would pray to the God of heaven through the gods (*òrìṣà, alálẹ̀ ilẹ̀, irúnmọlẹ̀*), and sometimes the ancestors. This stands in stark contrast to the mode of presenting petitions to God in the Bible. In the Old Testament times, national (and sometimes individual) petitions are made through a God-ordained priest (Lev 1–7).

In the New Testament times, the role of human priests is done away with and Christians can go to God without any intermediary. In contrast to the Yoruba prayer of peace, the New Testament people of God do not need any intermediary, be it *òrìṣà, alálẹ̀ ilẹ̀, irúnmọlẹ̀*, or the ancestors.

For Yoruba people, the only known way to secure peace with God is by offering petition through the gods or ancestors. The fundamental way to secure peace with God is through relationship with him, according to the perfected work of Christ on the cross (Rom 5:1; Eph 2:14–16; Col 1:20–23). In Christ we would be able to fulfil all the Law, and consequently be able to receive God's blessing of *shalom*.

The concept of *àlàáfíà lójù* teaches that some things are more important than material wealth. One of the proverbs that drives home this belief is, *"Bí a bá ń wá owó lọ, tí a bá pàdé iyì l'ọ́nà, ńse lóyẹ kí á padà s'ílé"* (When we set out of our house in search of money, and we come across dignity on our way, the right thing to do is to return home). It is true that money is needed to procure almost all material things as the writer of Ecclesiastes teaches (10:19), but the danger of uncontrolled pursuit of material wealth will lead us to do evil (1 Tim 6:10).

The concept of *àlàáfíà lójù* is therefore a teaching against materialism. It speaks to human tendency for undue competition and greed for power that make humanity to move helter skelter around the world. It speaks to the greed of capitalism that teaches people to measure achievements by skyscrapers, big castles, sophisticated automobiles, massive economic power, and so forth.

Healthy competition is good in that it brings about remarkable achievements in business, technology, science, etc. but it should not be at the expense of the inner peace and our soul. For the sake of pursuit of holistic wellbeing, although secondary, material prosperity is also necessary. While pursuing peace as the primary index of wellbeing and development, Africa can inculcate the biblical means of achieving the secondary indices, learning from modernization theory of development.

As I have suggested in chapter 5, it is time that Africans embrace work ethics that emphasizes hard work, thrift, and efficiency in one's worldly calling. Although work, thrift, and efficiency are not alien to African culture, modernization nevertheless challenges Africa to do more in those areas.

The dangerous pitfall that African nations need to watch out for in their greater efforts towards work, thrift, and efficiency is materialism, the belief that sums up all human wellbeing into physical pleasure. Nothing else can satisfy the human soul like the peace given by God (Ps 4:7). Things that give true happiness and joy are immaterial things; they are the transformation that our life experiences as we relate with God (2 Cor 3:18).

Àlàáfíà comes to our life when we grow in virtues, developing all the attributes that God wants us to have – love, honesty, courage, wisdom, and so forth, as particularly taught in God's word. *Àlàáfíà* also comes to our life when we obey God by giving ourselves to things that matter to our souls – service to humanity, quality moments with family and friends, obeying the principle of Sabbath which calls us to pause from our weekly busy engagement and spend time to renew our spirit and physical body (Exod 23:12).

Against the romance of materialism, deepened by African exposure to Western culture through modernization, one needs to realize that the most important things in life are immaterial, as I have indicated in the forgoing discussion. This is what must be the primary pursuit of both political leaders and the citizens of any nation. We all must be reminded of *àlàáfíà lójù*. We all must know as a community of people in Africa that rather than pursuing material things, we should pursue peace with God because "For what does it benefit a man to gain the whole world [with all its pleasures], and forfeit his soul?" (Mark 8:36, Amp). We all must remind ourselves, "A dry crust eaten in peace is better than steak every day along with argument and strife" (Prov 17:1, LB).

Political Society That Demands *Ìwà Rere* from Society Members

The root of poverty everywhere, any time is sin.[20] Sin implies alienation from God the Creator.[21] This alienation results in the loss of *shalom*. Human political system or society is obviously not without sin; therefore, the issue of sin is a paramount one to be discussed in contextual political theology of development. It is clear that sin, manifesting itself in human corruption and indiscipline, is endemic in African society as a political entity. According to research conducted in Nigeria to assess the state of corruption in the country, it was found that there is a high level of public awareness that both political leaders and the electorates are highly corrupt.[22] The research also reveals that in Nigeria, most political leaders use the public office for personal interest. It is also revealed that the electorates demonstrate a level of corruption in that majority of them vote for political candidates who paid for their votes. All these things have adverse effects on the wellbeing of the nation. Talking about corruption and one setback it causes, Osiyale writes:

---

20. Myers, 145.
21. Hughes, *Power and Poverty*, 28.
22. Adedayo, "Concept of Omoluabi."

> Corruption has resulted over time in the progressive and phenomenal enrichment of Nigerian rulers, the depletion of the national treasury and the huge foreign indebtedness of the country . . . thereby leading to lack of resources to invest in the critical sectors of that nation's economy like infrastructural development, health, agriculture etc.[23]

As we consider the manner in which people who have access to the public treasury have had it depleted, there is no way the society can experience any reasonable development. We should also remember the biblical injunction that:

> Righteousness [moral and spiritual integrity and virtuous character] exalts a nation,
> But sin is a disgrace to any people. (Prov 14:34, AMP).

What then do Yoruba traditional thoughts and practices have to say about dealing with sin, corruption, and indiscipline as the society pursues development-oriented politics?

Corruption is not a new phenomenon in any era of human history. Just as both contemporary leaders and their followers have tendencies to be corrupt, political leaders and their followers in the traditional Yoruba society have also had the tendency for corruption and all other forms of moral evils. Drawing from my discussion on sin in chapter 3, I shall highlight here some commendable ways through which the Yoruba people dealt with sin and other moral evils in their traditional society.

The first commendable Yoruba traditional practice in their approach to sin is that the sinners are called by names that provoke one's sense of shame and critically point out the graveness and repercussion of their acts: *ẹlẹ́sẹ̀, òdaràn, aṣebi, òṣìkà,* or *onílàabi.* To the ear and mind of an original speaker of Yoruba language, these words carry heavy meanings and undesirable tags, just like a sane English speaker would not desire to be called a "pig"; or would easily get a glimpse of what it is to be called a "viper."

Yoruba strongly believe that *ẹni bá lójú lojúú tì* (Whoever has a sense of shame is the one who would be ashamed). Hence, one of those ways to make people behave well in the society is to appeal to their sense of shame. One

---

23. Osiyale, "Indiscipline and Corruption," 252.

such way to appeal to people's sense of shame against bad habits is to call the perpetrator of the act by a shameful name.

Apart from the traditional practice of calling sinners by shame-inducing names, Yoruba are also forthright in calling sinful acts by shameful names. It is strongly held that *Oun tí ò dá'a kò lórúkọ méjì, oun tí kò dá'a kò dá'a* (What is bad does not have two names, what is bad is simply bad). Primarily, this is to say that bad habits and sinful acts do not deserve euphemisms.

English, the language of modernization, also tends to frown at the use of euphemism for bad habits when it says "Let us call a spade a spade." However, as we shall see later in this section on the analysis of Western education and its effect on character of the political leaders, many English words for bad things, being a second language, sound euphemistic to many African ears and hence fail to bring the knowledge of the intensity of the nature of their bad habits into their conscience.

Another noteworthy aspect is that there is both personal and communal responsibility in ensuring good character in the society. From the Yoruba concept of sin, it is realised that an individual human being has the responsibility to guard his/her behaviour so that he/she does not fall into sin. In order words, members of a community must seek to become an *ọmọlúàbí*, which is the Yoruba concept of an ideal human being.

This is partly in consonance with Paul's admonition to the Romans when he wrote to them, "Therefore do not let sin reign in your mortal body, that you should obey it in its lusts" (Rom 6:12, NKJV). With this, we learn that, according to Scripture, there is a place for personal responsibility when it comes to living a righteous life, a life above sin and corruption.

Yoruba tradition also has something to teach us from the word of God when it places responsibility on the community to hold one another accountable for their actions. When people have a hiding place for sin, then evil acts will thrive. However, the one who realizes that all eyes are watching will have a reason to caution himself/herself and think twice when on the verge of misbehaving.

Like the awareness of public eyes has the tendency to put an evildoer in check, so does public rebuke. Yoruba people would say, *ẹjẹ́ ká pa'nu pọ̀, ká b'ólè wí* (Let us put mouths together and rebuke a thief). Rather than, out of sycophancy, singing the praise of an evildoer, we would do the society good by "putting mouths together" and rebuking a sinner. From Yoruba culture, the modern-day society can learn how to bring out the graveness of the nature and repercussion of bad behaviours of people by appealing to their conscience. One effective way to do this could be using suitable language to tell the wicked it shall not be well with them (Eccl 8:13; Isa 3:10–11). The use of noneuphemistic words in talking about bad behaviours can bring to the conscience of sinners the truth that all is not well when they commit atrocities.

Although human beings are fallen in nature, they are created in the image of God, with the ability to share the communicable attributes of God, such as love, kindness, humility, and so forth. Although the human willpower is weakened by virtue of the fall, as Augustine noted, humans still have some ability to make efforts towards living a moral life. This can happen when a human being presents his/her will to God.[24]

Human beings can attempt on their own to attain some level of omolúàbí, a morally ideal human; Paul gave some imperative statements that suggest this (Rom 6:12; Phil 2:12). However, the aspect that is left out by Yoruba traditional belief is the aspect of God's willingness to help our willpower through the power of the Holy Spirit that comes upon people the day they received salvation (Rom 8:1–5). The level of omolúàbí that Yoruba traditional society wants to see in a human being can be fully attained only in Christ. This reality also becomes a critical component of contextual political theology of development.

As much as Yoruba belief in working out one's character finds a basis in the Scripture (cf. Phil 2:12b), that is not all that the Scripture teaches about forming good character. Beyond what Yoruba people believe as the way to possess and maintain good character, the Scripture further teaches that, "God is always at work in you to make you willing and able to obey his own purpose" (Phil 2:13, GNT).

Therefore, it is not enough for an individual to guard his/her behaviour through personal effort, it is also important that he/she taps into God's provision to help humanity do his will. Looking at the Yoruba concept of omolúàbí from the scriptural viewpoint, we find that the Bible holds that personal efforts alone cannot help anybody attain the height of "omolúàbí." The way to become an omolúàbí before God is through the righteousness of Christ that

---

24. Augustine, *City of God*, 605.

is imputed in us (2 Cor 5:21). Other than that, the demonstration of *ìwà rere* (good behaviour) that comes through personal effort, at its best, before God, is still like a filthy rag (Isa 64:6; Rom 3:10).

Although it does not totally agree with the biblical teaching, the basis for Yoruba appeal for good character is not as far away from the Scripture when compared to that of contemporary development theories. While contemporary development theories also acknowledge the place of good ethical standing (the Yoruba equivalence of "*ọmọlúàbí*") in ensuring wellbeing of humanity, their appeal for morality is based on humanistic ethics that is void of spirituality.

Yoruba's appeal for good character is not just based on "humanism" but also divinity. In the biblical term, divinity only entails the Trinitarian God – Olodumare minus ancestors and deities. While the shortcoming of Yoruba religious thought is evident in its placing of traditional deities and ancestors in the same realm with God, modernization theory can be critiqued for completely leaving out God.

In the biblical order, God is the reason humans should not do evil, since all evils are done against him (Gen 20:6; 29:9; Lev 5:19; 6:2; Ps 52:4). The way to be right with God is through the imputed righteousness of Christ. In fact, this can be appropriated when one gives oneself to spiritual activities (walking in the Spirit, cf. Rom 8:4; Gal 5:16).

The manifestation of *ìwà rere*, which makes a person *ọmọlúàbí*, otherwise known as kingdom lifestyle as taught by Christ, must be the primary focus in the pursuit of wellbeing. These can truly be manifested through spiritual walk with God; hence, the need for biblical restoration of Yoruba spirituality, putting God alone at the centre of morality, and all human activities.

Political Society Built on Spiritual, Value-Based Educational System

Education brings changes in human life. It offers knowledge that can bring about change of perspective and, ultimately, attitude. It creates awareness that leads people into helpful discoveries that enhance their safety and wellbeing, and bring about a better life. This is why education is a vital instrument in human development.

In the prophecy of Hosea, it is noted that people perish without knowledge (4:6). A careful examination of the book of Hosea brings us to the awareness that people did not just perish because of mere lack of knowledge, as it seems to appear in chapter 4:6a. The lack of knowledge that led to the peril of the people was their lack of knowledge of God: "My people are destroyed because of lack of knowledge. Because you have rejected knowledge . . . because you have forgotten the law of your God" (4:6, NKJV). Thus, the people were strongly rebuked by the prophet for their lack of "knowledge of God." The knowledge of God would have enabled them to live a lifestyle that demonstrated truth, mercy, and justice, human attributes that promote *shalom* (4:1, 6; 6:3, 6). Their situation was essentially the result of a failure in obeying the critical educational instruction given by Moses.

Moses told the people of Israel that the nation would be seen as a great nation if they followed the Law and commandments which he had *taught* them, as given by the Lord (Deut 4: 5, 6). They should not just follow the Law. This Law and commandment should therefore be *taught* to the children: "Impress them on your children. Talk about them when you sit at home and when you walk along the road, when you lie down and when you get up" (Deut 6:7, NIV). The people of Israel in Hosea's time failed in this regard.

In obedience to Moses' instruction in Deuteronomy, the writer of Psalm 78, perhaps on behalf of the people of his generation, made a promise that all those things they have *learnt* from the previous generation they would *teach* them to their children (vv. 3–4). As such, it is evident that the people of Israel in the psalmist's time knew the significance of education in the wellbeing of their nation.

In a general sense, educational system is an important aspect of a nation. Education entails seeking knowledge and information and passing them on to other persons. In Rather's opinion, "Education equips an individual for social, moral, cultural, and spiritual aspects and thus makes life progressive, cultured, and civilised."[25] This implies that education touches all the aspects of human life.

As we have seen in the case of the Israelites, the knowledge of God must be foundational to the content of educational instruction. In my discussion of Yoruba education in chapter 3, it was concluded that the underlying aim of education in Yorubaland is *ìwà rere* (good character), defined by the four-dimensional relationship – relationship with self, fellow humans, environment,

---

25. Rather, *Theory and Principle*, 1.

and God. This has a correlation in the Israelite's case: the basic educational objective is knowledge of God that manifests in godly character. In light of this awareness, this section shall discuss the Yoruba mode of education vis-à-vis Western education with the intention of drawing its implications on development and politics.

While discussing the scope of education, Rather gives two concepts which are: the narrower concept and the broader concept.[26] The narrower concept confines the scope of education to schools, colleges, and universities; whereas the broader scope of education refers to the experiences gained by human beings on a daily basis. The narrower concept of education is rather intentional and very systematic, limiting learning exercizes to the classrooms. It entails the relationship between students and teachers. Education in a broader sense goes beyond learning activities that take place in a formal setting such as classrooms.

One of the prevailing questions people would ask in the discourse on African education is whether the traditional Africa ever practiced formal education. By the contemporary characteristics of formal education, one can say that traditional Africa did not practice formal education. One would be correct to argue so because the mode by which learning took place in traditional setting did not entail reading and writing. However, in the broader sense of education, the African people, particularly Yoruba, were educated people, because teaching and learning took place among them.

Education is vital to the development of any nation. As much as Ayittey, in his *Africa in Chaos,* finds so many faults with many of the Western ideas and initiatives in Africa, he however honestly suggests that Africa could be said to be ignorant without Western education.[27] In the same vein, Nkansah-Obrempong gives prominent place to Western form of education when he proposed solutions to problem of underdevelopment in the developing societies.[28]

Through education, a nation can build its economic capacity and human resources, develop technology and creatives. Through education, all manners of professionals are trained for the betterment of the nation. In

---

26. Rather, 5.
27. Ayittey, *Africa in Chaos*, 31.
28. Nkansah-Obrempong, "Holistic Gospel," 211.

this subsection, I shall discuss African mode of education in face-to-face interaction with Western education. Nevertheless, my discussion shall be streamlined to education issues having to do with development and politics.

Historically, Western education was first brought to the Yoruba people of Nigeria in the fifteenth century by the Portuguese traders. This was without significant impact. Western education began to gain ground among the people in the late eighteenth century with the arrival of Christian missionaries.[29] The attempt of the Christian missionary was to "liberate the dark minds of the Africans from barbarism and idolatry."[30]

Keeping this short background of Western education among Yoruba in mind, one can deduce that one of its initial intentions among the Yoruba was to proselytize them into Christianity. Western education had one peculiarity: the use of the English language, since "children were expected to receive tuition in English . . . at [a] suitable age."[31]

Another peculiarity of Western form of education was the concept of reading and writing. The idea of reading and writing came with the advent of Western education. Western education considers ability to read and write as literacy, while inability to do so implies illiteracy.[32] It also approaches matters from logical perspective, arranging or following things in a sequence that makes meaning to the human five senses – hearing, sight, smell, taste and feeling, which is largely borne out of the consequence of eighteenth-century Enlightenment in Europe. On this note, I shall consider some critical implications of Western education on the spirituality and relational life of the Yoruba people.

Distortion of Meanings

It is worth noting that English, after becoming the official mode of communication, became the dominant language overriding the meaning of some words in Yoruba language. The use of English has made critical word-concepts in

---

29. "The Advent of Western Education in the Nature, Scope and Processes of Traditional Education in Nigeria," accessed 7 October 2019, https://kirusuf.wordpress.com/technology/by-period-and-geography/education/the-advent-of-western-education-in/.
30. "Advent of Western Education."
31. "Advent of Western Education."
32. Holme, *Literacy*, 1.

Yoruba language to lose the weight of their original meaning and implication. For instance, the word *ìmùlẹ̀* is frequently translated as "oath"[33] in English.

When people were assuming leadership offices in traditional Yorubaland, they undertook "*ìmùlẹ̀*," whereas in English concept they took an "oath." These are deemed as similar words in the respective languages. Therefore, when a leader is assuming a political office in the present-day Yorubaland the word used for the promises he makes to his people before the court of law is called "oath." According to English dictionary, "oath" means "the words said when making a formal pledge, especially when reciting a conventional formula such as that used in a court of law."[34]

In Yoruba cosmology, because such a pledge was made before the significant people in the land, and with the belief that the departed elders were watching, such pledge would be taken as *ìmùlẹ̀*. A promise made in such a solemn gathering is not a mere pledge among Yoruba people. It is seen as a commitment made to the "land" (*ilẹ̀*); and the people would say, "*Ẹni bá da'lẹ̀ á bá'lẹ̀ lọ*" (He who betrays [the land] would be swallowed by the ground).

Ìmùlẹ̀ is more than a mere pledge or promise but a serious commitment that has a life-and-death implication. It is spiritual in nature. It has the witness of the ancestors. As such, a traditional Yoruba man has more tendencies to stay faithful to *ìmùlẹ̀* he has made, because of its serious implication, than a modern-day Yoruba who sees it as a mere promise or pledge, without any spiritual implication.

The use of the word "oath" in place of *ìmùlẹ̀* among Yoruba political leaders did not help them to easily call to their mind the implication of the promise they made before the court of law and the people of the land. If the word *ìmùlẹ̀* was still used, it had the tendency to remind them that "*Ẹni bá da'lẹ̀ á bá'lẹ̀ lọ*." Saying it and committing it to mind in Yoruba language would remind them of the invisible eyes that are watching and waiting to administer justice to whoever breaks *ìmùlẹ̀*.

The use of the English word "oath" does not always call to the political leaders' mind the sacredness and consequence of their public promise. This is because the use of English as a second language among any people has the

---

33. Karade, *Handbook of Yoruba*, 116.
34. "Oath," *Microsoft Encarta 2009* [DVD] (Redmond, WA: Microsoft Corporation, 2008).

capacity to "play down fluidity and change in languages and ignore overlap and similarities of languages."[35]

Another effect of the use of English language is its distortion of some Yoruba worldviews. It is important to note that people's worldview is embedded in their language.[36] For instance Yoruba language, like many other African languages, does not have words such as cousin, niece, nephew, uncle and aunt; rather it only has father, mother, brother, sister, and children. One's cousin is one's brother or sister. One's uncle is said to be one's father. The implication of this in Yorubaland is the closeness of family ties. Cousins are not seen as distant family members, nor nieces and nephews seen as someone else's children.

The introduction of English words such as cousin, uncle and so forth has the tendency to build in the mind of a new-generation Yoruba person that cousins are not as close as one's brothers and sisters. This therefore creates a dent in the social system of the people, who hold the strong belief that, *èniyàn laṣọ mi* (people are my clothes).

Spirituality Insensitivity

Africans by nature are remarkably spiritual. None of their daily lives can be separated from spirituality. As it has been noted earlier in chapter 3, Yoruba worldview puts emphasis on the importance of the awareness of the invisible occurrences in one's surroundings. It is widely believed that beyond their five senses, human beings require another sense to be attuned to the events in the spiritual realm. This is synonymous to the concept of intuition in Greek philosophy, which implies "a form of knowledge or of cognition independent of experience or reason."[37]

In his *Emotional Intelligence*, Goleman highlights one of the deficiencies of Western education by noting that it emphasizes more on the development of intellectual ability than that of emotional ability.[38] This is an indication that there is an inner place of a man beyond his intellectual domain. The human existential makeup requires a psycho-spiritual element to be able to attune

---

35. Barton, *Literacy*, 70.

36. Walsh and Middleton, *Transforming Vision*, 22–30.

37. "Intuition." *Microsoft Encarta 2009* [DVD] (Redmond, WA: Microsoft Corporation, 2008).

38. Goleman, *Emotional Intelligence*, 161–62.

to what natural senses and intellect cannot fathom. Yoruba people are aware of this concept. Therefore, they hold that people must develop *ifura* as they grow. They must be in touch with the supernatural phenomenon that links humans' spiritual domain with their emotionality.

One's ability to develop his sixth sense is what makes a real leader in Yorubaland. A leader must be a man of intuition (*ifura*). Maxwell affirms this when he notes that leadership "requires intuition. Without it, you can get blindsided, and that's one of the worst things that can happen to a leader."[39]

The primary intention of Western education brought to Africa by Christian missionaries is to proselytize the people of the land. The effect of this is that while the missionaries were making attempts to proselytize the Africans, they (Africans) lost their African spirituality, that is, their spiritual commitment to the religious worldview,[40] and many of them did not attain Christian spirituality that was the aim of the missionaries. The result of this has been that they have bred a species of spiritually lukewarm people.[41]

This is quite evident in how the political leaders in Yorubaland are managing the affairs of the community without the fear of God. The spirituality of the leaders and followers in the traditional Yoruba community kept them from corruption and other delinquencies. The present-day leaders are found to be nonspiritual; hence, they lead without the fear of God. Likewise, the loss of African spiritual fervour also generally led to corrupt lifestyles. Biblical restoration of Yoruba spirituality would therefore imply that people will exhibit characters that are beneficial to the society, by the reason of their relationship with the Trinitarian God.

In contrast to African quest for spiritual ethics, modernization theory, operating through United Nations Educational, Scientific, and Cultural Organization (UNESCO), contends for humanistic ethics. Talking about UNESCO's commitment to humanism, its former director-general, Irina Bokova, submitted, "Humanism is a promise we must all keep."[42] This serves as a revelation to what underlies the educational practices that are globally regulated by UNESCO.

---

39. Maxwell, *21 Irrefutable Laws*, 88.
40. Bediako, *Christianity in Africa*, 97.
41. Pam, *African Concept of Sin*, 37.
42. Bokova, "Editorial," 5.

I have earlier noted in this chapter that humanity has the capability to guard their moral and ethical life, a claim that is in line with humanistic assertion. However, this study finds fault with humanism in that it holds the belief that humanity is at the centre of the universe, contrary to the biblical revelation that God is the centre of all things (cf. Rev 4:11). Hence, a prominent place is given to African spirituality-centred education that favours spiritual ethics and judgements, provided it undergoes biblical restoration.

Political Society Built on Sacred Kingship

Leadership like Fatherhood

Among the Yoruba people, a leader is a father. Almost all political leadership titles have a fatherhood implication. When loosely translated according to hearing, "*baálẹ́*" (*bàbá onílẹ̀*) means "father who owns the house." "*Baálẹ̀*" (note that *baálẹ́* is pronounced differently from *baálẹ̀*) is the contrasted form of "*bàbá onílẹ̀*" (father who is the owner of the land) which means "father in the land." In the Yoruba society, political leadership at whatever level is instituted to ensure everybody is catered to, just as the way a father caters to his household. The king, as the father of all, has his fatherly representatives at all levels of political units.

In both biblical and Yoruba context, fatherhood implies responsibility, the responsibility to ensure the wellbeing of his household. Jacob, during his years of servitude with Laban placed so much priority on providing for his own house, when he challenged Laban with the question, "When will I provide for mine own house?" (Gen 30:30, KJV). In Pauline teachings, fathers are required to provide for the needs of their houses (2 Cor 12:14; 1 Tim 5:8).

As depicted in the story of *Ìyá Alákàrà* in chapter 3, when problems arise, the one to call upon is always the head, the father. Hence, Adeyemo speaks in line with biblical Yoruba traditional belief when he argues in his book, *Africa's Enigma and Leadership Solutions*, that "leadership is problem solving."[43] The fatherhood of a king in Yorubaland is said to be sacred because everything he does is done because he is next to God, a human representation of the divine king, who is the Father of all.

It is also the responsibility of a father to ensure that members of the house are responsible. Both the Bible and Yoruba beliefs hold that it is required of

---

43. Adeyemo, *Africa's Enigma*, v.

a father to insist on right behaviour of his household. Repeatedly, Moses instructed the Israelites to teach their children the ways of God (Deut 4:9–10; 6:7; 11:19). The apostle Paul (Eph 6:4) and the writer of Proverbs (22:16) also state the importance of training up children in the way of God.

In my discussion of Yoruba concept of sin, I noted that the political system of the Yoruba society is structured in such a way that the king, as a father, has his watchful eyes everywhere. He has put the mechanism in place in order to know how people are behaving so that necessary actions can be taken in case of misconduct. This is of course applicable to "fathers" at all levels of the society.

The development implication of the fatherhood of the political leader among Yoruba people is therefore that, if leaders truly see themselves as fathers, they will sincerely prioritize people's wellbeing. Another implication is that when political leaders act as true fathers who lead by example and are very keen about good conduct of the people, there will be fewer moral atrocities in the society. As I have argued repeatedly in this book, human atrocities are the fundamental reason for underdevelopment.

Leadership by Divine Choice

The process of selecting a Yoruba king is worthy of mention. While in the contemporary political theories, as reflected in modernization, democratic election is romanticised, in Yoruba tradition, a choice of king is based on the choice of the gods. The discussion on the best kind of leadership is beyond the scope of this book; however, I shall emphasize the necessity of ensuring the right channel in selecting a leader. Whether in democracy or monarchy, it is believed that people can give room for God's providential choice of leadership, irrespective of the electoral system.

In the Yoruba electoral system, a king must be selected by the gods; otherwise, his reign would be chaotic. This is familiar too in the political story of Israel in the Bible. One case in point is the story of Abimelech (Judg 9). Abimelech manipulated his way into "kingship" (v. 6) and the story that follows his coronation depicts the picture of chaos. Athalia was another example who pushed her way to the throne against the precept of Yahweh (2 Kgs 11).

Her reign must also have been known for chaos since it is recorded that after her death the city was "quiet" (v. 20), which connotes peace.[44]

The need to select a leader through the right channel poses a challenge to African electoral process that is marked by bribery and violence. If our forebears, with their dim glimpse of God's revelation, could make the place of Olodumare a priority in the choice of a king, this places a bigger responsibility on contemporary Christian community to be more concerned about having a God-ordained leader in government. If nobody else picks up this responsibility, the church must, and all Christians must.

As earlier noted, while discussing the issue of sin and corruption, the order of the day, in many African countries during the time of election, is that the electorate, in many occasions, usually choose to vote for candidates who give handouts. Another popular phenomenon known to all, especially in multi-ethnic countries like Nigeria, is the tendency to vote along ethnic lines. Christian electorate should know differently that what matters in the choice of a political leader is that God is the one who makes the choice of the leader; anything otherwise would ruin the development and wellbeing of the nation.

Although God may allow any elected leader on the throne, but this does not imply he is pleased with him as a leader. The story of Saul should provide an important lesson for the people of God in times of political transitions. The people, out of some form of emotions, requested Samuel to anoint a king for them against the will of God, and God "gave" them Saul who messed up the Israelite's kingship (1 Sam 8; cf. Hos 13:11).

We could manipulate our ways against the will of God and secure a seat for a member of our ethnic group by virtue of our majority votes; however, the Israelite and Yoruba instances teach us that in such cases our land will not know peace. Political candidates may give handouts and buy their way to the political seat; nevertheless, we need to remember the anger of God against our unrighteousness.

It is time we became particular about God's choice of our leaders and their citizenship as *ọmọlúàbí* in the society. This is another critical lesson for our contemporary nation-state politics, as we seek to power it in the direction of

---

44. The primary meaning of the verb *Šāqaṭ* implies tranquillity experienced in the absence of war. It is the same word used in Joshua 11:23 depicting the extent of peace in the land.

national prosperity and development. It is grounded in the biblical laid-down principles for the Israelites' selection of a king as well.

> When you come to the land which the Lord your God is giving you, and possess it and dwell in it, and say, "I will set a king over me like all the nations that are around me," you shall surely set a king over you *whom the Lord your God chooses*; one from among your brethren you shall set as king over you; you may not set a foreigner over you, who is not your brother. But he shall not multiply horses for himself, nor cause the people to return to Egypt to multiply horses, for the Lord has said to you, "You shall not return that way again." Neither shall he multiply wives for himself, lest his heart turn away; nor shall he greatly multiply silver and gold for himself. (Deut 17:14–17, NKJV, italics added)

The fact that the democratic system is entailed in nation-state politics does not imply that God cannot use the process to make his choice for us. When the community of believers yield their will to God to be guided in the ballot, God will be pleased. This cannot happen until we give up all our prejudices and biases, and with an open heart cry out to God to make his choice for us (Acts 1:24).

It is also important that we honestly, without any sentiment, as individual voters, give our attention to the lifestyle of our political candidates to know whether they are above board or are people who live a ruthless life. The lifestyle of a leader can determine the course of the wellbeing of the nation. Therefore, a political leader must be an *ọmọlúàbí* in the society.

Leadership alongside Divinity

It is observed that almost all political activities among Yoruba entail some rituals, from activities that take place at the least political unit of the society to the ones in the palace. At this point, it is important to recognize the fact that all the political rituals (and perhaps other forms of ritual) in Yorubaland done to ensure peace in the society are an attempt to involve God in the state affairs. Although, as discussed earlier in chapter 4, the channel falls short of the biblical way of reaching God, all the *òrìṣà* worship is a sincere attempt to reach God.

Whereas this book condemns employing the *òrìṣà* as the medium to reach God, it nevertheless gives credit to the sincerity of our ancestors in their attempt to reach him. After all, God has overlooked this time of ignorance (Acts 17:30). As such, since this was their known way of reaching God, limited as it was, it is a commendable act. It leaves behind a lesson for us who have found the true way of calling upon the true God.

Again, worthy of note is also the requirement for a king to live a life devoted to the gods, through whom Olodumare can be reached, which is traditionally done daily and as special celebrations. A king must worship the *òrìṣà* all the time for the sake of himself and the entire nation. He must repatriate to the gods in times of trouble and in times of thanksgiving. He must always seek to receive guidance from the gods. The cause of the gods and ancestors must always guide his path.

In the biblical experience, the kings who related to Yahweh, in this manner that is traditionally expected of a Yoruba king to relate with the *òrìṣà* and the ancestors, were the kings whose reigns were remarkably prosperous. Such kings are: David (2 Sam 2–24; 1 Chr 11–29), Solomon (1 Kgs 1–11; 1 Chr 29:22–2 Chr 9:28), Asa (1 Kgs 15:9–24; 2 Chr 14– 16), Uzziah (2 Kgs 15:1–7; 2 Chr 26:3–23), Jehoshaphat (1 Kgs 22:41–50; 2 Chr 20:31–21:1), Hezekiah (2 Kgs 18–20; 2 Chr 29–32), and Josiah (1 Kgs 23:1–30; 2 Chr 34–36). They all learned to commit themselves to the Book of the Law and obedience to Yahweh and seek him first in times of need.

One significant distortion that has happened to the Yoruba, or rather African, sociopolitical thoughts, by virtue of modernization is secularism, which holds that "the physical universe is all that exists."[45] Although Africans still have the appearance of being religious in their daily lives, the grip of secularism has made African governments to address national issues from the secular point of view. This is different from the days of our ancestors, when consulting the gods was the quickest step to take in times of disasters.

This chapter was written during the time when the coronavirus (COVID-19) pandemic began to spread across Africa. The initial approach many African national governments took to the pandemic happened to be scientific. This is not to condemn the application of scientific solutions, but to point out how the contemporary era is different from the traditional era.

---

45. Miller, Moffitt, and Allen, *Worldview of the Kingdom*, 32.

Nothing is wrong with scientific intervention as long as it does not take the place of God. In fact, this is what largely happens in the modernization-driven political agenda for development: God is taken out of the scene.

God is the Olodumare, the One who has everything in bulk. Yoruba understand this and realize that to him they must all go in search of anything that spells their wellbeing. Like many other African communities, Yoruba believe that God is their ultimate king[46] to whom all human problems and challenges must be directed in order to receive solutions.

In Yoruba political practices, we learn about the role of divine power in the affairs of humans. We human beings are limited, not all problems are under our control. This is why leaders must learn to seek divine intervention. Seeking the wellbeing of humanity is a divine mission. God himself is concerned about it. As shown in the examples of the kings cited earlier, the biblical experiences reveal that leaders who are willing to genuinely seek God throughout the period of their reigns, not out of empty religious show-off, will have their reigns perpetually remembered for good. Seeking God and his will is part of Yoruba (or rather African) traditional political practice. If contemporary leaders seek God as required in his word, the nation will experience peace, prosperity, and wellbeing.

It is also an important realization that in Yoruba political practices, the unity of its diverse people is secured around the òrìṣà court. As discussed in chapter 4, the unifying factor of the Yoruba communities under the Oyo Empire was largely Sango worship. Although this strategy of unity, as suggested in the discussion, survives on mysticism, a threat that Sango the god of iron would vent his anger on whoever fails to comply with the demands of his worship, it is interesting to see the biblical parallel of this strategy among the Israelites.

The nation of Israel also encountered the problem of "tribalism." The Book of Judges gives a vivid picture of the state of anarchy in the land of Israel after the Israelites settled in Canaan. People lived in tribal communities and "everyone did as they saw fit" (Judg 21:25b). True unification of the nation only occurred when the nation had a leader who was anointed and awakened people to the course of Yahweh. David is a typical example (1 Chr 11–19).

---

46. Mbiti, *African Religions and Philosophy*, 44.

God must be the central figure of people's unity. People will only come together with an authentic sense of togetherness when God is the paramount reason for the assembly. Any other attempt to bring people together will only amount to a spurious expression of oneness. The effect never lasts in its authenticity. This is quite evident in the operations of the United Nations. At least, according to the realist views, the United Nations' effort in fostering unity among the nations of the earth is not resulting into genuine oneness.[47]

This is also evident in the situation on the ground in African political scenario. The African colonial leaders left the nations on the continent with a nation-state government. African governments today are struggling to unite the people groups within their countries. It is obvious in African nations how people commit their loyalty to their local community at the expense of the national government.[48]

There is scarcely a nation in Africa that experiences authentic oneness. In order to cater to this anomaly, many African nations put well-meaning policies in place to unite the people groups and tribes within their nations. These policies have been found ineffective. This is the idea behind the *Nyayo* philosophy in Kenya as being proposed by President Moi.[49] The same spirit gave birth to the National Youth Service Corps in Nigeria.[50] It is also the ultimate intention behind the political philosophy of *Ujamaa* in Tanzania, which was promoted by Julius Nyerere.[51]

All these political attempts by the leaders of African nations point us to the fact that the nations of Africa long for the spirit of unity. Africa will not succeed in bringing its people together in unity through a political philosophy. The only way by which people can burst out with the joy of brotherhood is when they climb the mount of God in worship. That is when we can truly see "how good and how pleasant it is for brethren to dwell together in unity" (Ps 131:1, KJV).

---

47. M. J. R. Norley, "Is the United Nations an Effective Institution?," *E-International Relations*, n.d., accessed 4 July 2017, http://www.e-ir.info/2013/02/23/is-the-united-nations-an-effective-institution/.

48. Kobia, *Courage to Hope*, 53; Hyden, *African Politics*, 51–52.

49. Moi, *Kenya African Nationalism*, 5.

50. "NYSC–Vision," accessed 4 July, 2017, https://www.nysc.gov.ng/vision.html.

51. Mwoleka and Healey, *Ujamaa and Christian Communities*, 9.

Yoruba kingship is said to be sacred because the king is next to the divinity. He acts as a father on behalf of the Father in heaven who is the Father of all. He acts as a king on behalf of the divine king who is the ultimate king. The development implication in Yoruba political thought and practice of sacred kingship is that the belief that king is a father of all instils in the mind of a leader the sense of responsibility to care for all. It also makes leaders take the responsibility to ensure good behavioural practices among the people, creating a suitable environment for wellbeing and development.

The sacredness of Yoruba kingship as rooted in the divine choice of a king sets a conducive political atmosphere for the society. The king's choice according to the will of God attracts the blessings of God, which is a basic criterion for peace and prosperity in the society. Leaders chosen through dubious electoral process are likely to bring about chaos in the society. In accordance with the biblical order of politics and development, when leaders seek God as exemplified in Yoruba political practice, the community enjoys the blessings of God and unity of the people. God is the giver of all blessings. Only his cause can truly unite humanity in the midst of diversity, as exemplified in the story of charismatic leaders like King David of ancient Israel.

The concept of sacred kingship in Yorubaland implies political pursuit of divinity, the only way through which the community can only enjoy true wellbeing and development. It teaches that God who is the Father and King of all ordains a human king to see to the welfare of all. When the human king fails in this regard, the society is tantamount to chaos.

Having given much commendation and premium to Yoruba spirituality, as I have noted repeatedly in my discussion, this study discredits the idea of having ancestors and deities as the means to reaching God. This Yoruba traditional belief is not in harmony with the Scripture. Yoruba spirituality, according to the cultural and political practices, also falls short of the biblical requirement, in that it does not reflect the knowledge of God's grace made available through Jesus Christ.

Conclusion

This chapter has sought to discuss the implications of Yoruba political practices and thoughts for development in Africa. I have examined these practices and thoughts in light of God's word and distortions caused to it by contemporary development theories. The implications of Yoruba traditional political practices and thoughts for development can be summarised as follows.

Yoruba political practices and thoughts on development are built upon the belief that peace, premised on good characters and relationship among the society members – leaders and followers, is the basis for development. Based on this belief, as I discussed in chapters 3 and 4, all the institutions in the society – social, educational, political, judicial, religious – are structured to achieve this peace goal. Yoruba are in line with the biblical principle that the conditions given by God the giver of peace (*àlàáfíà/shalom*) must be satisfied in order to experience wellbeing.

For Yoruba people, all that development entails is totally summed up in the concept of peace (*àlàáfíà*). Yoruba peace is the presence of cosmic order characterised by cordial relationship with oneself, others in the community, environment, and the divine. When all these are in place, every individual and the community experience "wellbeing," a variant name for peace and development.

The implication of this for development, according to the Scripture, is that one's life is not measured by material wealth (as is the order of the day in modernization theory). Considering this implication in a practical sense, having the awareness that one's life is not measured by material wealth saves people from unhealthy competition that materialism-driven free market promotes (a thinking that is embedded in contemporary development theories). Yoruba concept of peace puts the pursuit of the four-dimensional relationship, stated above, before any material thing (*àlàáfíà lójù*).

As I have argued in chapter 2, violation of relationships is a critical factor that pushes and keeps a society in poverty and underdevelopment. It is responsible for corruption, civil unrest and wars, cruel dealings with neighbours and environmental damages. Placing values on relationship, as taught in both biblical and Yoruba concepts of peace, fosters development and wellbeing of societies in that it tends to reduce factors that cause poverty and underdevelopment.

Development practitioners of all orientations agree that, "what is morally good and right is bound to the flourishing of human persons and human communities."[52] Yoruba traditional political thoughts and practices on development affirm and model this belief in their ways of dealing with sin. Dealing with ethical issues, as we learned from Yoruba context, sets a nation on the path of development. What would happen if a nation dealt with foundational ethical issues that escalated into a war? This would save the nation a huge amount of money that could have been spent on war at the expense of a nation's economic development.

What will happen if a nation becomes more proactive in dealing with corruption? This will translate into a big economic saving for a nation. According to Vishal Mangalwadi, corruption costs the world about 1 trillion dollars every year.[53] In Nigeria as of 2014, an average Nigerian was at a loss of about 1000 dollars every year due to corruption. If the situation is not salvaged the loss will rise to 2000 dollars in 2030. The country loses billions of dollars to corruption every year.[54] Therefore, in this way, applying Yoruba developmental-political thoughts and practices that centre on ethical living will lead to the economic development of a nation.

The second Yoruba developmental-political practice and thought that has positive implications for development in Africa is the concept of sacred kingship. This is explained in three perspectives: (1) the king who is a human representation of the divine king must serve his people like a father; (2) his choice must be divinely ordered; (3) he must reign in perpetual consultation with divinity. Examining these three perspectives from the biblical point of view, a typical Yoruba king who fits into these three, must have fulfilled God's description of an ideal king, equipped to bring wellbeing to his people.

A king who rules like a father is people-centred. He is genuinely concerned about the welfare of the people by creating conditions that will foster the community wellbeing. He is hands-on on matters of problem solving and ensuring good conducts and relationships (factors for ensuring peace) among his people. A king who rules like a father is convinced that it is his sole responsibility to ascertain the wellbeing of his nation.

---

52. Schweiker, "Theological Ethics," 359.
53. Mangalwadi, "Why Is the West?"
54. PricewaterhouseCoopers, "Impact of Corruption on Nigeria's Economy," *PwC*, accessed 17 April 2020, https://www.pwc.com/ng/en/publications/impact-of-corruption-on-nigerias-economy.html.

A leader whose choice is divinely ordered is the right king for the right situation. The implication of this for development is that, both in the biblical and Yoruba contexts, kings whose choices were determined by divine direction were the kings whose reigns were characterised by wellbeing. The reigns of the kings whose choices were manipulated by human actions were marked by chaos in the society. In both biblical times and Yoruba traditional context, the king is theocratically chosen, whereas in the contemporary time political leaders are democratically elected. Meanwhile, even in a democracy, God's providential choice can be allowed if the electorates let go of their personal biases as they go to the ballot.

Finally, Yoruba kinship reign must be in perpetual consultation with divinity, similar to the biblical requirement for a king. This one critical aspect is totally left out in modernization theory. It is depicted in the Scripture that the nation can only thrive in prosperity when its leader is under God's guidance. This is because God is our ultimate king and ruler.

However, this aspect of Yoruba kingship also holds a negative implication for development in Africa in that there are usually harmful covenants being made between the kings and the *alálẹ̀ ilẹ̀* (also known as *irúnmọlẹ̀*) who serve as intermediaries between God and the kings. The engagement of these deities is one of the strongest disparities between Yoruba spiritual-political practices and thoughts on development and the biblical teaching on the same.

CHAPTER 7

Way Forward

This book has focused on politics that fosters development; it draws biblical lessons from Yoruba culture. I have discussed Yoruba developmental-political thoughts and practices, pointing out their biblical correlations and antitheses. I have also, although briefly, discussed modernization theory in relation to its implications on development in Africa. This chapter provides the summary of these discussions, and suggests some way forward.

Lessons from Biblically Correlated Yoruba Developmental-Political Thoughts and Practices

According to this study, the two fundamental beliefs upon which Yoruba traditional developmental-political thoughts are rooted are: (1) the concept of peace (*àlàáfíà lójù*: peace is supreme); and (2) the peace-seeking responsibility of a king.

The Yoruba concept of peace (*àlàáfíà*) is similar to the biblical *shalom*. The concept of *àlàáfíà* underlies Yoruba developmental philosophy. It gives a prominent place to immaterial things as sources of wellbeing. Peace is supreme. When there is peace, that is when all individuals and the community experience wellbeing, a sum of what the heart of a human being desires. A community that experiences development has peace, characterised by cosmic order – "rats squeaking like rats, and birds chirping like birds." With this, it is therefore understood that the meaning of "peace," "development," and "wellbeing" are interrelated in Yoruba traditional thought. As such, the three words are used interchangeably in this book.

As in the biblical context, the Yoruba also holds that sin is the primary inhibitor of peace (i.e. wellbeing and development). It is the violation of the four-dimensional relationship with self, others in the community, environment, and the spiritual universe dominated by the supreme being, Olodumare. The Yoruba therefore place a high premium on good character (*iwà rere*). A person with *iwà rere* is an individual who does well in all the four dimensions of relationship. In fact, the four-dimensional relationship is held together by one's reverence for the spiritual universe. As such, Yoruba morality and spirituality go together.

Knowing that sin is the primary inhibitor of wellbeing, Yoruba society and the institutions in it are structured in such a way that people possess *iwà rere*. For instance, the (extended) family system is structured to ensure that all the members of the family are accountable to one another as per their moral lives. The educational system is also structured in such a way that all members of the society possess *iwà rere* and excel in their career, all for the wellbeing of the community.

The other principle learned as a foundational belief of Yoruba developmental-political practices and thoughts is the king's primary responsibility of pursuing the society's wellbeing. The king exists for nothing else other than ensuring the peace of the society. Hence, his success as a ruler is measured by how much wellbeing the community enjoys during his tenure of leadership. A king who fails to provide solution to the society's problem will not be remembered for good, because he is no king at all.

As peace is the grand total of human wellbeing, sin (i.e. bad characters and behaviours) is the primary factor that inhibits it. Therefore, one thing that the king must do to foster wellbeing of the society is to ensure good moral behaviour of the members of the society. Meanwhile, the political structure of the society is such that the king's network can fish out anyone with a bad behaviour in the society. In addition to ensuring good moral behaviour of the community members, the king must maintain the sacredness of the office. The elements of the sacredness of kingship are as follows:

A King Must Ensure Proper Political Coordination

The story of the Yoruba people all began from Ile-Ife, from where all the Yoruba race scattered broadly from the bank of the River Niger all the way to the Atlantic Ocean and Dahomey. Despite the vastness of the Yoruba communities under the Oyo Empire, the political system was organised in such a way that ensured the proper flow of political benefits.

A King Must Seek Spiritual Guidance and Help

All the Yoruba forms of worship centre around Olodumare. The wellbeing of a society is given by Olodumare. At the centre of all spiritual activities for the community stands the king himself. That is his primary obligation in order to ensure peace in the society.

A King Must Ensure Righteous Judgement

Yoruba judicial system caters for the naturally murky aspects of judgement, by seeking divine help in tracing the complicated roots of the matter under dispute. This has the tendency to provide a satisfactory verdict that will soothe the pain of an innocent person who otherwise could have been condemned. The ultimate implication of this on society's development is that there would be true peace.

A King Must Be Divinely Appointed

It is believed that proper procedure must be followed in choosing a king. Having followed such proper procedure, a king must be well oriented for the office.

These four above-mentioned activities of the king were critical for the wellbeing of the community. His failure to perform these activities would hamper the *àlàáfíà (shalom)* of the community. The nation-state political thoughts and practices have brought about underdevelopment because the political leaders have failed to observe these important biblical concepts, found in the Yoruba culture. This is not to say that everything about Yoruba thoughts and practices are biblical. Some of their thoughts and practices are found to be unbiblical.

Major Biblical Antitheses of Yoruba Traditional Developmental-Political Thoughts and Practices

The major biblical antitheses found in the Yoruba developmental-political practices and thoughts are:

Human Effort and Victory over Sin

One of the areas where the Yoruba got it wrong in their traditional beliefs is in the idea that victory over sin is found in personal and communal efforts for individuals to become *ọmọlúàbí*. The Bible teaches that all human righteousness are like filthy rags (Isa 64:6) and the only way they can be justified by God is through faith (Eph 2:8–9). Viewed through the biblical perspective, the Yoruba people also got it wrong in terms of their appeal to the gods for the atonement of sin. The only means of atonement given to humanity by God is the blood of Jesus (Eph 1:7).

The Place of the Ancestors and the Traditional Deities in Securing God's Help

While it is an acceptable practice in the Yoruba traditional society to reach God through intermediaries, the Bible condemns this practice. In addition to the fact that the Bible condemns the use of spiritual intermediaries, their activities among humans have negative development implications for the society. While the *irúnmọlẹ̀* (gods) have the power to act according to the petition of a community through the king, their willingness to act according to human request is based on the willingness of the community to enter a covenant. Meanwhile, all covenants have side effects with a negative implication on the community.

Lessons and Biblical Correlations of Modernization Theory

Modernization has wrought many wonders since its inception. It brought about industrialization, urbanization, and education that is based on critical thinking and scientific discoveries. The biblical correlation of modernization is found in the basis of its tenet grounded in Protestantism, which promotes hard work, thrift, and efficiency.

Negative Effects and Biblical Antitheses of Modernization Theory

The three fundamental problems of modernization: (1) deviation from divinity, which takes God out of the centre of everything; (2) overgeneralised idea of prosperity, which imposed Western taste for materialism on Africa; and (3) crisis of identity, the creation of two clashing Africas – the traditional and modern Africas, which are constantly colliding with each other.

Way Forward

With the gap that has been identified in the contemporary nation-state developmental-politics, what do we do? What are the ways to go forward for the general African society, church, and policymakers?

For the General African Society

1. Political Practices That Pursue Peace as the Basic Element for Development: The concept of peace stands out in Yoruba traditional political thoughts and practices, and it correlates with the biblical principle of *shalom*. However, this concept has been distorted by the influence of modernization. Africa in its political practices and thoughts should therefore restore a belief about development that places a premium on peace rather than on material wealth. Doing this implies that all institutions within the nation should be structured in a way that promotes the four-dimensional relationship, moral accountability, and respect for order. National institutions should all seek to promote African biblical values.

2. Upholding the Sacredness of Political Leadership: Yoruba political thoughts and practices have the distinctive belief of sacred kingship as a scripturally grounded development principle. Based on this finding, I thereby recommend the restoration of political leadership that truly cares for people like a father cares for his children and takes seriously the place of God as the divine ruler. Also based on this principle, I recommend electorate decision that is based on the character of a political candidate, rather than on personal bias or ethnicity.

For the African Church and Church Leaders

The following are some possible paths the African church can take as it seeks to fulfil its holistic mission:

1. Continued Biblical Teaching on Salvation:
I have emphatically stressed in this book how sin wages battle against human wellbeing. The only antidote offered by God to the problem of sin is salvation found in the death and resurrection of our Lord Jesus Christ. As such, the message of the cross is foundationally the answer to all the problems of humanity. When armed robbers come to the knowledge of the Lord Jesus Christ, when corrupt judges, lawmakers, law enforcement agents and politicians know Christ as their personal Saviour, when evildoers repent of their sin and turn to God, the society will enjoy unspeakable peace. This will also have economic development implications for the nation in that there will be no loss of funds due to corruption and other vices, as it would have been the order of the day, otherwise.

2. More Intensified Efforts in Disciple-making:
While so much is being done to bring people to the light of salvation, corresponding efforts also have to be taken so that they grow every day to become more and more like Christ. There are many Christians today in the society, people who have truly given their lives to Christ. However, the amount of evil, corruption, and indiscipline that are being perpetrated in the society betray this reality. Our society does not reflect the fact that there are reasonable numbers of people who are Christians. This is largely because many Christians are not growing to become like Christ in their characters.

3. Theology of Work Putting Emphasis on Work Ethics and Spirit of Excellence:
After people have committed themselves to the Christian faith, as they grow in character, it is also important that they grow in their attitude towards work. The prosperity of a society is not just about the people in political offices; it is about everyone in the society. Whatever vocation we engage in, it contributes to the society. Researchers should undertake the job with biblical guiding principles; teachers should teach the pupils in their custody with the fear of God; nurses and all medical practitioners should do their job knowing that one day they will give account to the Lord. Everyone should do their work as they ought to and develop necessary capacity to meet the challenges of the day by virtue of their work.

4. Individual and Communal Repentance for Our Sins and That of the Past Generations:

So much evil has been perpetuated by our forebears for the sake of sustaining their political powers. In fact, so much blood has been shed. Not just with our forebears, so much evil still takes place in our time. The repercussion of such evil will always catch up with us if we fail to repent. With all the atrocities committed on a daily basis in our society, with all the sin of commission and omission, conscious or unconscious sin, our society may not experience a lasting forward movement in a positive direction. Therefore, a call for national repentance is important.

5. A Call for Potential and Incumbent Politicians to Desist from Occultism:

The demons of the days of our ancestors are still here with us. Many of our political leaders still pay allegiance to them with serious covenant and heavy side effects that have bound our African nations. By engaging in secret cults, political leaders or aspirants are giving up the prosperity and wellbeing of our land to gods who should not have a say over the destiny of our nations.

6. Prayer of National Healing and Deliverance against the Curses and Holds of Traditional Gods:

Until and unless God delivers our land from the territorial gods, the human hearts will be held captive in wickedness. We have once given them power, through our forebears, to act on us, now as Christians we need to denounce them. They are no longer the gods of our land. They may not lose their grip unless we undertake prayer and fasting (Matt 17:21). We should not shy away from talking about this kind of prayer in our political quest to proffer solutions to our national predicaments. As God promises to answer the prayer of the Israelites if they pray for their land and turn from their evil way (2 Chr 7:14), the same promises apply to us since the God of Israel is the same God we call upon.

For National Policymaking in Africa

1. Strategic Implementation of Transnational Organizations' policies:

In their interactions and dealings with the transnational organizations, political leaders and national policymakers in Africa are advised to consider critically the sociocultural realities of their nations before buying into proposals from foreign and international agencies.

2. Educational Policy that Fosters Spiritual Growth and Godly Values:
African moral characters are based on their spirituality. This has a correlation in the Scripture whereby kingdom lifestyle is based on the Christian spiritual walk with God. On this note, this study recommends that national educational curriculum should be formulated in such a way that African godly values would be inculcated into students' lives.

Bibliography

Books and Dictionaries

Acemoglu, Daron, and James A. Robinson. *Why Nations Fail: The Origins of Power, Prosperity and Poverty*. London: Profile Books, 2012.

Abimbola, Wande. "Ifa: A West African Cosmological System." In *Religion in Africa: Experience and Expression*, edited by Thomas D. Blakely, Walter E. A. Van Beek, and Dennis L. Thomson. London: James Currey, 1992.

Adeleye, Femi. *Preachers of a Different Gospel: A Pilgrim's Reflections on Contemporary Trends in Christianity*. Grand Rapids: HippoBooks, 2011.

Adeyemo, Tokunboh. *Africa's Enigma and Leadership Solutions*. Nairobi: World Alive Publishers, 2009.

———. *Salvation in African Tradition*. Nairobi: Evangel Publishing, 1979.

Agbaje, Bode. *Alo Ninu Asa Yoruba*. Ilesa: Elyon Publishers, 2013.

Apter, Andrew. *Black Critics and Kings: The Hermeneutics of Power in Yoruba Society*. Chicago: University of Chicago Press, 1992.

Asante, Molefi Kete, and Emeka Nwadiora. *Spear Masters: An Introduction to African Religion*. Maryland: University Press of America, 2007.

Asaolu, Taiwo Olufemi. *Privatization in Nigeria: Regulation, Deregulation, Corruption and the Way Forward*. Inaugural Lectures Series 278. Ile-Ife: Obafemi Awolowo University Press, 2015.

Augustine. *The City of God against the Pagans*. Edited by R. W. Dyson. Cambridge: Cambridge University Press, 1998.

Awobuluyi, Oladele. *Essentials of Yoruba Grammar*. Ibadan: University Press Limited, 1979.

Ayandele, E. A. "Ijebuland 1880–1891: Era of Splendid Isolation." In *Studies in Yoruba History and Culture*, edited by G. O. Olusanya, 88–107. Ibadan: University Press, 1983.

Ayittey, George B. N. *Africa in Chaos*. Basingstoke: Palgrave Macmillan, 1999.

———. *Indigenous African Institutions*. Leiden: Brill, 2006.

Babade, Tope. *Egberun Ijinle Owe Yoruba Pelu Itumo Ati Iloo Won Ni Ede Geesi: 1000 Yoruba Proverbs with Their Translation and Usage in English Language.* Yoruba Research Project Publications. Lagos: Onas B. Printing Press, 2008.

Babu, A. M. "Postscript." In *How Europe Underdeveloped Africa*, by Walter Rodney, 311–16. London: Bogle-L'Ouverture Publications, 1972.

Balogun, M. J. *Public Administration in Nigeria: A Developmental Approach.* London: Macmillan Nigeria, 1983.

Banerjee, Abhijit V., and Esther Duflo. *Poor Economics: A Radical Rethinking of the Way to Fight Global Poverty.* 1st ed. New York: PublicAffairs, 2011.

Barton, David. *Literacy: An Introduction to the Ecology of Written Languages.* Oxford: Blackwell, 1994.

Bediako, Kwame. *Christianity in Africa: The Renewal of a Non-Western Religion.* Edinburgh: Edinburgh University Press, 1995.

———. *Theology and Identity: The Impact of Culture upon Christian Thought in the Second Century and Modern Africa.* Regnum Studies in Mission. Oxford: Regnum Books, 1993.

Castells, Manuel. *The Power of Identity.* Information Age: Economy, Society and Culture Vol. 2. Malden: Blackwell, 2002.

Chamberlain, M. E. *The Scramble for Africa.* 3rd ed. New York: Routledge, 2014.

Chanda, Nayan. *Bound Together: How Traders, Preachers, Adventurers, and Warriors Shaped Globalization.* New Haven: Yale University Press, 2007.

Chomsky, Noam. *Hegemony or Survival: America's Quest for Global Dominance.* 1st ed. New York: Metropolitan Books, 2003.

———. *How the World Works.* New York: Soft Skull Press, 2011.

Chossudovsky, Michel. *The Globalization of Poverty and the New World Order.* 2nd ed. Ontario: Global Outlook, 2003.

Chua, Amy. *World on Fire: How Exporting Free Market Democracy Breeds Ethnic Hatred and Global Instability.* New York: Doubleday, 2003.

Coetzee, Jan K. "Modernization Theory." In *Development: Theory, Policy, and Practice*, edited by Jan K. Coetzee, Johann Graaff, Fred Hendricks, and Geoffrey Wood, 27–43. Oxford: Oxford University Press, 2001.

Cole, Victor. "Africanising the Faith: Another Look at the Contextualisation of Theology." In *Issues in African Christian Theology*, edited by Samuel Ngewa, Mark Shaw, and Tite Tienou, 12–23. Nairobi: East African Educational Publishers, 1998.

Collier, Paul. *The Bottom Billion: Why the Poorest Countries Are Failing and What Can Be Done about It.* Oxford: Oxford University Press, 2007.

Crowther, Samuel A. "Idagba." *Vocabulary of the Yoruba Language: Part I. English and Yoruba. Part II. Yoruba and English. To Which Are Prefixed, the Grammatical Elements of the Yoruba Language.* London: Church Missionary Society, 1843.

Crowther, Samuel A. *A Vocabulary of the Yoruba Language*. London: Seeleys, 1852.
Crowther, Samuel A. A Brief History of the Yoruba People. 2015. Kindle.
Davis, Ellen F. Scripture, Culture, and Agriculture: An Agrarian Reading of the Bible. New York: Cambridge University Press, 2009.
Delano, Isaac O. *Atumo Ede Yoruba: A Short Yoruba Grammar and Dictionary*. London: Oxford University Press, 1958.
Dixon, Peter. *Peacemakers: Building Stability in a Complex World*. Nottingham: InterVarsity Press, 2009.
Eagles, Munroe. *Politics: An Introduction to Modern Democratic Government*. Toronto: University of Toronto Press, 2008.
Elizondo, Virgillio. "Culture, the Option for the Poor, and Liberation." In *The Option for the Poor in Christian Theology*, edited by Daniel Groody. Indiana: University of Notre Dame Press, 2007.
Falola, Toyin. *Yoruba Gurus: Indigenous Production of Knowledge in Africa*. Trenton & Asmara: Africa World Press, 1999.
Falola, Toyin, and Matthew M. Heaton. *A History of Nigeria*. Cambridge: Cambridge University Press, 2008. Kindle.
Farrow, Stephen S. *Faith, Fancies and Fetich or Yoruba Paganism*. New York: Negro University Press, 1926.
Ford, Leighton. Transforming Leadership: Jesus' Way of Creating Vision, Shaping Values & Empowering Change. Downers Grove: InterVarsity Press, 1991.
Friedman, Thomas L. *The World Is Flat: A Brief History of the Twenty-First Century*. 1st ed. New York: Farrar, Straus and Giroux, 2005.
Garraty, John A. *The American Nation: A History of the United States*. 3rd ed. New York: Pearson/Longman, 1975.
Gehman, Richard J. *African Traditional Religion in Biblical Perspective*. Nairobi: East African Educational Publishers, 1993.
Gener, Timoteo D. "Contextualization." Edited by William A. Dyrness and Veli-Matti Karkkainen. *Global Dictionary of Theology*. Illinois: InterVarsity Press, 2008.
Gifford, Paul. *African Christianity: Its Public Role*. London: Hurst, 1998.
Goleman, Daniel. Emotional Intelligence: Why It Can Matter More Than IQ. New York: Brantan Books, 2006.
Goudzwaard, Bob. *Idols of Our Time*. Illinois: InterVarsity Press, 1984.
Groody, Daniel. *Globalization, Spirituality, and Justice*. Theology in Global Perspective Series. Maryknoll: Orbis Books, 2007.
Grudem, Wayne A. Politics according to the Bible: A Comprehensive Resource for Understanding Modern Political Issues in Light of Scripture. Grand Rapids: Zondervan, 2010.
———. Systematic Theology: An Introduction to Biblical Doctrine. Grand Rapids: Zondervan, 2009.

Gugler, Josef, and William G. Flanagan. "The Yoruba." In *Urbanization and Social Change in West Africa*, edited by Kenneth Little, 16–19. Urbanization in Developing Countries. Cambridge: Cambridge University Press, 1978.

Guinness, Os. *The Call: Finding and Fulfilling the Central Purpose for Your Life.* Nashville: Thomas Nelson, 2003.

Gyekye, Kwame. *The Unexamined Life: Philosophy and the African Experience.* Accra: Ghana University Press, 1988.

Hanks, Patrick, ed. "Politics." *Collins Dictionary of The English Language*. London: Collins, 1986.

Harrison, Paul. *Inside the Third World: The Anatomy of Poverty.* 3rd ed. London: Penguin Books, 1993.

Hastings, James. "Blessing." *Dictionary of the Bible*. Edinburgh: T&T Clark, n.d.

Healey, Joseph, and Donald Sybertz. *Towards an African Narrative Theology.* Nairobi: Paulines Publications Africa, 1996.

Herbst, Jeffrey Ira. *States and Power in Africa: Comparative Lessons in Authority and Control.* Princeton Studies in International History and Politics. Princeton: Princeton University Press, 2000.

Heuser, Andreas. "Religio-Scapes of Prosperity Gospel: An Introduction." In *Pastures of Plenty: Tracing Religio-Scapes of Prosperity Gospel in Africa and Beyond*, edited by Andreas Heuser, 15–29. Frankfurt: Peter Lang, 2015.

Hoelzl, Michael, and Graham Ward, eds. *Religion and Political Thought.* London: Continuum, 2006.

Holme, Randal. *Literacy: An Introduction.* Edinburgh: Edinburgh University Press, 2004.

Hughes, Dewi. *Power and Poverty: Divine and Human Rule in a World of Need.* Nottingham: Inter-Varsity Press, 2008.

Hyden, Goran. *African Politics in Comparative Perspective.* Cambridge: Cambridge University Press, 2006.

Ihonvbere, Julius O. "Democratization in Africa: Challenges and Prospects." In *Issues and Trends in Contemporary African Politics: Stability, Development and Democratization*, edited by George Akeya Agbango, 1:287–320. Society and Politics in Africa. New York: Peter Lang Publishing, 1997.

Ikenga-Metuh, Emefie. *Comparative Studies of African Traditional Religions.* Onitsha: Imico Publishers, 1987.

Jejeniwa, G. B. S., and G. O. Babatunde. *Akojopo Owe Yoruba Fun Orundun Kokanlelogun: A Compendium of Yoruba Proverbs for the 21st Century.* Vol. 1. Akure: Bendunny Plus, 2013.

Johnson, Samuel. *The History of the Yorubas: From the Earliest Times to the Beginning of the British Protectorate.* Edited by Obadiah Johnson. New York: Cambridge University Press, 2010.

Karade, Baba Ifa. *The Handbook of Yoruba Religious Concept*. Newburyport: Weiser Books, 1994.

Kato, Byang. "Theology of Eternal Salvation." In *Issues in African Christian Theology*, edited by Samuel Ngewa, Mark Shaw, and Tite Tienou, 192–209. Nairobi: East African Educational Publishers, 1998.

Katongole, Emmanuel. *The Sacrifice of Africa: A Political Theology for Africa*. Grand Rapids: Wm. B. Eerdmans Publishing, 2011. Kindle.

King, Philip J., and Lawrence E. Stager. *Life in Biblical Israel*. Edited by Douglas A. Knight. Library of Ancient Series. Louisville: Westminster John Knox Press, 2001.

Kinoti, George. *Hope for Africa: And What the Christian Can Do*. Nairobi: AISRED, 1994.

Kiwanuka, Semakulia. "The Three Traditional Foundations of African Nationalism: A Study of the Western Impact on African Politics 1900–1960." In *Politics and Leadership in Africa*, edited by Aloo Ojuka and William Ochieng, 37–52. Nairobi: East African Literature Bureau, 1975.

Kobia, Samuel. *The Courage to Hope: The Roots for a New Vision and the Calling of the Church in Africa*. Risk Book Series No. 102. Geneva: WCC Publications, 2003.

Koyzis, David T. *Political Visions and Illusions: A Survey and Christian Critique of Contemporary Ideologies*. Downers Grove: InterVarsity Press, 2003.

Kunhiyop, Samuel Waje. *African Christian Theology*. Grand Rapids: Zondervan, 2012.

Lahey, Benjamin B. *Psychology: An Introduction*. 10th ed. New York: McGraw-Hill Higher Education, 2009.

Laitin, David D. Hegemony and Culture: *Politics and Religious Change among the Yoruba*. Chicago: University of Chicago Press, 1986.

Lloyd, P. C. *Africa in Social Change*. Penguin African library, AP22. Middlesex: Penguin Books, 1974.

Magesa, Laurenti. *Christian Ethics in Africa*. Christian Theology in African Scholarship. Nairobi: Acton Publishers, 2002.

Maggay, Melba Padilla. *Transforming the Kingdom and Politics*. Quezon: The Institute for Studies in Asian Church and Culture, 2004.

Maté, Gabor. *When the Body Says No: Understanding the Stress-Disease Connection*. Hoboken: J. Wiley, 2003.

Maxwell, John C. *21 Irrefutable Laws of Leadership*. Nashville: Thomas Nelson Publishers, 1998.

Mbiti, John S. *African Religions and Philosophy*. Reformatted. Nairobi: East African Educational Publishers, 2015.

McKenzie, Peter. *Hail Orisha!: A Phenomenology of a West African Religion in the Mid-Nineteenth Century*. Edited by Adrian Hastings and Marc R. Spindler. Studies of Religion in Africa. Leiden: Brill, 1997.

McKim, Donald K. "Ontology." *Westminster Dictionary of Theological Terms*. Louisville: Westminster John Knox Press, 1996.

Mentan, Tatah. *The State in Africa: An Analysis of Impacts of Historical Trajectories of Global Capitalist Expansion and Domination in the Continent*. Bamenda: Langaa Research and Publishing Common Initiative Group, 2010.

Miller, Darrow L., Bob Moffitt, and Scott D. Allen. *God's Remarkable Plan for the Nations*. Seattle: YWAM Publishing, 2005.

———. *The Worldview of the Kingdom*. Seattle: YWAM Publishing, 2005.

Mitchell, Robert Cameron. *African Primal Religions*. Allen: Argus Communications, 1977.

Moi, Daniel Arap. *Kenya African Nationalism: Nyayo Philosophy and Principles*. London: Macmillan, 1986.

Moltmann, Jurgen. "Political Theology." In *Global Dictionary of Theology*, edited by William A. Dyrness and Veli-Matti Karkkainen, 669–72. Downers Grove: InterVaristy Press, 2008.

Moon, W. Jay. *African Proverbs Reveal Christianity in Culture: A Narrative Portrayal of Builsa Proverbs Contextualizing Christianity in Ghana*. Eugene: Wipf and Stock Publishers, 2009.

Moss, Todd J. *African Development: Making Sense of the Issues and Actors*. 2nd ed. London: Lynne Rienner Publishers, 2011.

Mugambi, Jesse Ndwiga Kanyua. *From Liberation to Reconstruction: African Christian Theology after the Cold War*. Nairobi: East African Educational Publishers, 1995.

Mugambi, J. N. K. "Religion and Social Reconstruction in Post-Colonial Africa." In *Church-State Relations: A Challenge for African Christianity*, edited by J. N. K Mugambi and Frank Kuschener-Pelkmann, 13–50. Nairobi: Acton Publishers, 2004.

Muia, Daniel M. "Concepts and Theories of Development and Underdevelopment." In *Introduction to Development Studies for Africa*, edited by Daniel M. Muia and J. E. Otiende, 1–14. Nairobi: Acacia Publishers, 2014.

Mulin, Robert Bruce. *A Short World History of Christianity*. London: Westminster John Knox Press, 2008.

Mumford, Debra J. *Exploring Prosperity Preaching: Biblical Health, Wealth & Wisdom*. 1st ed. Valley Forge: Judson Press, 2012.

Mutonono, Dwight S. M. *Stewards of Power: Restoring Africa's Dignity*. Bukuru: Hippo Books, 2018.

Mwoleka, Christopher, and Joseph Healey, eds. *Ujamaa and Christian Communities*. Eldoret: Gaba Publications, 1976.

Myers, Bryant L. "Poverty." In *Global Dictionary of Theology*, edited by William A. Dyrness and Veli-Matti Karkkainen, 687–96. Downers Grove: InterVarsity Press, 2008.

———. *Walking with the Poor: Principles and Practices of Transformational Development*. Rev. and updated ed. Maryknoll: Orbis Books, 2011.

Narayan, Deepa, Robert Chambers, Meera Kaul Shah, and Patti Petesch. *Crying Out for Change: Voices of the Poor*. Oxford: Published by Oxford University Press for the World Bank, 2000.

Nixon, R. E. "Poverty." Edited by I. H. Marshall, A. R. Millard, J. I. Packer, and D. J. Wiseman. *New Bible Dictionary*. Leicester: InterVarsity Press, 1996.

Njoh, Ambe J. *Tradition, Culture and Development in Africa: Historical Lessons for Modern Development Planning*. Hampshire: Ashgate Publishing, 2006.

Nkansah-Obrempong, James. *Foundations for African Theological Ethics*. Carlisle: Langham Monographs, 2013.

Oakley, Nigel W. *Engaging Politics?: The Tensions of Christian Political Involvement*. Milton Keynes: Paternoster Press, 2007.

Oduyoye, Modupe. *The Vocabulary of Yoruba Discourse*. Ibadan: Daystar Press, 1971.

Ogungbile, David. "African Pentecostalism and the Prosperity Gospel." In *Pentecostal Theology in Africa*, edited by Clifton R. Clarke, 132–48. Eugene: Wipf and Stock Publishers, 2014.

Ogunmefu, M. I. *Yoruba Legends: 40 Myths, Legends, Fairy Tales and Folklore Stories from the Yoruba of West Africa*. London: Abela Publishing, 2009.

Ojo, G. J. Afolabi. *Yoruba Culture: A Geographical Analysis*. London: University of London Press, 1971.

Okullu, Henry. *Church and State in Nation Building and Human Development*. Nairobi: Uzima Publishing House, 2003.

Olupona, Jacob K. "Orisa Osun: Yoruba Sacred Kingship and Civil Religion in Osogbo, Nigeria." In *Osun across the Waters: A Yoruba Goddess in Africa and the Americas*, edited by Joseph M. Murphy and Mei-Mei Sanford, 46–67. Indiana: Indiana University Press, 2001.

Osiyale, B. O. "Indiscipline and Corruption in Nigeria." In *Themes in Nigeria as a Nation*, edited by R. O. Ajetunmobi and B. O. Osiyale, 242–64. Lagos: Gabby Printing (Nig.), 2009.

Paget-Wilkes, Michael. *Poverty, Revolution and the Church*. Exeter: The Paternoster Press, 1981.

Pam, Gyang D. *A Compendium of Theology*. Jos, Nigeria: Sele Printing and Publishing House, 2012.

———. *African Concept of Sin: A Theological Appraisal*. Jos, Nigeria: Sele Printing and Publishing House, 2009.

Parrinder, Edward Geoffrey. *African Traditional Religion*. 3rd ed. London: Sheldon Press, 1974.

Pemberton III, John, and Funso S. Afolayan. *Yoruba Sacred Kingship: A Power Like That of Gods*. Washington, DC: Smithsonian Institution Press, 1996.

Phiri, Isaac. *Proclaiming Political Pluralism: Churches and Political Transitions in Africa*. Religion in the Age of Transformation. Westport: Praeger, 2001.

Rather, A. R. *Theory and Principle of Education*. New Delhi: Discovery Publishing House, 2004.

Ray, Benjamin C. *African Religions: Symbol, Ritual, and Community*. Englewood Cliffs: Prentice-Hall, 1976.

Rodney, Walter. *How Europe Underdeveloped Africa*. London: Bogle-L'Ouverture Publications, 1972.

Rosen, Michael, and Jonathan Wolff, eds. *Political Thought*. New York: Oxford University, 1999.

Ross, Kenneth R., ed. *God, People and Power in Malawi: Democratization in Theological Perspective*. Kachere Monograph 3. Blantyre, Malawi: CLAIM, 1996.

Sachs, Jeffrey. *The End of Poverty: Economic Possibilities for Our Time*. New York: Penguin Press, 2005.

Schanbacher, William D. *The Politics of Food: The Global Conflict between Food Security and Food Sovereignty*. Santa Barbara: Praeger Security International, 2010.

Sen, Amartya. *Development as Freedom*. Oxford: Oxford University Press, 1999.

Shaw, Mark R. *Work, Play, Love: A Visual Guide to Calling, Career, and the Mission of God*. Illinois: InterVarsity Press, 2014.

Sims, Walter Hines, ed. *Baptist Hymnal*. Nashville: Convention Press, 1956.

Spechler, Martin C. "The Trouble with Globalization: It Isn't Global Enough!" In *Globalization and Sustainable Development in Africa*, edited by House-Soremekun Bessie and Toyin Falola, 22–42. Rochester Studies in African History and the Diaspora. Rochester: University of Rochester Press, 2011.

Stanssen, Glen H. *Just Peacemaking: Transforming Initiatives for Justice and Peace*. Louisville: Westminster Press, 1992.

Steger, Manfred B. *Globalization: A Very Short Introduction*. Oxford: Oxford University Press, 2013.

Storkey, Alan. *A Christian Social Perspective*. Leicester: InterVarsity Press, 1979.

———. *Jesus and Politics: Confronting the Powers*. Grand Rapids: Baker Academic, 2005.

Subair, Kola. "Globalization and Industrial Development in Nigeria." In *Globalization and Sustainable Development in Africa*, edited by Bessie House-Soremekun and Toyin Falola, 257–75. Rochester Studies in African History and the Diaspora. Rochester: University of Rochester Press, 2011.

Tétreault, Mary Ann, and Robert Allen Denemark, eds. *Gods, Guns, and Globalization: Religious Radicalism and International Political Economy*. International Political Economy Yearbook Vol. 13. Boulder: Lynne Rienner Publishers, 2004.
Thompson, William R., and Rafael Reuveny. *Limits to Globalization: North-South Divergence*. Rethinking Globalizations 21. Abingdon: Routledge, 2010.
Tracy, David. *Blessed Rage for Order, the New Pluralism in Theology*. San Francisco: Harper & Row Publishers, 1988.
Turaki, Yusufu. *Foundations of African Traditional Religion and Worldview*. Nairobi: WordAlive Publishers, 2006.
Umeasiegbu, Rems Nna. *The Way We Lived*. Ibadan: Heinemann Educational Books, 1969.
Usman, Aribidesi, and Toyin Falola. *The Yoruba from Prehistory to the Present*. Cambridge: Cambridge University Press, 2019.
Walsh, Brian J., and J. Richard Middleton. *The Transforming Vision: Shaping a Christian World View*. Illinois: InterVarsity Press, 1984.
Watt, Patrick. *Social Investment and Economic Growth: A Strategy to Eradicate Poverty*. Oxfam Insights. Oxford: Oxfam, 2000.
Wolters, Albert M. *Creation Regained: Biblical Basics for a Reformational Worldview*. Grand Rapids: Wm. B. Eerdmans Publishing, 2005.
Wright, Christopher J. H. *The Mission of God: Unlocking the Bible's Grand Narrative*. Illinios: InterVarsity Press, 2006.
Villa-Vicencio, Charles. *Theology of Reconstruction: Nation-building and Human Rights*. Cambridge: Cambridge University Press, 1992.
Zodhiates, Spiros, and Warren Baker, eds. *Hebrew-Greek Key Word Study Bible: Key Insight to God's Word, King James Version*. 2nd rev. ed. Chattanooga: AMG Publishers, 2009.
Zulu, Edwin. "'Fipelwa Na BaYahweh': A Critical Examination of Prosperity Theology in the Old Testament from a Zambian Perspective." In *In Search of Health and Wealth: The Prosperity Gospel in African, Reformed Perspective*, edited by Hermen Kroesbergen, 21–28. Eugene: Wipf and Stock Publishers, 2014.
Globalisation, Growth, and Poverty: Building an Inclusive World Economy. A World Bank Policy Research Report. Washington, DC: The World Bank, 2002.

Journals

Adedayo, Muyiwa Samuel. "The Concept of Omoluabi and Political Development in Nigeria: The Missing Gap." *IOSR Journal of Humanities and Social Science* 23, no. 3 (March 2018): 1–7.

Adelowo, Dada. "Rituals, Symbolism, and Symbols in Yoruba Traditional Religious Thought." *African Journal of Theology* 4, no. 1 (1990): 162–73.

Ademowo, Adeyemi, and Noah Balogun. "Proverbs, Values and the Development Question in Contemporary Africa: A Case Study of Yoruba Proverbs." *Antropologij* 14 (2014): 149–61.

Ajayi, Adeyinka Theresa, and Lateef Oluwafemi Buhari. "Methods of Conflict Resolution in African Traditional Society." *An International Multidisciplinary Journal, Ethiopia* 8, no. 33 (April 2014): 138–57.

Akinade, Akintunde E. "The Enduring Legacy: Christian-Muslim Encounter in Yorubaland." *Studies in World Christianity* 3, no. 2 (1 October 1997): 138–53.

Alokan, P. O. "The Impact of Religion on the Promotion of Peace and Economic Integration in Yoruba Land." *Journal of Sociology, Psychology and Anthropology in Practice* 2, no. 1–3 (2010): 9–20.

Awolalu, J. Omosade. "The Yoruba Philosophy of Life." *Presence Africaine Editions*, no. 7. Nouvelle Serie (1er Trimestre 1970): 20–38.

Balogun, Oladele Abiodun. "The Concepts of Ori and Human Destiny in Traditional Yoruba Thought: A Soft-Deterministic Interpretation." *Nordic Journal of African Studies* 16, no. 1 (2007): 116–30.

Bassey, Magnus O. "Missionary Rivalry and Educational Expansion in Southern Nigeria, 1885–1932." *The Journal of Negro Education* 60, no. 1 (1991): 36–46.

Berman, Sheri E. "Modernization in Historical Perspective: The Case of Imperial Germany." *World Politics* 53, no. 3 (April 2001): 431–62.

Biobaku, Subari. "The Effect of Urbanisation on Education in Africa: The Nigeria Experience." *International Review of Education* 13, no. 4 (1967): 451–60.

Buck, Robert Enoch. "Protestantism and Industrialization: An Examination of Three Alternative Models of the Relationship between Religion and Capitalism." *Review of Religious Research* 34, no. 3 (March 1993): 210–24.

Cafferky, Michael E. "The Ethical-Religious Framework for Shalom." *Journal of Religion and Business Ethics* 3, no. 1. Article 7 (21 February 2014): 1–36.

Collier, Paul. "Poverty Reduction in Africa." *Proceedings of National Academy of Sciences of the United States of America* 104, no. 3 (23 October 2007): 16763–68.

d'Orville, Hans. "New Humanism and Sustainable Development." *Cadmus* 2, no. 5 (October 2015): 90–100.

Daniel, Kasomo. "An Investigation of Sin and Evil in African Cosmology." *International Journal of Sociology and Anthropology* Vol. 1, 8 (December 2009): 145–55.

Easterly, William. "The Big Push Déjà Vu: A Review of Jeffery Sach's 'The End of Poverty: Economic Possibilities for Our Time.'" *Journal of Economic Literature* 44, no. 1 (March 2006): 96–105.

Fadamiro, Joseph Akinlabi and Joseph Adeniran Adedeji. "Cultural Landscapes of the Yoruba of South-Western Nigeria Demystified as Solidified Time in Space." *Space and Culture* 19, no. 1 (2016): 15–30.

Folarin, George O. "Contemporary State of the Prosperity Gospel in Nigeria." *Asia Journal of Theology* (April 2007): 68–95.

Garuba, Harry. "The Good, the Bad, and the Beautiful: Discourse about Values in Yoruba Culture." *Philosophia Africana* 6, no. 1 (March 2003): 59–62.

Huntington, Samuel P. "Transnational Organizations in World Politics." *World Politics* 25, no. 3 (April 1973): 333–68.

Jiafeng, Wang. "Some Reflections on Modernization Theory and Globalization Theory." *Chinese Studies in History* 43, no. 1 (Fall 2009): 72–98.

Kalu, Kelechi A. "Globalization and Its Impact on Indigenous Governance Structures." *Southwestern Journal of International Studies* (March 2004): 29–60.

Law, R. C. C. "The Chronology of the Yoruba Wars of the Early Nineteenth Century: A Reconsideration." *Journal of the Historical Society of Nigeria* 5, no. 2 (1970): 211–22.

Law, Robin. "Early Yoruba Historiography." *History in Africa* Vol. 3 (1976): 69–89.

———. "Making Sense of a Traditional Narrative: Political Disintegration in the Kingdom of Oyo." *Cahiers d'Études africaines* 22, no. 87 (1982): 387–401.

Lloyd, P. C. "Sacred Kingship and Government among the Yoruba People." *Journal of the International African Institute* Vol. 30, no. 3 (July 1960): 221–37.

———. "Craft Organization in Yoruba Towns." *Journal of the International African Institute* 23, no. 1 (January 1953): 30–44.

Morton-Williams, Peter. "The Yoruba Ogboni Cult in Oyo." *Journal of the International African Institute* 30, no. 4 (October 1960): 362–74.

Myers, Bryant L. "Progressive Pentecostalism, Development, and Christian Development NGOs: A Challenge and an Opportunity." *International Bulletin of Missionary Research* Vol. 39, no. 3(July 2015): 115–20.

Ndlovu, Mbulisi, and Bhekezakhe Ncube. "The Philosophy of Sustainable Development as Depicted in the Proverbs of Amandebele." *Journal of Emerging Trends in Educational Research and Policy Studies* 5, no. 8 (1 January 2014): 209–13.

Nkansah-Obrempong, James. "Holistic Gospel in a Developing Society: Biblical, Theological, and Historical Backgrounds." *Evangelical Review of Theology* 33 (2009): 191–212.

Obidi, S. S. "Skill Acquisition through Indigenous Apprenticeship: A Case Study of the Yoruba Blacksmith in Nigeria." *Comparative Education* 31, no. 3 (November 1995): 369–84.

Odebode, Idowu. "Naming Systems during Yoruba Wars: A Sociolinguistic Study." *Names* 58, no. 4 (1 December 2010): 209–18.

Oladosu, Olusegun A. "Ethics and Judgement: A Panacea for Human Transformation in Yoruba Multi-religious Society." *International Journal of Theology & Reformed Tradition*, April 2012: 137–164.

Guo, Yan-Rong, Qing-Dong Cao, Zhong-Si Hong, Yuan-Yang Tan, Shou-Deng Chen, Hong-Jun Jin, Kai-Sen Tan, De-Yun Wang, and Yan Yan. "The Origin, Transmission and Clinical Therapies on Coronavirus Disease 2019 (COVID-19) Outbreak – An Update on the Status." *Military Medical Research* 7, no. 1 (13 March 2020): 1–10. https://doi.org/10.1186/s40779-020-00240-0 137 – 164.

Olanipekun, Olusola Victor. "Omoluabi: Re-Thinking the Concept of Virtue in Yoruba Culture and Moral System." *Africology: The Journal of Pan African Studies* 10, no. 9 (2017): 217–31.

Olurode, Lai. "Ifa, the Deity of Wisdom, and Importance of Work among the Yoruba People." *Journal of Enterprising Communities: People and Places in the Global Economy* 1, no. 2 (5 June 2007): 135–41.

Oyeshile, Olatunji A. "Traditional Yoruba Social-Ethical Values and Governance in Modern Africa." *Philosophia Africana* 6, no. 2 (2003): 81–88.

Parrinder, Edward Geoffrey. "Divine Kingship in West Africa." *Numen* 3 (1956): 111–21.

Pemberton III, John. "Art and Rituals for Yoruba Sacred Kings." *Art Institutes of Chicago Museum Studies* 15, no. 2 (1989): 97–174.

Peng, Yuan. "Modernization Theory: From Historical Misunderstanding to Realistic Development: A Review of a New Thesis on Modernization." *Chinese Studies in History* 43, no. 1 (Fall 2009): 37–45.

Schweiker, William. "Theological Ethics and the Question of Humanism." *The Journal of Religion* 83, no. 4 (2003): 539–61.

Stepin, Vyacheslav S. "Philosophy as Cultural Self-Awareness." *Russian Studies in Philosophy* 53, no. 2 (October 2015): 151–58.

Thompson, Robert Farris. "The Sign of the Divine King: An Essay on Yoruba Bead-Embroidered Crowns with Veil and Bird Decorations." *African Arts* 3, no. 3 (Spring 1970): 8–17, 74–80.

Togarasei, Lovemore. "The Pentecostal Gospel of Prosperity in African Contexts of Poverty: An Appraisal." *Exchange* 40, no. 4 (October 2011): 336–50.

Trieber, J. Marshall. "Creation: An African Yoruba Myth: An Adaptation." *CLA Journal* 18, no. 1 (1974): 114–18.

Theses, Dissertations, Magazines and Unpublished Materials

Adeyemi, Lamidi. "Civilisation Started from Yoruba Kingdom." *Oranyan Festival 2017 Brochure*, September 2017.

Aladejana, Tony Idowu. "An Axiological Analysis of Yoruba Education." PhD Thesis, Loyola University of Chicago, 1979.

Bokova, Irina. "Editorial." *The UNESCO Courier*, December 2011.

Kasera, Basilius. "The Biblical and Theological Examination of Prosperity Theology." MTh Thesis, South African Theological Seminary, 2012

Larbi, E. Kingsley. "Theological Examination of Poverty Relief Models in the African Context." MA thesis, Nairobi Graduate School of Theology, 1990.

Nkansah-Obrempong, James. "Visual Theology: Some Akan Cultural Symbols, Metaphors, Proverbs and Myths about God and Their Implications for Doing Christian Theology." PhD Thesis, Fuller Theological Seminary, Pasadena, 2002.

———. "Lecture Notes: Christian Ethics" presented at the TH605: Christian Ethics Lectures, Africa International University, Nairobi, April, 2016.

Ojo, Samuel. "Brochure: Oranyan Festival 2017." Oranyan Festival Committee, September 2017.

Pam, Gyang D. "Christian View of Poverty" presented at the Theology and Poverty (TH704) weekly lectures, Africa International University, Nairobi, 15 October 2015.

Seth, Sanjay. "Where Is Humanism Going?" *The UNESCO Courier*, December 2011.

Turaki, Yusufu. "A Christian Vision for Africa: Towards a Conception of Development and Transformation." Unpublished article, 2011.

Internet Sources

Chigozie, Emeka. "10 Fun, Interesting Facts About Nigeria." *Answers Africa*. Last modified 28 February 2013. Accessed 20 September 2018. https://answersafrica.com/facts-about-nigeria.html.

Dada, Peter. "South-West Records Low Crime Rate –IGP." *Punch*. Lagos, September 2019. Accessed 4 December 2019. https://punchng.com/swest-records-low-crime-rate-igp/.

Elwell, Walter A. "Wickedness." *Baker's Evangelical Dictionary of Biblical Theology*. Grand Rapids: Baker Book House, 1997. Accessed 5 March 2020. https://www.biblestudytools.com/dictionary/wickedness/.

Gbenda, Joseph S. "Age-Long Land Conflicts in Nigeria: A Case for Traditional Peacemaking Mechanisms." *Ubuntu: Journal of Conflict and Social*

Transformation 1, no. 1_2 (2012): 156–176. Accessed 9 December 2015. http://aceser.net/journals/download.php?aid=27&action=download.

Mangalwadi, Vishal. "Why Is the West the Least Corrupt?" Youtube video presented at the Truth Matters Youtube channel, 10 November 2017. Accessed 17 April 2020. https://www.youtube.com/watch?v=-sNFukJr7HA.

Oborji, Francis Anekwe. "Archbishop Tutu & South African Black Theology." *TheCable*. Last modified December 27, 2021. Accessed April 18, 2023. https://www.thecable.ng/archbishop-tutu-south-african-black-theology.

Opande, Isaac Nilson, and Margaret Nasambu Barasa. "Locating Sustainable Development in Africa: Discourses on EkeGusii and LuBukusu Proverbs in Kenya" (2017). Accessed 4 March 2020. http://41.89.196.16:8080/xmlui/handle/123456789/311.

Pricewaterhouse Coopers. "Impact of Corruption on Nigeria's Economy." *PwC*. Accessed 17 April 2020. https://www.pwc.com/ng/en/publications/impact-of-corruption-on-nigerias-economy.html.

SAHRC. "Whites Are Not an Oppressed Minority Group in SA, Says SAHRC." Last modified November 23, 2020. Accessed April 1, 2023. https://www.sahrc.org.za/index.php/sahrc-media/news/item/2525-whites-are-not-an-oppressed-minority-group-in-sa-says-sahrc.

Sowole, James. "Nigeria: South-West Has Lowest Crime Rate – IG." This Day, 6 September, 2019. Accessed 4 December 2019. https://www.thisdaylive.com/index.php/2019/09/06/south-west-has-lowest-crime-rate-says-ig/.

Movies

Andy, Amenechi. *Oduduwa*. Infinity Films Production, 2008. Accessed 9 November 2019. https://www.youtube.com/watch?v=0q_6X6bXRb4.

Bamiloye, Mike. *Esin Ajoji* (The Strange Religion). All Nigeria Conference of Drama Ministries (ANCEDRAM), 2003.

Quadri, Lateef. *Opa Oranmiyan*. Fam Multipurpose Limited, 2017.

Adesina, Olayinka J. *Orisun Yoruba*. Yoruba Hood. 2018.

Lasode, Obafemi. *Sango: The Legendary African King*. Accessed 7 December 2019. https://www.youtube.com/watch?v=XpduBzMpPHw.

Paimo, Lere. *Ogbori Elemosho*. Afelele & Brothers. Accessed 9 December 2019. https://www.youtube.com/watch?v=1Q5PPIVvLUg.

Oral Sources

Adeyemi, Hazzan, presently a royal chief in Alaafin's palace (Mogaji). Interviewed together with other five elderly princes who requested anonymity. 13 June 2019.

Adekunle, Kadewole, former Oyo State politician. 3 July 2019.

Ajuwon, Samuel. Yoruba lecturer at Federal College of Education Obudu, River State, WhatsApp interview, 5 October 2019.

Awoyeye, Moshood, Emese, a member of judicial council in the Ooni of Ife's palace, 1 August 2019.

Fatokun, Lawrence, a retired major in Nigerian army. 29 July 2019.

Gbadegesin, Omooba. Prince of a former Alaafin of Oyo, Oba Ladigbolu II. 12 June 2019.

Kofoworade, Kunle, a Yoruba youth leader, WhatsApp conversation, 9 June 2018.

Makinde Femi, a royal chief in the Ooni of Ife's palace. 31 July 2019.

Oke, Zion Adeola, Community Development Association leader, Alimosho Local Government, Lagos. 4 July 2019.

Oladipo J.A. retired civil servant. 22 June 2019.

Omoboye, Olumide. A Yoruba missionary to Kenya. 29 November 2017.

Onaolapo, Victor, legal practitioner and youth leader, 9 June 2019.

Onaolapo, Folusho Anna, History lecturer at Ogunsanya College of Education Ijanikin, Lagos State. 8 July 2019.

Oroja, Samuel Ismaila Adisa Adewale. "Oral Interview." Palace of Onimeiran of Meiranland, Meiran, Lagos, 9 July 2019.

Tella, Ben, a descendant of Oyo Local chief, Ona Isokun, also a senior Baptist pastor. 23 May 2018.

Glossary of Yoruba Terms Used

Abúlé: a small village
àdìrẹ: tie and dye, literally means "tied and soaked"
àdúrà: prayer or petition
àgbà (àgbàlagbà): adult person; old age; a senior person; an elder
àgbẹ̀: a farmer; *iṣẹ́ àgbẹ̀*: farming
àgbẹ̀dẹ: blacksmith, or any form of smithery
Alaafin: the political head of Oyo kingdom, both Old Oyo, and present-day Oyo
àlàáfíà: peace, cosmic order
alálẹ̀-ilẹ̀: the spiritual owner of the land; also refers to the gods of the land
Awujaale: the political head of Ijebu kingdom
àyàn (aláyàn): expert in playing and making drums
baálé: title given to the head of an extended family, living in a family compound
baálẹ̀: title given to the head of a hamlet or village
èjè: blood
èsan: vengeance, the negative repercussion of moral evil
èṣè: generally refers to sin
Esu: the name of the trickster god in Yoruba pantheon
gbẹ́nà-gbẹ́nà: a carpenter
ìdàgbàsókè: growth; development
Ifa: the name of the god of wisdom in the Yoruba pantheon
ìfura: spiritual sensitivity or alertness
ilọsíwájú: progress, moving forward; development
irúnmọlẹ̀: a variant name for the deities
iṣẹ́: chronic poverty, also *òsì*
iṣẹ́: daily job, vocation
iṣẹ́ ọwọ́: handiwork; or craft; vocation
ìtura: comfort; relief
ìjòyè: chief, either serving in the king's court as a minister or head of a small community
ìletò: hamlet

ìlú: a town or city
ìwà: refers to human behaviour
ìwà rere: good behaviour, socially acceptable character
ìwèfà: a eunuch; a former slave whose status was upgraded to serve as a king's minister. He is usually castrated.
ìyekan: a relative, mostly not a close relative
kábíyèsí: a traditional title of all Yoruba kings
ọba: king, the political head of a Yoruba major town
Obatala: the name of Yoruba god of purity
ọdẹ (ọlódẹ): a hunter, who may also, in addition to his game hunting vocation, serve as a community guard
Oduduwa: the progenitor of the Yoruba race
Ogun: the name of the Yoruba god of iron. He is the god in charge of all ferrous vocations.
Ojútùú: solution; order
Okanbi: the only son of Oduduwa
Olokun: wife of Oduduwa
ọlọ́nà: an artist, carpenter, or woodworker
olú ìlú: the capital city, a city with a crowned king
ọmọdé: a child or young person
ọmọlúàbí: the term used for a human being of noble character; popularly used to refer to an ideal human being
òògùn: spiritual power; juju
Oranmiyan: one of the grandsons of Oduduwa
Orí: the name given to the god of good fortune; orí also used to refer to "head"
òrìṣà: traditional deities or gods, emissaries of Olodumare
ọrọ̀: material wealth
òsèlú: politics or statecraft
òwò: trade
owó: money
Sango: the god of thunder; formerly a king in the Old Oyo Empire before being raised to the status of divinity after his death

APPENDIX

Some Yoruba Cities in the Middle Ages

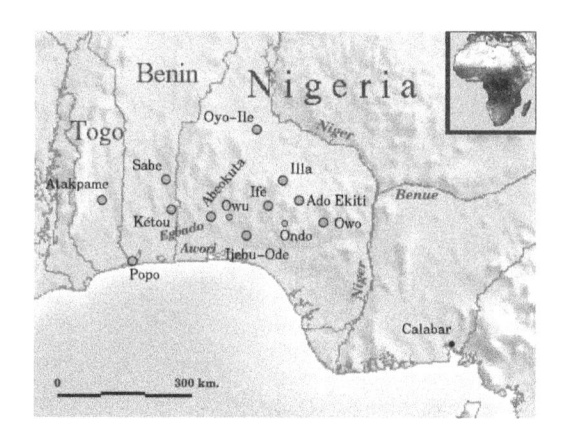

Source: "Some Yoruba cities of the Middle Ages." Accessed 13 April 2020. https://en.wikipedia.org/wiki/Yoruba_people#/media/File:HistoYoruba.jpeg, CommonRollebon, CC BY-SA 3.0 https://creativecommons.org/licenses/by-sa/3.0/, via Wikimedia Commons

Langham

Langham Literature, with its publishing work, is a ministry of Langham Partnership.

Langham Partnership is a global fellowship working in pursuit of the vision God entrusted to its founder John Stott –

> *to facilitate the growth of the church in maturity and Christ-likeness through raising the standards of biblical preaching and teaching.*

Our vision is to see churches in the Majority World equipped for mission and growing to maturity in Christ through the ministry of pastors and leaders who believe, teach and live by the word of God.

Our mission is to strengthen the ministry of the word of God through:
- nurturing national movements for biblical preaching
- fostering the creation and distribution of evangelical literature
- enhancing evangelical theological education

especially in countries where churches are under-resourced.

Our ministry

Langham Preaching partners with national leaders to nurture indigenous biblical preaching movements for pastors and lay preachers all around the world. With the support of a team of trainers from many countries, a multi-level programme of seminars provides practical training, and is followed by a programme for training local facilitators. Local preachers' groups and national and regional networks ensure continuity and ongoing development, seeking to build vigorous movements committed to Bible exposition.

Langham Literature provides Majority World preachers, scholars and seminary libraries with evangelical books and electronic resources through publishing and distribution, grants and discounts. The programme also fosters the creation of indigenous evangelical books in many languages, through writer's grants, strengthening local evangelical publishing houses, and investment in major regional literature projects, such as one volume Bible commentaries like the *Africa Bible Commentary* and the *South Asia Bible Commentary*.

Langham Scholars provides financial support for evangelical doctoral students from the Majority World so that, when they return home, they may train pastors and other Christian leaders with sound, biblical and theological teaching. This programme equips those who equip others. Langham Scholars also works in partnership with Majority World seminaries in strengthening evangelical theological education. A growing number of Langham Scholars study in high quality doctoral programmes in the Majority World itself. As well as teaching the next generation of pastors, graduated Langham Scholars exercise significant influence through their writing and leadership.

To learn more about Langham Partnership and the work we do visit **langham.org**